COLESVILLE

MARYLAND

*The Development of a Community,
Its People and Its Natural Resources,
Over a Period of Four Centuries*

Ned Bayley

HERITAGE BOOKS
2008

HERITAGE BOOKS
AN IMPRINT OF HERITAGE BOOKS, INC.

Books, CDs, and more—Worldwide

For our listing of thousands of titles see our website
at
www.HeritageBooks.com

Published 2008 by
HERITAGE BOOKS, INC.
Publishing Division
100 Railroad Ave. #104
Westminster, Maryland 21157

Copyright © 1997 Ned Bayley

All rights reserved. No part of this book may be reproduced or transmitted in any form or by any means, electronic or mechanical, including photocopying, recording or by any information storage and retrieval system without written permission from the author, except for the inclusion of brief quotations in a review.

International Standard Book Numbers
Paperbound: 978-1-58549-004-2
Clothbound: 978-0-7884-7709-6

DEDICATED TO

the Colesville Community Strawberry Festival,

that for more than a decade has made important

contributions to a spirit of unity

and cooperation among Colesville residents,

churches, and businesses.

Contents

TABLE OF FIGURES ix

ACKNOWLEDGEMENTS xi

INTRODUCTION xii

Chapter I: BEFORE THE SETTLERS 1
    The Precontact Period 1
    Indians in the Colesville Area 2
    Contact with the British 4

Chapter II: GEORGE CALVERT'S LEGACY 7

Chapter III: EARLIEST LANDOWNERS IN THE COLESVILLE
    AREA 12
    James Beall, Sr. 13
    Charles and William Beall 14
    James Beall, Jr. 15
    Richard Snowden 24

Chapter IV: THE SETTLERS 30
    The Lazenbys 30
    Samuel and Mary Thomas 35
    John Berry 36
    James Odell 38
    More Turnover of Farms 39

Chapter V: EVAN THOMAS, MOUNT RADNOR'S EMINENT
    QUAKER 43
    Plantation Owner 43
    Public Servant 44
    Dissenter 49
    Freer of Slaves 53
    Land Disperser 55
        Peaches Lot 55
        Two Farms 57
    Family Man 57
    Evan Thomas's Legacy 60

Chapter VI: 18TH CENTURY ROADS 64
    The Road to Bell Town 64
    Private Roads 66

INTO THE 19TH CENTURY
Page 69

Chapter VII: EARLY MILLS 71
    A Grist and Saw Mill on Northwest Branch 71
    The Mills on Paint Branch 72
        Ninian Edmonston's *Hamburgh* 72
        Kemp's Mill Seat 74
        Dr. Washington Duvall Buys Peter Kemp's Mill 76
        Later Owners of the Mill 77
        The Lansdale Mill 78
        Fawcett's Woolen Mill 78

Chapter VIII: EARLY STORES AND A POST OFFICE 80
    Edward Berry's *Coalsville* Store 80
    Rawlings' Store 82
    Edward Dawes's Store 83
    Colesville Post Office 84

Chapter IX: 19TH CENTURY ROADS 87
    The Washington-Colesville-Ashton Turnpike 87
    A Public East-West Road 87
    Good Hope Road 87
    Bonifant Road 89
    Notley Road (West) 89
    Fairland Road 89

Chapter X: FEDERAL METHODIST EPISCOPAL CHURCH 91

Chapter XI: SCHOOLS 94

Chapter XII: TWO PROMINENT FAMILIES 98
    The Bonifants - Their First Century in Colesville 98
    James and Laura Bonifant of *Drumeldry* 100
    The Washington Duvalls 102

Chapter XIII: CIVIL WAR BRINGS CHANGE 106
    Smith Town 107
    Good Hope Methodist Episcopal Church 107
    Schools for African-American Children 108
    Joseph Burr - Affluent Resident 108
    Allen Reed's Blacksmith Shop 108
    A Saloon at the Crossroads 110

THE 20TH CENTURY
Page 113

Chapter XIV: CHANGING PLACES AND FACES 114
    In the Cemetery 114
    The Bradford Store and Post Office 115
    Cissel's General Merchandise Store 116
    Ed Reed's Blacksmith Shop 116
    Judge Alfred C. Tolson 118
    The Bonifants 119
    The Hobbs Family 120
    William Smith of Smithville 123
    Elizabeth McCulloch - Colesville's Venturous Farmer 124
    Helen Vierling 127
    The Hutchisons 129
    Smitty's Esso 129
    Colesville's Mr. 4-H 131

Chapter XV: DEVELOPMENT 134
    Subdivisions 134
    Roads 136
    Police and Fire 137
    Utilities 138
    Protection of Natural Resources 139

Chapter XVI: SCHOOLS AND CHURCHES 144
    Schools 144
    Churches 146
        Methodists 146
        Catholics 147
        Baptists 148
        Presbyterians 148
        Episcopalians 149

Continued Development of Churches 150

Chapter XVII: CIVIC ORGANIZATIONS 153
    W.C.T.U. 153
    Lions Club 154
    Citizen's Associations 155
    The Colesville Council of Community Congregations 157
    The Colesville Community Strawberry Festival 158

Epilogue 162

Appendix I: TWILIGHT 166

Appendix II: PERIPHERAL PATENTS 167

Appendix III: EVAN THOMAS'S LAND ACQUISITIONS
             AND SALES 171

Appendix IV: ORIGINAL CHURCH CEMETERY 173

Index 185

Table of Figures

Figure

1. Site of Indian Hunting Camp 3
2. Location of Nacotchtank Tribe 4
3. George Calvert 8
4. James Beall, Sr.'s, Patents 14
5. Nine Earliest Patents in Colesville 16
6. *Easy Purchase* 17
7. *Drumeldry* 18
8. *Beall Christie* 19
9. *Addition to Easy Purchase* 20
10. *Wolfs Den* 21
11. *Beals Manor* 22
12. *The James and Mary* 23
13. *Snowdens Fourth Addition to His Manor* 26
14. *Snowdens Mill* 27
15. Robert Lazenby's 217 Acres of *Wolfs Den* 30
16. The Lands of Samuel Thomas 35
17. The Lands of John Berry 37
18. James Odell's Portion of *Beall Christie* 39
19. Evan Thomas's *Beaver Dam* 46
20. *Mount Radnor* 47
21. Evan Thomas's Plantation 48
22. The Oldest House in Colesville 56
23. The 18th Century Roads in the Colesville Area 67
24. Location of Evan Thomas's Mill 71
25. The Triangular *Hamburgh* Patent 72
26. Example of Single Geared Breast Mill 73
27. Peter Kemp's House 75
28. 1859 Etching of the "Old Mill" 76
29. The Michael Peter House 81
30. Location of *Berrys Chance*, 1804 *Coalsville*, and Michael Peter's House 82
31. 19th Century Roads in the Colesville Area 88
32. Andrew Chapel Methodist Church 93
33. Colesville School, 1899 97
34. Bonifant Family Cemetery 99

35.	Bonifant House	101
36.	Early Bonifant House	102
37.	*Drumeldra*	104
38.	Valley View	109
39.	Allen Reed's Blacksmith Shop	111
40.	1996 View of Original Colesville Cemetery	114
41.	Emma and Harold Bradford	115
42.	Cissel's Store	117
43.	Ed Reed's House	118
44.	Charles Hobbs and Grace Hobbs Suthard	122
45.	William Smith	124
46.	Elizabeth McCulloch	127
47.	Smitty's Esso	130
48.	Smitty Holds a Tire Sale	131
49.	Traffic Zones in the Colesville Area	135
50.	Colesville Intersection, 1996	136
51.	1915 Class of Colesville School	145
52.	W.C.T.U. Hall	153
53.	Colesville Strawberry Festival Scenes	159
54.	Peripheral Patents	170

ACKNOWLEDGMENTS

Over the past 14 years, many persons have contributed information for this book. Special recognition is due Robert Barendsen for years of participation in mapping the early tracts, and his suggestions and critical review of this and earlier manuscripts. Michael Dwyer, Park Historian for the Maryland National Capital Park and Planning Commission (MNCPPC), reviewed this manuscript. Jim Sorensen, also of MNCPPC, reviewed information and helped interpret data. Eveleen Carter provided a wealth of information and photographs of 20th century families and the early Methodist church. Joyce Bayley provided contemporary photographs of historic sites. Robert Hutchings, Joyce Barendsen, and Roberta Kurtz reviewed this manuscript and made important suggestions. Jane Sween, Librarian for the Montgomery County Historical Society, other members of the staff, and Eleanor M. V. Cook, Editor of *The Montgomery County Story*, have been very helpful in locating references. In addition, the following persons helped in gathering and assembling data: Nancy Bonifant, John Bowen, Mrs. George Robert Cole, Winifred and Don Dickson, James Elliott, Mary Goodman, Betty Haslip Fling, Sallie Gridley, Culver and Lois Hutchison, W. C. Leyshon, Joan Mann, Grace and Quentin Melander, Martha C. Nesbitt, Susan G. Pearl, Russell Reed, Thelma Reed, Solomon Rosenthal, Dan Wilhelm, and George Wilson.

An additional acknowledgment is appropriate. When I started this study of history, I quickly learned that the search for facts is never ending. There always is some information that eludes the seeker of final truth. Therefore, a history is never complete. Also, the names of people and places included in the text are those that could be found. There may be others of equal importance that were not available. Nevertheless, I believe the data, names and places in the text, tables, appendices, and notes are adequate to tell the story.

INTRODUCTION

Colesville, Maryland, is an unincorporated community with an estimated population of 17,000. It is on the southeast edge of the Piedmont Plateau in eastern Montgomery County. It surrounds the intersection of two arterial routes - New Hampshire Avenue and Randolph Road. The community reaches out to a rectangular perimeter that extends over a mile north to today's Bonifant and Good Hope Roads and south to White Oak. Northwest and Paint Branches bound the community on the west and east, respectively. Topography is rolling and rainwater drains into small streams that lead to the branches and then to the Anacostia River.

Because the community is not incorporated, these boundaries are based on judgement of the author. During most of the 19th century, reference to Colesville related to the intersection plus a few stores and homes in the immediate vicinity. Farms, settlements, and stores a half mile or more away were called "near Colesville."*

Early in the 18th century, today's Colesville area was part of Prince George's County. In 1748, the area became part of Frederick County, and in 1776, it was included in the newly formed Montgomery County.

The story of Colesville is a case history covering more than three centuries. It depicts how an uninhabited land of forest, meadows and streams developed into several tracts owned or leased by farmers. The population slowly increased, then exploded in the 20th Century. The story shows how, with the building of mills, stores, post offices, roads, schools, churches, and the creation of civic organizations, a community emerged.

This history illustrates the interaction of people with each

---

* An expansive but not very useful reference to Colesville is the Colesville Election District which extended from the B & O Railroad on the south to the Patuxent River on the north, and from Norbeck on the west to the county line on the east.

other and with their natural, economic, and societal environment. It is a story of Indians, land speculators, farmers, storekeepers, tradesmen, slaves, slave-holders, freemen, patriots, and dissenters. This is a story of arrivals and departures, prosperity and failure.

Throughout its recorded history, turbulent economic and political events have surrounded and affected the Colesville area. Indians settled peacefully in a village on the Anacostia River and used the Colesville area for hunting grounds. Then they left, their numbers decimated by intertribal wars, white settler conflicts and disease. Kings of England established a proprietary colony of Maryland, made it a royal colony, then reestablished the proprietorship. Frontier skirmishes culminated in the French and Indian Wars. The American Revolution created a new form of government. The port of Baltimore boomed. President George Washington chose the area of Washington, D.C., as the Federal capital. British invaded Bladensburg and Washington. A bloody civil war tore America apart. An amendment to the Constitution banished slavery. The United States fought the Mexican War, Spanish-American War, World Wars I and II, Korea, Vietnam, and the Persian Gulf War. Although the community was never directly in the path of these hurricanes of violence and change, people in the Colesville area experienced all of the events, reacted to them and modified their lives accordingly. This book is also about water abundance and the way people used it, a story of siltation, pollution and efforts toward restoration. It is about land exploitation, depletion, restoration and conservation.

Hopefully, the book will not only inform the reader about people and events, but also provide an understanding of the way people in local communities react to change. It is hoped the book will generate an understanding of the elements needed for a sense of community. Finally, it is hoped that this understanding will be helpful when local communities, states, and the Federal Government address local needs and plan future changes.

Chapter I

BEFORE THE SETTLERS[1]

The Pre-Contact Period

During the Ice Age, glaciers covered most of northern United States down to the Pennsylvania border. Grasses and sparse stands of pine and spruce covered nearly all the land south of the ice. Bands of hunters from the west followed herds of mastodon and mammoth as they moved south ahead of the glaciers.

Perhaps as much as 15,000 years ago, these bands came into the area of today's Montgomery County, Maryland. They brought survival technology and religious traditions that had developed over thousands of years. They were few in numbers and stayed in one place only long enough to make use of the flesh, hide and bones of their kill. Thus they were more creatures of their environment rather than modifiers of it.

Then, over more thousands of years, the ice slowly melted. Water formed rivers and filled deep gorges such as the Chesapeake Bay. Dense forests of oak, hickory and gum replaced pine and spruce and encroached upon the grasslands. Mastodons and mammoths either migrated north with the glaciers or became extinct. The woodlands supported caribou, elk, moose, black bear, wolf, beaver, lynx and musk-ox.

The hunters that remained near the Potomac River had to change their means of survival and their culture. Plant food sources became varied and abundant for gathering in specific seasons. To take advantage of these resources, the people set up seasonal camps, constructed shelters and made tools for hunting and fishing from raw materials nearby.

Modern climatic conditions stabilized from about 8,500 to 3,000 years ago, improving the supply of plants and animals for food, clothing and shelter. The human population increased and slowly became more sedentary. They developed heavy cooking utensils such as mortars and millstones that were difficult to carry from place to place. They cleared wooded areas and dressed timber with stone axes, adzes, chisels and gouges, probably to build shelters and possibly water craft. They constructed fish traps in the island channels of the Potomac River, remains of which can still be seen today.

Trade between native settlements became an important motivation for economic and social change. Natives in today's Washington, D.C., area had an abundant supply of soapstone that they used to make a variety of tools and utensils. There is reason to believe that the area was a regional source of these products.

As far back as 3,000 years ago, local Indians had domesticated plants such as sunflower, goosefoot, marsh elder and pigweed. Then during the first century A.D., traders from tribes to the west brought in the most important food crop of all: domesticated strains of maize. With this productive food crop, the local Indians increased their agricultural prowess, settled in villages, and obtained their game in designated hunting grounds.

Indians in the Colesville Area

When Captain John Smith made his historic voyage up the Potomac River in 1608, he found villages of Piscataway Indians scattered along the Potomac River and its Eastern Branch (now known as the Anacostia).* Approximately 35 miles from the head of the Chesapeake Bay, a community of Susquehannock Indians lived along the west bank of the Susquehanna River.

An Indian trade route ran between the Patuxent and Eastern Branch of the Potomac. It was part of a major trade route extending from the Northeast to Florida. Another trade route ran along the lower Appalachian mountains in lands occupied by Seneca tribes.

The area that is now Colesville lay north of the Potomac villages, south of Susquehannock territory and between the two trade routes. At the time of John Smith's voyage and until the beginning of the 18th Century, it was pristine and undisturbed except for seasonal hunting.

The rolling hills and stream valleys were mostly covered by dense stands of oak interspersed with hickory, maple, yellow poplar and dogwood.[2] Black bear, bobcat and panther made trails in the woods. White-tailed deer browsed on young trees and shrubs and grazed in meadows near streams. Wild turkey fed on seeds in the forest understory. Beaver cut down trees with their teeth to dam streams, to build lodges and for food. Fish filled the pools of larger streams. Muskrat, raccoon, gray fox, squirrel, rabbit and a host of other small animals and birds thrived in the forest.

In 1689, a British surveyor noted a "great Indian field" on the western edge of today's Colesville area.[3] It was located at a fork of the Northwest Branch, a few hundred feet north of the bridge on present-day

---

* Anacostia is an Indian name for River of Trade.

Randolph Road.[4] Recent soil samples taken at that location by staff of the Maryland National Capital Park and Planning Commission revealed evidence that a hunting and fishing camp had once been there.

Figure 1

Indians usually used such camps seasonally. They dried skins from the hunt and preserved the meat for winter. They gathered nuts, berries and other wild fruits and prepared them for storage.

Hunters for large animals used spears and bows and arrows. They made spearheads of chipped or flaked stone - usually quartzite that they obtained from a quarry located near Piney Branch. Bows were hickory, ash and locust with strings of sinew or strips of deer hide. Arrow heads were bone, horn or stone, and the shafts of arrows were from strong reeds or light wood. Feathers were added to the ends of arrows to guide the missiles in flight. The Indians often caught smaller animals in snares and used hooks made from bone and spears and nets for catching fish.

Wigwams in the seasonal camps were temporary and called hunting lodges. They were circular at the base and made of sapling poles thrust into the ground and tied together at their tops with vines. Grass mats, leafy boughs, bark and skins covered the framework. In cool weather, an opening in the roof allowed smoke to escape from a fire on the floor. Mats on the floor provided places to sit and sleep.

These Indians were slender, of medium height, and could withstand considerable exposure to heat, cold and other discomforts. Their eyes were dark, their hair black, coarse and straight. They wore clothes of softened skins, decorated with shells, beads, animal teeth and feathers. They draped the skins around their waist like an apron, or over their shoulders as a cloak. Moccasins and leggings, crafted from strips of hide and sometimes from bark protected their feet and legs. They applied bear grease to the skin to avoid insect bites and for protection from the cold. Red and blue pigment in plants and berries painted their faces and bodies.

Indians that hunted in the Colesville area probably lived in a village called Anacostank at a major fork of the Anacostia River. They were part of a group of tribes known as Nacotchtanks which were a part of the still larger Piscataway Complex. The Piscataways in turn were members of a still larger family of tribes, the Algonquins. All these tribes spoke related Algonquin languages.

Besides hunting and fishing, the men made dugout canoes by burning and scraping the insides of huge logs. Women and children took care of the meat and hides, carried out domestic chores and raised crops. After the men cleared an area in the forest by burning trees, the women planted squash, melons, pumpkins, maize, beans, peas, sunflowers and tobacco. Harvests were stored in large pits within the village grounds.

Figure 2: Location of Nacotchtank tribe

Social life consisted of music, dances, games and feasts. Their religion assumed an interdependency of humans, animals, plants, and inanimate objects such as land, air and water. They did not consider themselves separate from their environment but a part of it. Although they believed in many spirits associated with corn, sun, fire, thunder, stones, animals and other objects, they also believed in an overall spirit, Manito. They sacrificed to him the first of their returns from harvests, hunting and fishing. If they had led a good life, they expected another in a place of bliss. Only rulers of tribes and the Piscataway Complex were assured of taking their wealth with them into the hereafter. Evil persons were punished with suffering.

<u>Contact with the British</u>

When he visited them in 1608, Captain John Smith found the Indians on the Anacostia friendly and cooperative. The British valued beaver pelts for furs and a brisk trade developed.

In the 1620s, a raiding party led by two British captains from Jamestown burned the village of Anacostank. In the same decade, the Susquehannocks, who had built up a thriving trade with the British in their territory north of the Patuxent River, took to the warpath to eliminate competition from tribes along the Potomac. They overran villages and drove many inhabitants farther southeast. The Anacostanks, perhaps remembering the consequences of the earlier British attack, struck a deal with the Susquehannocks. They put themselves under the protection of the invaders from the north, and became go-betweens in trade with white men.

Beginning with the first emigration to Maryland in 1634, British settlers occupied more and more of the Indian hunting grounds. This deprived the natives of an important source of food, and many of them fled the area. Tribal wars and exposure to new diseases such as smallpox further decimated their numbers. Although 5,000 to 6,000 Indians lived in Maryland in the early 1600's, only a few hundred remained by 1700.

When the Anacostanks abandoned their hunting and fishing camp on the west bank of Northwest Branch is not known. The 1689 survey did not say if the site was still in use. However the description of it as a "great Indian field" would suggest that occupancy had been recent enough to leave noticeable evidence of Indian activity.[4]

What is certain is that the Indians no longer had a hunting camp in the Colesville area at the time of the survey. They had left only a small scar on the landscape that, barring further disturbances, probably would have healed completely over time. The flora and fauna of the area were not permanently affected in either quantity or quality.

Even though they worshiped the bear, corn, and other natural objects, there is no evidence that the Indians consciously applied environmental conservation practices. They exploited the natural resources around them. They destroyed trees and other plant life to raise crops. They did not hesitate to set fires to aid them when hunting big game. The minimal impact that Indians had on the area's environment was due primarily to their few numbers relative to the vast natural resources.

Notes for Chapter I: Before the Settlers

1. Unless otherwise noted, material in this chapter was compiled from:
   - T. H. S. Boyd, *The History of Montgomery County*, Regional Publishing Co., Baltimore, MD. Published 1879; reprinted 1968.
   - Robert J. Brugger, *Maryland, A Middle Temperament*, The Johns Hopkins University Press and Maryland Historical Society Baltimore, MD, 1988.
   - Thomas Francek, *An Illustrated History of the City of Washington*, The Junior League of Washington, D.C. Alfred A. Knopf, New York, NY, 1977.
   - Francis Jennings, "Indians and Frontiers in Seventeenth-Century Maryland," *Early Maryland in a Wider World*, edited by David B. Quinn, Wayne State University Detroit, MI, 1982, pp. 216-241.
   - Harold R. Manakee, *Indians of Early Maryland*, Maryland Historical Society Baltimore, MD, 1959.
   - Frank W. Porter III, *Maryland Indians Yesterday and Today*,

Museum and Library of the Maryland Historical Society Baltimore, MD, 1983.
- Stitt Robinson, "Conflicting Views on Landholding: Lord Baltimore and the Experiences of Colonial Maryland with Native Americans," *Maryland Historical Magazine, Vol. 83, No. 2, Summer 1988,* pp. 85-97.
- Carl Waldman, *Atlas of the North American Indian,* Facts on File, New York, NY, 1985.
- Stephen G. Hyslop, "Life in America 400 Years Ago," *Washington Post,* June 14, 1995, pp. H1, 4, 5.

2. E. D. Matthews, E. Z. W. Company, and J. C. Johnson, *Soil Survey of Montgomery County, Maryland,* Soil Conservation Service in cooperation with Maryland Agricultural Experiment Station October 1961, p. 58.

3. Patent C 3, pp. 557-559, 1695, MD Archives.

4. Frank W. Porter III, Op. Cit., p. 7. We do not know what evidence the 1689 surveyor found for a "great Indian field," but Porter states that "Indian field" was the European term for clearings made by killing trees with fire or cutting grooves around the trunk. Todd H. Barnett, *Ibid.*

Chapter II

GEORGE CALVERT'S LEGACY

While Indians seasonally occupied their hunting camp on the edge of today's Colesville area, political and religious turmoil in far away England set the stage for the area's future. When Queen Elizabeth died in 1603, the flamboyant period of British sea power began to wane. James I succeeded Elizabeth. He was 37 years old and had ruled Scotland as James VI since he was an infant. A "good-natured, conceited, garrulous King, wise in book-learning but a poor judge of men,"[*] he claimed divine hereditary right for himself and his heirs to the Crown.

He imprisoned Sir Walter Raleigh, a favorite of Queen Elizabeth, in the Tower of London for 13 years. He then released Raleigh for a gold-seeking expedition to South America. Raleigh had promised not to pick a fight with the Spanish, but he did and the king executed him for treason.

James I quarreled frequently with a parliament that continuously demanded more power. The king also was at odds with Puritans and others who refused to give allegiance to the Established Church of England and steadily increased their influence.

James I proclaimed the Church of England to be the only legitimate religious body and set himself up as its supreme leader. He also gave the Church powers in the courts, a move that further incensed the lawmakers in the parliament.

James tried to develop peaceful relations with England's enemies, particularly Spain, but the onset of the Thirty-Years' War interrupted these efforts. He still tried to placate Catholic Spain by offering to marry his son, Charles, to the Spanish infanta. When this effort turned into a fiasco, Charles was married to Henriette Maria of France, a zealous Roman Catholic. The Protestant - dominated parliament was infuriated.

During the reign of James I, settlement of Jamestown started and became the Royal Colony of Virginia. Because of the King's intolerance of dissident religions, there were many in England who looked to the New World for freedom. James I did not prevent their departure, provided they promised to live peacefully as English subjects. In allowing them to colonize the New World, James I not only rid England of their

---

[*] G. M. Trevelyan, *History of England, Volume Two*. Doubleday & Company, Inc., New York, NY, 3rd edition, 1952, p. 154.

troublesome presence, but also created overseas markets for England's growing manufacturing industry.

When James I died in 1625, his son obtained the throne as Charles I. The son was even more intolerant of dissident religions than James I. Bishops replaced noblemen and commoners as councilors to the Crown. After three attempts to work with his parliament, he dissolved the body and ruled without it. Opposition to his policies intensified. Oliver Cromwell, a Puritan, led an armed rebellion that overthrew the King, and in 1649, Charles I was executed.[1]

In this furnace of controversy, George Calvert spent his professional life, and by all accounts, he thrived in it.[2] The son of a Catholic Yorkshire gentleman , a 1597 graduate of Oxford, he followed the fashion of his times and traveled in continental Europe before entering public service. Although he first served in minor posts, his keen political acumen, ability to adopt and promote the policies of a Protestant king, and his unusual command of the language, attracted the help of influential patrons. He rose rapidly through the ranks. In 1613, King James I appointed him clerk of the Privy Council. After 1619, he was one of the two most important secretaries of state and a close adviser to the king. In 1621, Calvert served in the House of Commons as representative from Yorkshire. He used his persuasive powers trying to win the militant Puritans over to the king's hope of an alliance with Spain. He also strongly supported the failed effort to marry Prince Charles to the Spanish Infanta.

Figure 3: George Calvert (Maryland Historical Society)

James I rewarded Calvert generously for his services. He knighted his loyal councillor and made him a commissioner of the treasury with a pension of L 1000 a year plus a considerable subsidy on imported raw silk. As part of a policy to encourage settlement by British gentlemen on lands seized from Irish inhabitants, the King granted Calvert 2,300 acres in County Longford, Ireland. By developing estates, Calvert's grants grew to 5,000 acres, part of them in County Wexford. Calvert built a home in Ireland known as the Manor of Baltimore.

GEORGE CALVERT'S LEGACY

Calvert's ventures in Ireland were only part of his involvement with colonization efforts. His residence in London and his professional activities in affairs of state provided him with opportunities to make profitable investments in settlements outside England. As early as 1609, he invested in the Virginia Company and made a series of profitable investments in the East India Company. In 1621, he financed a fishing settlement on the Avalon Peninsula of Newfoundland.

Calvert's personal life underwent major changes in the 1620s. His wife, Anne, who bore him eleven children, died in childbirth in 1622. He married again and his second wife bore him several more children.[3]

Sometime before 1625, Calvert converted or reconverted to Catholicism. After helping to formulate and carry out the policies of a Protestant king for more than two decades, the reasons for his becoming a Catholic are not clear. Obviously he no longer could remain in a government post that would require his taking the Oath of Supremacy, which denied the ecclesiastical power of the pope. Was he tired of public service or disillusioned with the rule of James I? Were his rivals threatening his standing with the king and in the royal court? If so, did he use his conversion to a new faith as an excuse for leaving the government? Or was the reason even more personal - such as the possibility that his second wife was a Catholic and he converted to consummate the marriage? Or was his change of faith entirely a result of spiritual soul searching?

Whatever the reason, he could no longer accept the king as the ultimate authority in English religious affairs and submitted his recognition to James I in 1625. Grateful for Calvert's efforts, the king took no punitive action but gave the born-again Catholic the title of Baron of Baltimore (Lord Baltimore).

In 1623, Calvert had obtained a charter for his Avalon settlement in Newfoundland that gave him complete control. After his resignation from the government, he made a serious effort to develop Avalon into a thriving colony. He made two trips to Newfoundland, taking settlers with him, hoping to establish a successful plantation. During the second visit, he, his family and prospective settlers suffered through a frigid, debilitating winter that blasted his hopes and in 1629, he abandoned Avalon to the fishermen.

James I had died in 1625, and Calvert petitioned Charles I for a grant in the Royal Colony of Virginia. Calvert was a member of the Board of the Virginia Company, and he and Lady Baltimore visited Jamestown. His reception was cool to say the least, and the visit ended when Calvert, the Catholic, refused to take the Oath of Supremacy. Returning to

England, Calvert, despite failing health, successfully used his influence in the Royal Court to obtain a grant for the northern portion of the Virginia colony.

George Calvert died in early 1632 before the grant was signed. Throughout his adult life, he had worked within the political and religious environment of England to his professional and financial advantage. Although death barred him from the rewards of his greatest endeavor, the Calvert family did not lose. In June 1632, Charles I granted the land to Cecil Calvert, the second Lord Baltimore.

The new colony, named Maryland, after Queen Henrietta Maria, was not a royal colony like most of the other English territories in America. It was a gift to Lord Baltimore, a fiefdom, much like that bestowed by medieval English kings on loyal subjects. Cecil Calvert was Lord Proprietor of Maryland, answering only to the king for his actions. He owned all the land in the territory. He received all rents, taxes and fees, appointed officials needed to enforce laws and had final political and judicial authority in his domain. He had the power to grant lands in the same manner as the king had made the grant to him.

Within the terms of his proprietorship, he provided settlers in his colony all the rights of Englishmen. He established Maryland as a place of refuge for Catholics, Presbyterians, Quakers and those of other religions who suffered because they failed to conform to the orthodoxy of the Church of England. In doing so, he was following a policy of James I, which Cecil's father, George, may have helped formulate - to reduce the number of religious dissents in England and increase the overseas markets for English manufactured goods.[4]

Cecil Calvert and his descendants continued to be Lord Proprietors of Maryland until 1692, when William and Mary declared Maryland a royal colony. The Church of England became the official faith of Maryland. Colonists were subjected to the union of church and state that many of them had experienced in the home country. Parishes were established in every county. Taxes, paid in tobacco, were levied to support Anglican priests. Some Quakers refused to pay the tax; others joined with Presbyterians and Puritans in paying with the lowest grade of tobacco. Counties heavily populated by Presbyterians became known "to produce a very mean tobacco." Quakers, opposed to fighting, resisted demands that they swear allegiance to the state and support or join the militia. Many Quakers, who had been prominent in Provincial and local governments, retired from public life.

Catholics were major targets of the Anglican Church. Anglican clergy protested vehemently and repeatedly to the continuing activities of the

"Romish" priests. Catholic priests were not allowed to say mass in churches, but they bypassed this restriction by using private homes or dwellings in communities of priests.

In March of 1715, King George I returned proprietary privileges to Benedict Leonard Calvert, the fourth Lord Baltimore, who was an Anglican convert. Benedict died in April of the same year, and his 16-year-old successor, Charles Calvert, became the Lord Proprietor. Charles's guardians continued the oppression of non-Anglican religions. The ideal of religious tolerance promoted by Cecil Calvert ceased to exist. However, despite the hostility of the Anglican Church and restrictions on their social and political activities, Catholics, Quakers, Presbyterians and members of other non conforming sects adopted a variety of techniques for continuing the practice of their beliefs.

Notes for Chapter II: George Calvert's Legacy

1. These paragraphs on English history are drawn from G. M. Trevelyan, *History of England, Volume Two*, Doubleday & Company, Inc., New York, NY, 3rd edition, 1952, pp. 146-197.

2. With the exceptions noted below, the information on George Calvert and his son, Cecil, is drawn from Robert J. Brugger, *Maryland, a Middle Temperament*, Johns Hopkins University Press and Maryland Historical Society, Baltimore, MD, 1988, pp. 3-6, 12, 48-56, 80.

3. • Vera Foster Rollo, *Your Maryland: A History*. Maryland Historical Press, Lanham, MD, 1965, pp. 11-13. Photograph of George Calvert adapted from p. 12.
   • Russell B. Manard & Lois Green Carr, "The Lords Baltimore and the Colonization of Maryland," *Early Maryland in a Wider World*, edited by David B. Quinn, Wayne State University Detroit, MI, 1982.

4. G. M. Trevelyan, *Ibid*.

Chapter III

EARLIEST LANDOWNERS IN THE COLESVILLE AREA

To make their holdings profitable, the Lords Baltimore encouraged settlement of persons who would turn the wilderness into productive agriculture. At first they granted patents for land to gentlemen who transported five yeomen of working age to the new colony. Over the years, the acreage allotted was reduced, and in 1682, cash payments were required. The Lords Baltimore and their agents collected many fees for awarding the patents, including an annual quitrent* of four shillings per 100 acres. Gentlemen who acquired patents often resold them. To cash in on this activity, the Lords Baltimore collected an alienation transfer fine that was equivalent to one year's quitrent every time the land changed hands.[1]

The nine earliest patents in today's Colesville area were issued between 1714 and 1724. The holders of these patents were Archibald Edmonston, James Beall, Sr., James Beall, Jr., Charles and William Beall, and Richard Snowden. All were absentee owners.

They, or their immediate ancestors, had emigrated from Scotland and Wales. Some came to escape the intolerance of the King toward their religion. All came to exploit the opportunities for riches in a new environment. They were vigorous, enterprising men. Although some may have brought wealth with them from England, all of them accumulated it. By the early 18th Century, they were influential members of Maryland's rural gentry.

Specific information on these early landowners is not fully available, but as members of the rural gentry, they probably lived a life that would be envied by relatives in Britain. On their extensive plantations, they raised tobacco, other crops, and livestock. They first built clapboard houses with a single great room and an upstairs divided into bedrooms. Later they added rooms and a full second story. They often added wings of either clapboard or brick. A characteristic structure evolved that was two rooms deep and had chimneys at both ends. The homes were furnished as elegantly as their wealth would allow. Many furnishings were imported from England.

---

* Derived from the Medieval practice that required a tenant to pay a fee in lieu of services.

EARLIEST LANDOWNERS IN THE COLESVILLE AREA 13

Their food included luxury items such as coffee, sugar, spice, imported wines, rum, and bread made from wheat flour. Like those who were not so affluent, corn was a basic part of their diet. They baked it in tasty hoe cakes or served it as porridge. They served beef, ham, bacon, mutton, and chicken along with several vegetables, such as carrots, turnips, cabbage, parsnips, sweet potatoes, squash, and watermelon. Apples, pears, peaches, and quinces were eaten fresh or made into cider and other drinks. Added to all this, they served game and fish.

The members of the Snowden family were Quakers. They had a comfortable standard of living that reflected their wealth, but their social life was in accordance with the austere requirements of their religion.

The other early landowners in the Colesville area were Presbyterians. Besides participating in church activities, whole families visited from one plantation to another. The men gathered in groups for talk and gambling with cards. A popular sport was horse racing over a quarter mile stretch. Rules were few and wagering heavy. A man's reputation could rise or fall according to his willingness to accept challenges, the size of his bets, and the promptness with which he paid his debts.[2]

Labor for their plantations, field work, livestock care, and domestic services were supplied by slaves. Slave quarters were single room sheds with dirt floors and crude wood furniture.

Figure 5 shows the location of the patents obtained by these early landowners.[3]

James Beall, Sr.

James Beall, Sr., acquired his first land in the Colesville area in 1715 when he bought the 900-acre tract, known as *Easy Purchase*.

James Beall, Sr., owned a total of 1,989 acres. Besides *Easy Purchase*, they included *Addition to Easy Purchase*, *Drumeldry*, *Ballchrist* and part of *Beall's Manor*. (See Figure 4 for the location of these tracts. Overlays of these tracts on a 1987 map are shown in Figures 6-9.)

James Beall, Sr., also patented *Lahill*, containing 1,298 acres next to other Colesville tracts on the north and west.[4]

Born about 1665, James Beall, Sr., emigrated with two brothers from Fifeshire, Scotland, sometime after 1684. It was a time when the Church of England was making life difficult for Scotch Presbyterians. James and his brothers were land speculators. They accumulated patents, renting or selling their large tracts in smaller parcels, and amassing enough wealth to put them among the elite gentlemen of Prince George's County.

Before 1700, James Beall, Sr., married Sarah Pearce, daughter of John and Sarah Sprigg Pearce. James and his family enjoyed a high economic and social standard of living at their Prince George's County home on *Rover's Content* and *Fife*. (*Fife* is now a part of Washington, D.C.). Wealthy enough to ignore the hostility of the Anglican church, James was a trustee in the local Presbyterian church. When he died in 1725, he left eight children and Sarah, his widow.[5]

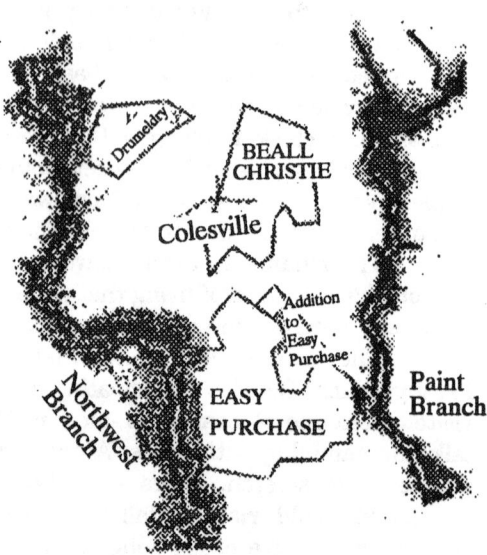

Figure 4: James Beall, Sr.'s, Patents

Charles and William Beall

Charles and William Beall were first generation descendants of immigrants from Scotland. Charles, a son of the colorful Ninian Beall,** was born in 1672 and died in 1740. His first wife was Mary Walstad, his second wife, Mary Price. He had six children. He had the title of captain for his service in the Colonial Militia. Charles also was known as a gentleman for his life style and as a carpenter (a term in those days for an architect). Unlike many Bealls, he was an Anglican and a founder of St. Paul's Church. His home was near the fork of the Eastern Branch (Anacostia River).[6]

** Ninian Beall emigrated from Scotland as an indentured servant. He eventually became a wealthy landowner, patriarch of a large family, and honored by the Provincial Assembly for his exploits as a leader in the Colonial Militia. His relationship to James and the other Bealls is not known.

EARLIEST LANDOWNERS IN THE COLESVILLE AREA   15

William Beall was a son of Alexander Beall, a brother of James Beall, Sr. Before 1712, he married Elizabeth Magruder, widow of Ninian Beall II. They had seven children. He is recorded as living in Frederick County in 1753 and died in 1756.[7]

In 1718, William patented a 317 acre tract known as *Wolfs Den*. It was on the Northwest Branch in the northwest corner of today's Colesville area.[8]

Charles and William patented *Beals Manor* in 1724.[9] It contained 1,787 acres and its irregular boundaries spread north and east from the heart of today's Colesville. (Overlays of these two tracts are shown in Figures 10 and 11.)

James Beall, Jr.

James Beall, Jr., a son of Alexander Beall, was born in 1698 and married Mary Ann Edmonston, daughter of Archibald Edmonston. They had seven children. He was known as James Jr. until his uncle, James Beall, Sr., died in 1725.

James Beall, Jr., obtained a patent for *The James and Mary* in 1720. This tract occupied the southeast portion of today's Colesville area. The original patent for 145 acres was resurveyed in 1728 and the area increased to 874 acres. (An overlay map of the tract is shown in Figure 12.)

James Beall, Jr., died in 1733, and his son, James, inherited *The James and Mary*.[10]

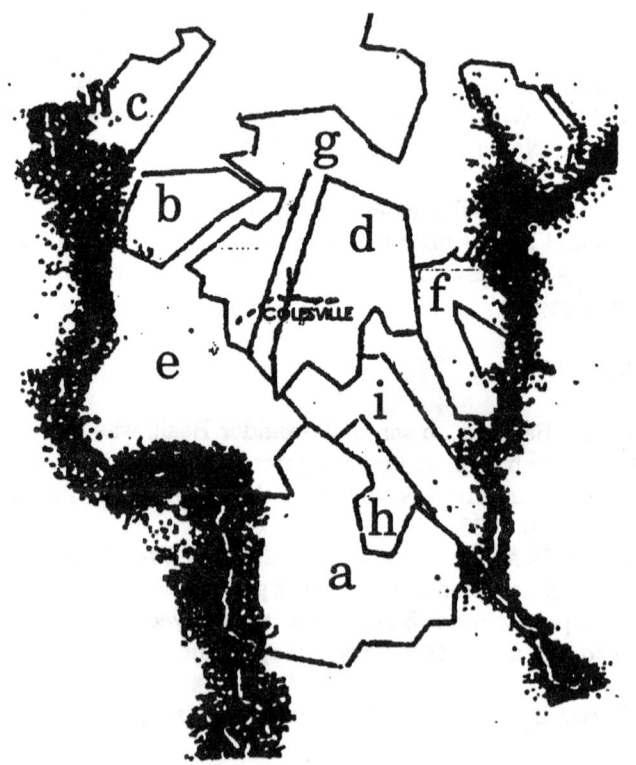

Figure 5:
Nine Earliest Patents in Colesville

	TRACT NAME	ACREAGE	YEAR PATENTED
a.	Easy Purchase	900	1714
b.	Drumeldry	225	1715
c.	Wolfs Den	317	1718
d.	The James & Mary	145	1720
	(resurveyed)	374	1728
e.	Ballchrist (Beall Christie)	503	1721
f.	Snowdens Fourth Additon to his Manor	6,449	1723
g.	Snowdens Mill (Certificate of Survey)	525	1723
h.	Beals Manor	1,787	1724
i.	Addition to Easy Purchase	153	1724

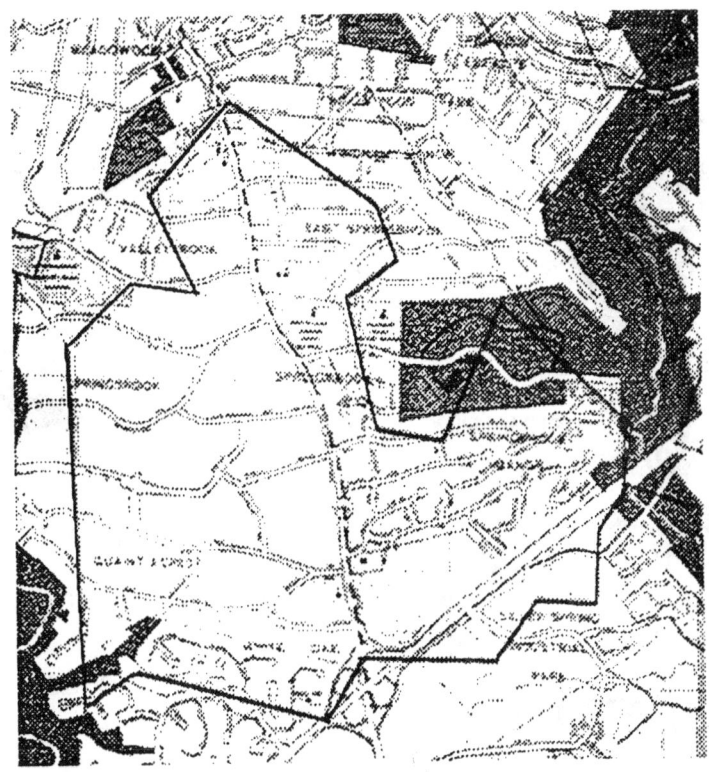

Figure 6: James Beall, Sr.'s,
Easy Purchase

Archibald Edmundson patented the tract in 1714. Beall bought it a year later. Containing 900 acres, it extended from just north of today's Seventh Day Adventist Church on New Hampshire Avenue, southward through the Valleybrook, East Springbrook, Springbrook, Springbrook Villa, Springbrook Manor, and Quaint Acres subdivisions to White Oak. (Dotted line follows the route of New Hampshire Avenue.)

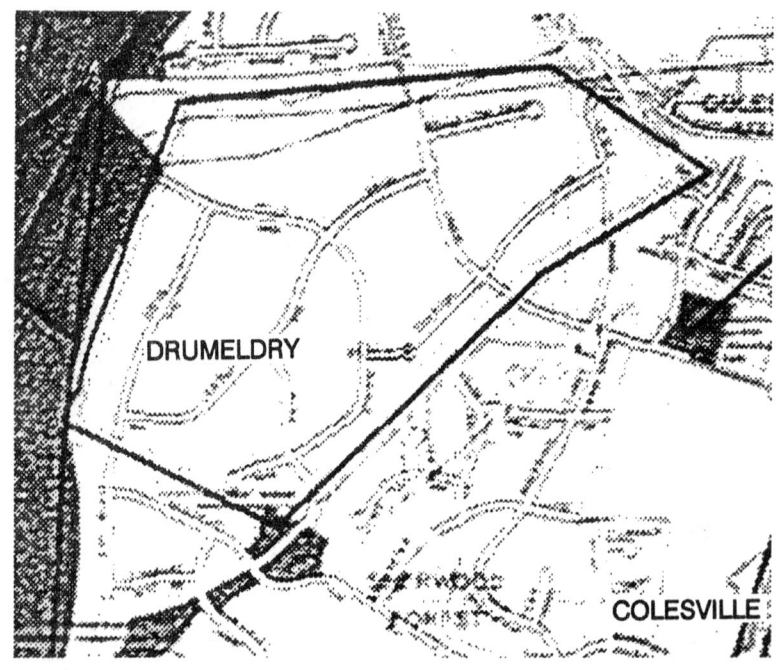

Figure 7: James Beall, Sr.'s,
Drumeldry

Patented in 1715 and containing 225 acres, it extended from Northwest Branch, near the Indian Spring Country Club, across Notley Road to Shannon Drive.

EARLIEST LANDOWNERS IN THE COLESVILLE AREA 19

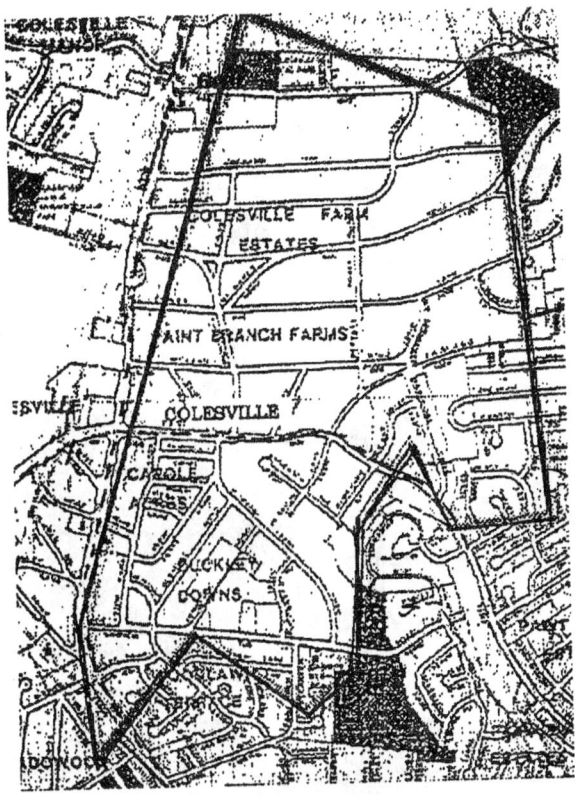

Figure 8: James Beall, Sr.'s,
Beall Christie

Patented in 1721 and containing 503 acres, it extended from north of Hobbs Drive southward through Colesville Park Estates, Paint Branch Farms, Carole Acres, and Buckley Downs, to Woodlawn Terrace subdivisions. It covered an area east of New Hampshire Avenue to Page Elementary School. (North-south dotted line follows route of New Hampshire Avenue. East-west dotted line follows route of Randolph Road.)

Figure 9: James Beall, Sr.'s
Addition to Easy Purchase

Patended in 1724, it contained 153 acres. Attached to the northeast border of *Easy Purchase*, it encompassed the Jackson Road Elementary School, part of the adjacent recreation center, and a narrow strip extending northwest to the vicinity of Rosemere Avenue.

EARLIEST LANDOWNERS IN THE COLESVILLE AREA 21

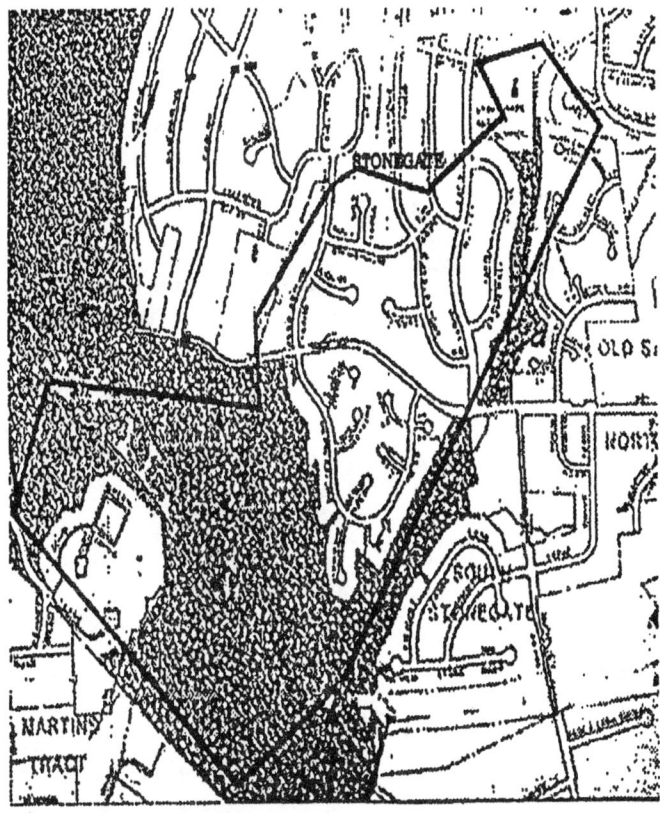

Figure 10: William Beale's *Wolfs Den*

Patented in 1718 for 317 acres, it straddled Bonifant Road in the Stonegate Subdivision area, extending from Stonegate Elementary School in the north, southward across Northwest Branch.

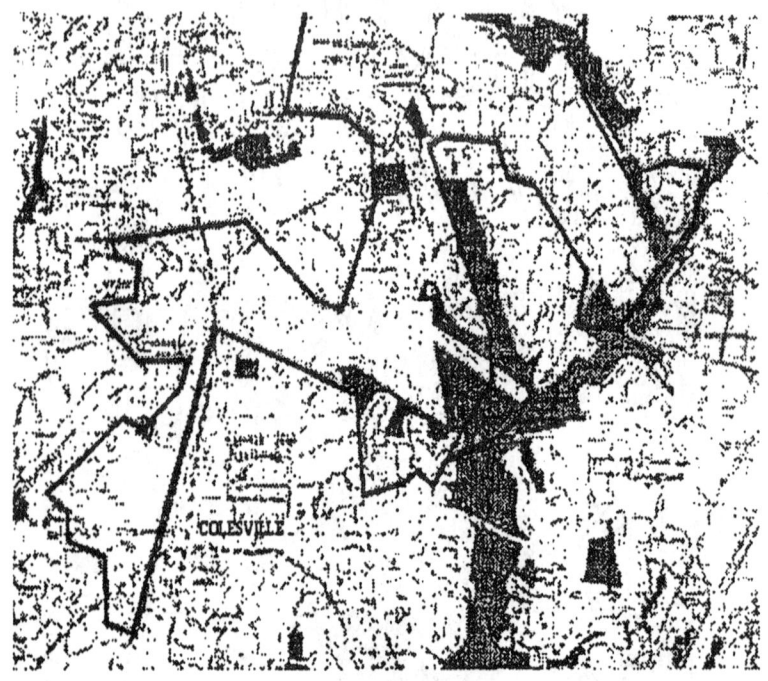

Figure 11: *Beals Manor*

Patented in 1724 by Charles and William Beall, it contained 1,787 acres. In the Colesville area, the tract extended from south of the Colesville United Methodist Church northward to Cape May - Good Hope Roads. Then it angled eastward into the valley Paint Branch.

EARLIEST LANDOWNERS IN THE COLESVILLE AREA

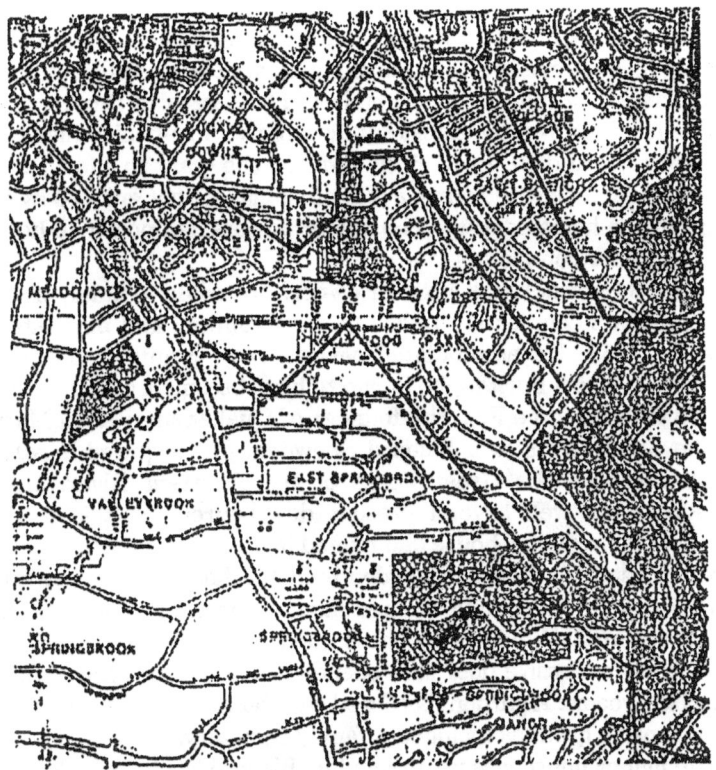

Figure 12: James Beall, Jr.'s, *The James and Mary*

Patented in 1720 and resurveyed in 1728, it contained 874 acres. One section ran from Woodlawn Terrace through Hollywood Park, Windham Manor, and East Springbrook subdivisions, and across Paint Branch. The second section started north of Randolph Road, ran southeast through Paint Branch Estates and across the branch.

Richard Snowden

When Cecil Calvert first promoted the development of his colony, he not only made provisions for awarding patents but also made possible the establishment of manors. He promised 2,000 acres to those who would provide for their own transport and that of five able-bodied men between the ages of 16 and 50. In 1635, he reduced the grant to 1,000 acres. The grantees could build and name a Manor similar to that enjoyed by English gentry in the home country. The manor owners had power to hold court to settle minor complaints.[11]

Richard Snowden was a manor owner. According to family history, he held a major's commission under Oliver Cromwell and emigrated from Wales in 1658. He accumulated several large grants from the Lords Baltimore. Once a Puritan, he is said to have become a convinced Quaker in 1672 when George Fox, the founder of Quakerism, visited Maryland.

The immigrant's son, Richard Snowden, Jr., acquired a patent for 16,068 acres on the Great Forks of the Patuxent River. His lands extended west well beyond present day Laurel. On this land,[***] in 1690, he built a manor house and named it *Birmingham Manor* after the Snowden estate in Wales. Snowden built the house in the English style with bricks to the second floor, then shingles formed the sidewalls leaning toward the roof. Windows on the second story were recessed. A front porch led to a massive door that opened into a hallway. Large fireplaces heated the rooms. A garden, bordered with boxwood, was near the house. The extensive grounds included a family cemetery.

The manor house was maintained by Richard Snowden's descendants until fire destroyed it in 1801.

The grandson of the immigrant Richard Snowden was born in 1688 and died in 1763. He was known as Richard Snowden "the youngest" or "the ironmaster." He acquired the latter cognomen because, before 1736, he engaged in the manufacture of iron. By his first wife, Elizabeth Coale Snowden, he had three daughters: Deborah, the first born, married James Brooke; Elizabeth, one year younger than Deborah, married John Thomas, and their two families were early settlers in the vicinity of Sandy Spring; and Mary, the third daughter, married Samuel Thomas and settled in the Colesville area. All three families were founders of the Sandy Spring Meeting of Friends.[12]

[***] The land is now part of the Patuxent Wildlife Sanctuary.

Richard Snowden, "the youngest," added 6,449 acres to the lands he had inherited by obtaining a patent for *Snowdens Fourth Addition to His Manor* in 1723.[13] Figure 13 shows how this tract related to other patents in the Colesville area. It is obvious that the surveyor had instructions to include as much vacant land as he could find among already patented lands.

The portion of *Snowdens Fourth Addition to His Manor* north of the eastern most point of *Drumeldry* became part of a 1753 resurvey which contained 9,265 acres. It was known as *Snowden's Manor Enlarged*.[14] The revised tract extended northward to Cloverly and beyond.

Snowden deeded the southern portion of this tract, containing 1,029 acres, to his son-in-law, Samuel Thomas, in 1748. It is known as *Part of Snowden's Fourth Addition to His Manor*.[15] It was located in the heart of today's Colesville area west of New Hampshire Avenue.

The process of obtaining a patent required the applicant to request a warrant for an approximate area of land. When the warrant was granted, the land was surveyed and a certificate of survey filed in the patent office. The filing of the certificate reserved the land for the holder of the warrant, but no quitrent was charged until a patent was awarded. Some land speculators took advantage of this procedure by filing a certificate of survey and avoiding quitrent by never obtaining a patent. Such was the case with the Certificate of Survey for *Snowdens Mill* filed by Richard Snowden in 1723.[16] It contained 546 acres, five acres of which were "cultivated with a small mill thereon." This mill, probably located where today's Fairland Road crosses Paint Branch, is the earliest known mill in Montgomery County.[17]

Another Certificate of Survey was filed in 1776 to reconcile the boundaries with those of *The James and Mary*.[18] The resurvey was ordered by Richard Snowden's estate and the tract contained 525+ acres. Figure 14 shows the relationship of this tract to 1987 subdivisions.

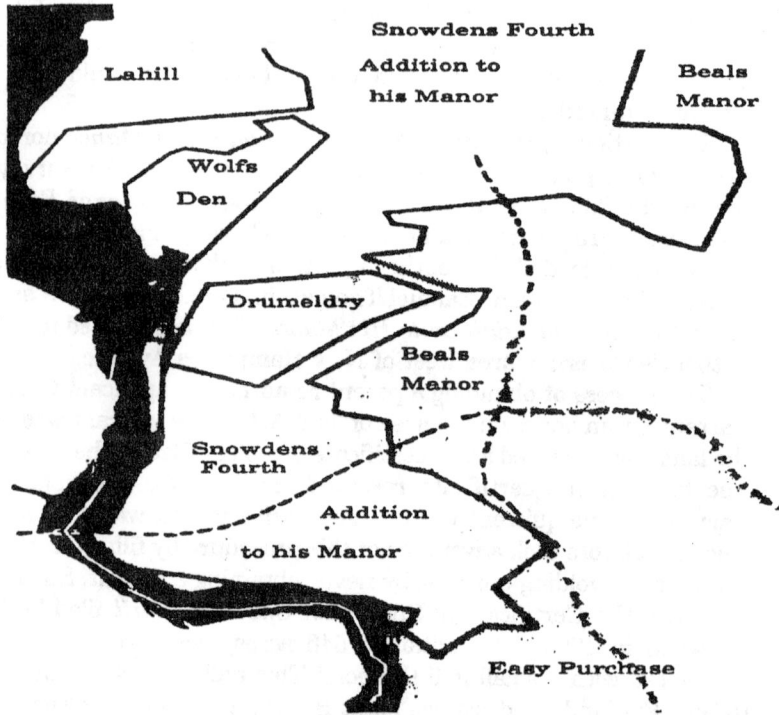

Figure 13: *Snowdens Fourth Addition to His Manor*

Patented in 1723 by Richard Snowden, the whole tract contained 8,449 acres. In the Colesville area, the tract started in the south with today's subdivision of North Springbrook and went north through Sherwood Forest Manor, Colesville Manor, South Stonegate, Stonegate, and Old Salem Village. (The north-south dotted line is the route of New Hampshire Avenue. The east-west line is the route of Randolph Road.)

EARLIEST LANDOWNERS IN THE COLESVILLE AREA 27

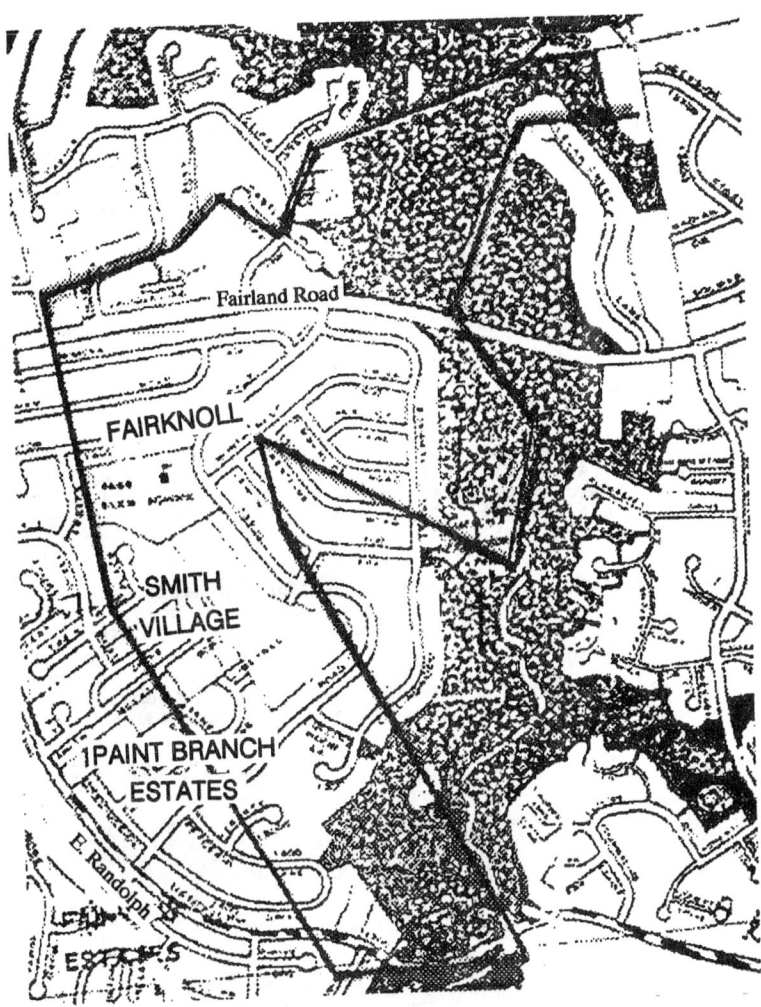

Figure 14: *Snowdens Mill*

Richard Snowden obtained a Certificate of Survey for this 325-1/4 acre tract in 1723. The original boundaries were modified in 1776. The southernmost point of the tract was just west of today's Valley Mill Park on East Randolph Road. The tract ran north through Paint Branch Estates, Smith Village, and Fairknoll. Above Fairland Road, it turned east and crossed Paint Branch.

Notes on Chapter III: The Earliest Landowners of the Colesville Area

1. Further details on the land system of early Maryland may be found in:
   - Robert J. Brugger, *Maryland, A Middle Temperament*, pp. 14-18.
   - Clarence P. Gould, *The Land System of Maryland 1720-1765*, Johns Hopkins University Press, Baltimore, MD, 1913.
   - Richard Walsh and William Lloyd Fox, *Maryland, A History 1632-1974*, Maryland Historical Society, Baltimore, MD, 1974.

2. Robert J. Brugger, Op. Cit., pp. 70-75.

3. The author is especially grateful to Robert Barendsen for the years of cooperative effort in developing the map for Figure 4. Without his participation, the map could not have been completed.

4. Patent EE 6, pp. 35-36, 1714, MD Archives. Rent Rolls 1651-1772, Bk. 4, p. 396, 449, MD Archives. Patent EE 6, p. 304, 1715, MD Archives. Patent FF 7, p. 199, 1716, MD Archives. Patent PL 4, p. 492, 1721, MD Archives. Patent PL 5, pp. 784-785, 1724, MD Archives.

5. - Louise Jorner Heinton, *Prince George's Heritage - Sidelights on the Early History of Prince George's County, Maryland, from 1696 to 1800*, The Maryland Historical Society, Baltimore, MD, 1972, p. 97.
   - Harry Wright Newman, *The Bealls of Maryland with Sketches of Allied Families of Edmonston and Beddo*, Unpublished Manuscript, MD Archives, MDHR G 2233, pp. 431-433.

6. Harry Wright Newman, Op. Cit., pp. 222, 303, 307, 415.

7. Harry Wright Newman, *Ibid*.

8. Patent FF 7, p. 370, 1718, MD Archives.

9. Patent PL 5, pp. 669-671, 1724, MD Archives.

10. - Patent PL 5, pp. 52-53, 1720, MD Archives. Patent PL 7, pp. 229-230, 1728, MD Archives.
    - Harry Wright Newman, Op. Cit., p. 375.

11. Robert J. Brugger, Op. Cit., p. 14.

12. Information drawn from:
    - Lawrence B. Thomas, *The Thomas Book*, The Henry J. Thomas Co., New York, NY, 1896. Reprinted by Heritage Books, Bowie, MD, 1994, Volume 2, pp. 508-509.
    - William G. Cook, *Montpelier and the Snowden Family 1976*.
    - Martha C. Nesbitt, Mary Reading Miller, et al., *Chronicles of Sandy Spring Friends Meeting and Environs*, Sandy Spring Monthly Meeting of the Religious Society of Friends, Sandy Spring, MD, 1987.

13. Patent LG & E, pp. 105-197, 1723, MD Archives.

14. Patent BY & GS, 4 pp., 577-581, 1753, MD Archives.

15. Deed, Prince George's Couty, EE 1, pp. 445-447, 1748.

16. Certificate of Survey 337, 1723, MD Archives.

17. Eleanor M. V. Cook, *Early Water Mills in Montgomery County*, The Montgomery County Story, Volume 33, p. 132, 1990.

18. Certificate of Survey 338, 1776, MD Archives.

Chapter IV

THE SETTLERS

As mentioned in the previous chapter, the earliest landowners were speculators, willing to sell their holdings for whatever purpose would bring them the greatest return. Their primary interest in the natural resources was timber, grasslands, and water. They paid particular attention to the availability of streams for navigation because roads were nonexistent. They also had water power in mind for the construction of mills. However, they did not directly change the environment. This was left to the settlers, who came in to establish farms.

The Lazenbys - Frontier Farmers

Robert Lazenby, thought to be a son of Henry Lazenby, High Sheriff of Anne Arundel County, was the person from whom most of the Lazenbys in the United States descended.[1] He purchased 217 acres of *Wolfs Den* from William Beall in 1723. Because he was living on the land at the time,[2] he and his family were the first known settlers in the area of today's Colesville.

Lazenby's property occupied the southern portion of *Wolfs Den*. It straddled today's Bonifant Road and lay between the Northwest Branch and one or more of its tributaries. Much of the land near the river and streams would have been marshy and/or permanently covered with brush and trees, making the land available for crops relatively small. However, the at-hand opportunity to hunt, trap and fish probably offset the disadvantage of small crop acreage. Whether

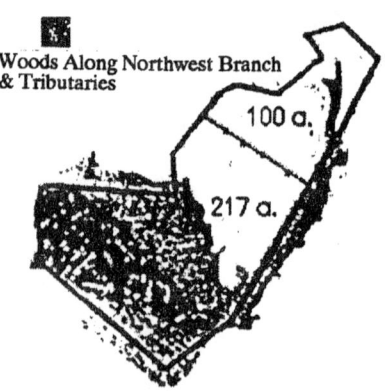

Figure 15: Robert Lazenby's 217 acres of *Wolfs Den*

THE SETTLERS

Lazenby leased the other 100 acres of *Wolfs Den* from the owner, Ignatius Perry, is not known.*

Robert and his wife, Ann, had two sons: Robert, born about 1719, and Henry, born in 1721.[3] We do not know exactly how the Lazenbys lived. However, like other frontier families, their life would have been a sharp contrast to that of the landed gentry.

Their first need was water. A bubbling spring provided drinking water. The nearby headwaters of Northwest Branch provided water for other needs, including, in those days, navigation by canoe, dugout, or raft.

Except for grass meadows that may have been close to the river, timber covered their property. The Lazenbys' house was of wood, probably a one room cabin with a loft above. Logs of yellow poplar (tulip poplar) were smoothed on one side and made into puncheon floors. Logs also were split and matched pairs laid horizontally to form flat inside walls. Sometimes logs were sawed with one edge wider than the other to form clapboards that could be overlapped as siding for a cabin. The green boards often shrank as they dried and required constant chinking with clay. White oak shingles, split-rail fences, fuel for their fires, furniture and many cooking utensils were hand hewn from native timber.

Chimneys sometimes were made of clay over sticks and poles. More permanent structures were of stone, which was often found far from the house and hauled on sleds by oxen.

A woodshed, nearby or attached to the cabin, stored hickory, maple, and oak. Pine wood and pine knots made good kindling. Poplar and chestnut were seldom used for fire because the former gave off little heat and the latter "popped" so much it threatened to set a cabin aflame.

The early frontier family had a log building to store and preserve meat. When hogs, deer, or bears were butchered in the fall, the meat was laid on a shelf at the far end of the building. It was cured by covering each layer with a thick coat of imported salt. To protect it from "varmints" and keep it dry, the cured meat was hung from poles that spanned the interior of the meat house.

An apple house, made with thick rock walls, had two floors. The upper floor stored soft, summer apples and other fruit from the orchard, while the lower floor held winter apples. Sometimes sliced apples were

---

* Ignatius Perry purchased his 100 acres of *Wolfs Den* from William Beall in 1723 - the same time Robert Lazenby purchased his share. However, no evidence has been found indicating that Perry lived on the land.

dried on homemade scaffolds and then tied in clean clothes and hung from the rafters.

The family had a log crib to store their most important food crop - Indian maize or corn. Corn was not only a feed for livestock, but also the chief item in the family's diet. It was eaten as roasting ears and ground into corn meal and served as hoe cakes, corn bread, and corn meal mush.

A picket fence surrounded the garden to keep deer and other animals from foraging on the beans, cabbage, lettuce, onions, peppers, cucumbers, beets, turnips, potatoes, and pumpkins. Even that protection did not always keep out all rabbits, squirrels, woodchucks, and crows. A farmyard dog dealt with those pests.

Other buildings on the farmstead included a log springhouse that protected the drinking water supply. Evaporation from the running water cooled the air to keep melons, sweet milk, and crocks of buttermilk for days. Still other buildings included a blacksmith shop and sheds for livestock and for drying tobacco, the most important cash crop. Also a barn with stalls and hay mow to house oxen, horses and cattle would be added. Essential to the food supply was a dairy cow for milk and butter.

Women and children not only carried out chores around the house, but also tended the garden and milked the cows. They also worked in the fields with the men. When farm activity increased, a single-room log cabin or two with dirt floors and crude furnishings would be built to house one or more families of slaves or indentured servants.[4]

The family added to their food supply by hunting, trapping, and fishing. Furs and skins of beaver, bear, and deer as well as rough cloth were used for clothing. Because of the location among the tributaries of Northwest Branch, the Lazenbys may have sold pelts of trapped animals for cash.[5]

The main cash crop was tobacco. The Lazenbys, like other Maryland pioneers, sewed tobacco seeds in beds and transplanted the seedlings to the field. There, they hoed and hilled the soil around the plants to destroy weeds and hold the soil around the base of the stems. They topped the plants to provide the most growth for leaves and "suckered," i.e. removed, lower leaves and side stems to allow maximum growth for the upper six or eight leaves.

At harvest time, the Lazenbys cut the stalks and left them in the field to wither for a short time in the sun. They tied the stems on poles and hung them in a shed to dry. At the proper time, they removed the stems from the poles and piled them in a covered heap. The next jobs were removing the leaves from the stems, called "stemming," and stripping out the long fibers from the leaves. After tying the leaves in bundles, they packed them into large barrels known as hogsheads. Each hogshead contained about 1,100 pounds of tobacco.[6]

Because the production of tobacco was handwork, it required a large amount of labor. Unless a pioneer family, on a farm the size of the Lazenbys', included several children of working age, a family of slaves, or one or more indentured servants, would be kept to do the work.

Robert Lazenby died in 1724, only one year after purchasing his portion of *Wolfs Den*.[7] The cause of his death is unknown. It could have been a farm or hunting accident or illness. Of the diseases that permeated the early settlers environment, bloody flux (influenza), smallpox, diphtheria, yellow fever, and malaria were common.[8] Whatever the cause, Robert's widow, Ann, and the two small boys were left to fend for themselves.

Nothing is known of the years between Robert's death and the time when the boys reached adulthood. Did Ann farm the land herself, possibly with the help of a family of slaves and such help as the boys could give? She may have lived with her parents, but they are unknown. Her father-in-law, Henry Lazenby of Anne Arundel County, died in 1723, but she might have lived with his family while the boys were growing. If she remarried, there is no record, and if she did, the boys retained the Lazenby name.

Records do show that in 1748, at ages of 29 and 27 years respectively, Robert and Henry were members of Captain George Beall's Troop of Horse. This was a unit of the Provincial Militia that helped protect settlers from the Indians, probably in western Maryland.[9] For their services, the two Lazenbys would have received pay in pounds of tobacco.[10]

Records also show that, in 1760, Henry purchased 100 acres of land just outside the west edge of today's Colesville area. He built a home there, and added 82 acres during later years. He died in 1788, but his family remained on the property until 1920.[11]

Robert inherited the 217 acres of *Wolfs Den* and lived there until his death in 1785. In 1748, he married Lucy Harding.[12] The size of the Lazenby farm operations was typical of the early settlers in the area. They kept a few slaves, probably grew tobacco and corn, had several horses for work and travel, and grazed between 15 and 20 head of cattle. The records show that 67 acres were cleared in 1783.[13]

Robert served on juries in Frederick County in 1753 and 1755.[14] His wife, after giving birth to seven sons and two daughters, died sometime in the late 1760s or early 1770s. About 1777, Robert married Martha Brewer Odell. She was a widow and, at the time of her marriage to Robert, had two sons and five daughters, all of the latter already married.[15]

Records show that six of Robert and Lucy's sons saw action in the Revolutionary War: Robert, the eldest, served in the Maryland Militia; Elias was an ensign with the Maryland forces; Thomas was in the 7th Company, Upper Battalion of the Montgomery County Militia; Alexander and Henry were with the Maryland Flying Camp (a unit of the Continental Army); and Joshua belonged to Company 1, 29th Lower Battalion of the Maryland Militia.[16]

All six sons survived their service in the armed forces. At the war's end, they, like many others, may have had high expectations of a better life, but these could not be realized without drastic personal adjustments. Except for freedom from British rule, life became even more difficult. Taxes climbed higher to pay the war's expenses. Also, like many Maryland farmers, the Lazenbys undoubtedly experienced economic hardship caused by a depressed price for their main crop, tobacco. Also, like others, they no doubt had been obtaining low yields from soils depleted by growing tobacco year after year. The technologies of soil conservation were still unknown. The growing of tobacco and other row crops not only drained the soil of fertility but eroded it severely. Run-off silted the Northwest Branch and reduced its use for navigation. The use of fertilizers was still many years off, and the only method for restoring soil was to let it rest for several years. With only 68 acres of cleared land, the Lazenbys could not have managed that.

Even if the 68 acres of cleared land had been highly fertile, the Lazenby farm could not have supported a livelihood for seven sons and two daughters. Fortunately, the third generation was young enough at the end of the war to take on the challenges of change in their economic and physical environment.[17]

All the sons and daughters of Robert and Lucy Lazenby moved out of the Colesville area. Before the end of the war, young Robert was reported living in Georgetown, and from there is thought to have moved to Bedford County, Virginia. John, Thomas, Henry, Joshua, and their sister, Elizabeth, joined the Maryland migration to the more fertile lands of North Carolina and were living there by 1790. Elias became the founder of the Lazenby family in Georgia. Alexander is thought to have settled in Nashville, Tennessee.[18]

Robert's will of 1785 provided that his 217 acres of *Wolfs Den* be sold within 12 months of his death. The proceeds were to be divided among his children, with dower's rights to his widow and a child's share to Thomas Odell, one of her sons. Accordingly, Wolfs Den was sold to Samuel Bonifant (Bonnifield) in 1787.[19]

Samuel and Mary Thomas - Plantation Owners

Samuel Thomas's grandfather was a founder of the Herring Creek and West River Meetings of Friends in Anne Arundel County. His grandmother and father were Quaker ministers. Born in 1702, Samuel also became a Quaker minister. In 1730, he married Mary Snowden, daughter of the wealthy Quaker, Richard Snowden.[20]

Samuel's first land holding was a 1737 patent on *Saint Winexbergh*, a tract of 493 acres west of Northwest Branch. In 1748, he bought *Part of Snowdens Fourth Addition to His Manor* from his father-in-law, Richard Snowden. It contained 1,029 acres. In 1757, he bought 216 acres of *Beals Manor*, bringing his holdings to 1,738 acres.[21]

Although Samuel and Mary Thomas's plantation was large compared to other holdings in the Colesville area, it was not nearly as large as the plantation of their brother-in-law, James Brooke. Starting in 1728 with 889 acres in the Sandy Spring area, he increased the acreage of his holdings to 22,834.[22]

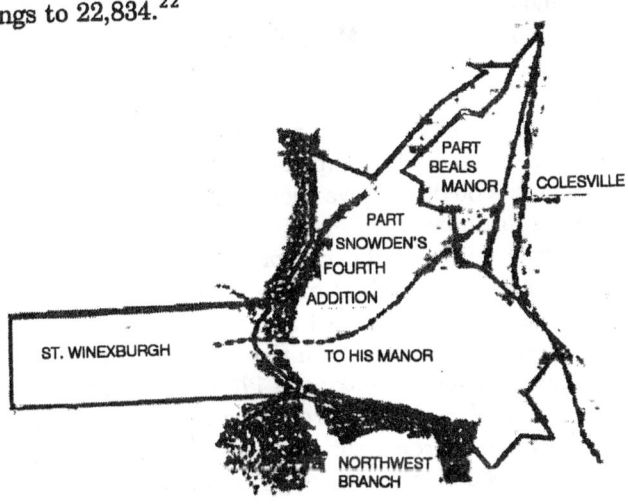

Figure 16: The Lands of Samuel Thomas

When Samuel and Mary Thomas settled in the Colesville area is not known. Except for the recorded existence of houses on the *Saint Winexbergh* tract some fifty years after the 1737 patent, there is no evidence that they ever lived there.[23] On the other hand, they did live on the *Part of Snowdens Fourth Addition to His Manor* purchased from Richard Snowden and could have lived there as tenants before the purchase.[24]

The exact location of their house has been a subject for considerable speculation. However, the first parcel of the 1,029 acres was sold two years after Samuel Thomas's death. The 1785 deed specified the existence of houses. The location of the parcel strongly suggests that the houses were on present-day Randolph Road. One of them could have been the residence of Samuel and Mary Thomas.

The outbuildings on the plantation could have included livestock barns, tobacco drying sheds, a blacksmith shop, crop storage, and other buildings. They would have been similar to those on the Lazenby farm, but probably more substantial and numerous. Log cabins for slave quarters probably were part of the farmstead and scattered in outlying fields. The largest acreage in crops would have been divided between tobacco and corn.

Both Samuel and Mary Thomas were active Quakers. Samuel is considered to be a founder of the Sandy Spring Meeting of Friends. At the weekly and monthly meetings, they were joined with other Quakers, many of whom were in-laws and cousins. As Quakers, their life style was austere and simple with emphasis on the work ethic. However, their financial status no doubt gave them comforts not known to small farmers such as the Lazenbys.

Their affluence did not protect them from diseases and other causes of death so prevalent in the frontier environment. Of their four children, one died as an infant and a second son died at the age of 19. They were more fortunate with the other two children. Elizabeth, born in 1735, married Johns Hopkins in 1758, and became the grandmother of Johns Hopkins II, the Baltimore financier and philanthropist. Evan, born in 1738, became a prominent and controversial Quaker, not only in the Sandy Spring Meeting but throughout Maryland.[25]

John Berry - Mid-Sized Planter

John Berry was born in 1736, the son of Benjamin Berry, known in Prince George's County as the "planter" and the "innholder."

John bought *Drumeldry* from Josias Beall** when he was twenty-five.²⁶ He married Eleanor Bowie Clagett six years later and they had four sons and two daughters.²⁷

John Berry, like Robert Lazenby, started as a small planter. He owned 225 acres of *Drumeldry*, to which he later added 25 acres. In the 1783 tax assessment, his cleared land of 123 acres on *Drumeldry* was one of only two tracts in the Colesville area for which the soil was rated "good." The soils in all the other tracts were considered either "middling" or "thin."

However, the 1783 "good" rating does not mean that the soil type on *Drumeldry* was superior to that of other tracts in the area. To the contrary, a 1961 soil survey of Montgomery County shows that the soils of *Drumeldry* were gravelly or silt loams commonly found throughout the Colesville area. The most likely reason for the "good" rating of *Drumeldry* soils in 1783 is that John Berry was the first person to farm the tract. This conclusion is substantiated by the fact that there is no evidence any of the prior owners lived on *Drumeldry*. Because John Berry probably was the first to farm *Drumeldry*, then his "good" soils would have been cropped for only 15 years by 1783. In contrast, the "thin" soils of the area had been cropped for thirty or more years.

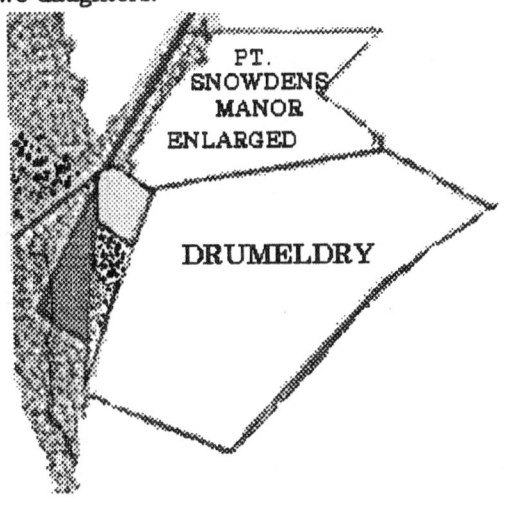

Figure 17: The Lands of John Berry

** Josias Beall was a grandson of James Beall, Sr., who patented *Drumeldry*. See Chapter III.

Like others in the area, tobacco would have been John Berry's major crop. It was common practice to raise tobacco continuously on a field for about three seasons and then let the land lay fallow (idle) for as many as twenty years. The idle land grew up in brush and sapling trees, giving rise to the "sapling" description of it. John Berry apparently did not have enough "sapling" land in 1783 to have it classified in the survey. This is additional evidence that Berry could have been the first person to clear and farm *Drumeldry*.

Still further evidence is the existence of wooded land considered "timber" in 1783. This suggests that some original forest of *Drumeldry* had not been cut.

John Berry and his family lived in a frame house. They cured and stored tobacco in a 30 x 20 foot shed. In addition, they probably raised several acres of corn. He had a family of slaves for field and domestic work, kept half a dozen horses for work and travel, and maintained a herd of about 20 cattle.[28]

John Berry served in the Colonial Militia. He was a justice for the Frederick County court that had jurisdiction over civil cases and many criminal cases. The court levied taxes for local projects, laid out and maintained public roads, policed weights and measures, and licensed taverns. The justices heard disputes between masters and servants, supervised election of delegates to the Provincial assembly and oversaw the placement and welfare of orphans.[29]

When John Berry died in 1786, his wife, Eleanor, inherited *Drumeldry* and the added 25 acres. His will provided that the land should go to his eldest son, Benjamin, when Eleanor died.[30]

James Odell - Also a Mid-Sized Planter

James Odell was a grandson of James Beall, Sr. In 1747, his parents, Thomas and Mary Odell, deeded him 300 acres of a tract known as *Beal Christie*.[31] It was located in the central part of today's Colesville area and east of New Hampshire Avenue.

Although his parents were absentee owners, James lived on his 300 acres. Like John Berry, he would have been a mid-sized planter, raising tobacco and corn, keeping several head of livestock and having a few slaves.

In 1748, James was a corporal in Thomas Sappington's unit of the Colonial Militia.[32] He served as a juror for Frederick County in 1750. From 1754-1756, he was the county road supervisor for the route of the current New Hampshire Avenue through the Colesville area.[33]

THE SETTLERS

James's son, Thomas, was born in 1753, and inherited the 300 acres owned by his father. Thomas's first wife was Elizabeth Garrett; his second was Gracie Austin. He had more than seven children.[1]

Thomas Odell was an active patriot before and during the Revolutionary War. When the Second Maryland Convention met in the fall of 1774, the members organized the Association of Free Men. They established a Council of Safety to carry out their resolutions. At the county level, extra legal Committees of Observation took on the power of justices of the peace and enforced the Association's actions. In 1775, Thomas Odell was a member of the Committee of Observation for Frederick County. In 1776, he was commissioned a lieutenant in the Frederick County Militia.[2]

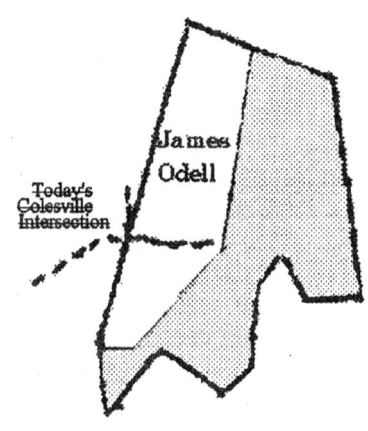

Figure 18: James Odell's portion of *Beall Christie*

Like the Lazenbys, perhaps for the same reasons of a large extended family and a worn out farm, the Odells had fled Maryland by 1790. Thomas Odell was living in Virginia in 1785 and he sold 100 acres in the southwestern corner of *Beall Christie* to Richard Jones. In 1792, Odell sold his remaining 200 acres to Jeremiah Berry. He died in Decatur, Illinois, in 1827.[3]

More Turnover of Farms

The changes in land ownership in the Colesville area during the 18th Century were not confined to the Lazenbys, Berrys, and Odells. The tracts called *Beals Manor* and *Easy Purchase* are representative of the others.

As mentioned in Chapter III, Charles and William Beall patented *Beals Manor* in 1724. It contained 1,787 acres. The tract originated in the central part of today's Colesville area and extended north and east. James

Beall, Sr., purchased 216 acres and gave them to his daughter, who sold them to Samuel Thomas. They were in the heart of the Colesville area.

Other parcels were sold to persons who established farms. Families such as the Williamses and Cases held on to their lands for more than one generation before they sold them. Others, including John Davis, Wm. Dunkin, Valentine Myers, Wm. Waters, John Trundle, and Alexander Estep lived on their properties for a relatively short time. (Admittedly, a "relatively short time" of 10 to 20 years could have been a lifetime in the 18th century.)

James Beall, Sr., bought the 900-acre tract of *Easy Purchase* in 1715. The pattern of ownership for the parcels that Beall and his family sold was similar to that for *Beals Manor*. Some of the 18th century owners were John Ramsey, Chris Sowndes, and Jeremiah Orme. Only Orme would still be an owner in the century to follow.

During the 18th century, the Colesville area was transformed from a wilderness, not even used by Indians for hunting, to large tracts held by land speculators. They sold the land to frontier farmers who felled much of the forest, bled the soil of its fertility, silted streams from eroded fields, and sold out. These farmers were not greedy nor were they deliberately destructive of natural resources. Farming was a risky venture. Early settlers struggled against adverse weather, floods, and diseases of plants, animals, and humans for which there were no known controls. They experienced economic hardship because of depressed or volatile prices for tobacco. They were impacted by an unstable political system and the turmoil of the Revolutionary War. Those who survived had large land and financial resources, and the most notable of these was Evan Thomas.

Notes on Chapter IV: The Settlers

1. Mary Lazenby, *Lazenby Notes on the American Families*, copied in 1933 by Addie Bell Baggerly Chase at D.A.R. Library, Washington, D.C. Copy is in Montgomery County Historical Society Library, Rockville, MD, p. 5.

2. Rent Rolls 1651-1772, Book 4, MD Archives, p. 433. Deed, Prince George's County, Book I, p. 400, 1723.

3. Mary Lazenby, Op. Cit., pp. 5, 6.

4. Indentured servants were persons who placed themselves under contract to work for another over a period of years, usually seven. The contract was accepted in exchange for transportation to America. Convicts also were transported to America as indentured servants. It has been reported that Ninian Beall, who became a wealthy landowner in Maryland and a prominent citizen, started as an indentured servant.

5. Information drawn from:
   * Robert J. Brugger, Op. Cit., p. 25.
   * Jane C. Sween, Montgomery County, *Two Centuries of Change*, Windsor Publications, Inc., Woodland Mills, CA, 1984, pp. 19-20.
   * Great Smoky Mountains Natural History Society in cooperation with the National Park Service, *Pioneer Farmstead*, pp. 1-10.

6. Paul Wilstach, *Potomac Landings*, Tudor Publishing Co., New York, NY, 1937, pp. 89-91.

7. Mary Lazenby, Op. Cit., p. 6.

8. * Robert J. Brugger, Op. Cit., pp. 22-23.
   * John Duffy, *Epidemics in Colonial America*, Louisiana State University Press, 1953, 274 pp.

9. Mary Lazenby, *Ibid*.

10. Maryland Assembly Proceedings Archives of Maryland II, 1666-1676, p. 464.

11. Mary Lazenby, Op. Cit., p. 9.

12. Mary Lazenby, Op. Cit., p. 6.

13. Assessment Book, Montgomery County, 1783.

14. Millard Milburn Rice, *This Was the Life*, Monocacy Book Co., Redwood, CA, 1979.

15. Mary Lazenby, Op. Cit., p. 8.

16. Mary Lazenby, *Ibid*.

17. Todd H. Barnett, *Ibid*.

18. Mary Lazenby, *Ibid*.

19. Deeds, Montgomery County, Book C, p. 424, 1786. Deeds, Montgomery County, Book C, p. 683, 1787.

20. * Martha C. Nesbitt, et al., Op. Cit., pp. 9-11.
    * Lawrence B. Thomas, *The Thomas Book*, Henry F. Thomas Co., New York, NY, 1895. Reprint by Heritage Books Bowie, MD, 1994, Vol 1, p. 60.

21. Patent E 1, pp. 528-529, 1737, MD Archives. Deed, Montgomery County, Book EE 1, pp. 445-447, 1748. Deed, Montgomery County, Book F, pp. 323-324, 1757.

22. * Martha C. Nesbitt, Op. Cit., p. 34.
    * Ray Eldon Hiebert & Richard K. MacMaster, *A Grateful Remembrance, The Story of Montgomery County, Maryland*, Montgomery County Government & Montgomery County Historical Society, Rockville, MD, 1978, p. 11.

23. Deed, Montgomery County, Book D, pp. 56-57, 1788.

24. Deed, Frederick County, Book L, pp. 211-213, 1768. This deed transfers the 1,029 acres of *Part of Snowdens Fourth Addition to*

His Manor from Samuel Thomas to Evan Thomas, but exempts the house in which Samuel Thomas lived.

25. • Martha C. Nesbitt, et al., Op. Cit., p. 35.
    • William C. Cook, *Ibid.*

26. Deed, Prince George's County, Book EE, p. 199, 1761. Deed, Frederick County, Book G, pp. 355-367, 1761.

27. George F. Griffiths, "The Berrys of Maryland," December 1976, pp. 18-22.

28. • Assessment Book, Montgomery County, 1783-1797, p. 166.
    • E. Z. W. Company, et al., Op. Cit., p. 105 and Map 39.
    • Todd H. Barnett, "Planters, Tenants, and Slaves: a Portrait of Montgomery County in 1783", Maryland Historical Magazine Baltimore, MD, Volume 89, Summer 1994, pp. 184-203.

29. • Millard Milburn Rice, Op. Cit., p. ?.
    • George F. Griffiths, Ibid.

30. Abstracts of Wills, Montgomery County, 1776-1865, p. 15.

31. Deed, Prince George's County, Book EE, p. 364, 1747.

32. Louise Jorner Heinton, Op. Cit., p. 157.

33. • Millard Milburn Rice, Op. Cit., p. 53.
    • Court Minutes, Frederick County, 1750-1772, November 1754, 1755, 1756.

34. Gen. Rec. Comm. Serv., Volume 2, p. 53.

35. *Journal for Council of Safety*, Volume 2, 1775-1776, MD Archives.

36. • United States Census 1790.
    • Deed, Montgomery County, Book C, p. 342, 1786.
    • Deed, Montgomery County, Book E, p. 111, 1792.
    • Journal for Council of Safety, *Ibid.*

Chapter V

EVAN THOMAS
MOUNT RADNOR'S EMINENT QUAKER

Evan Thomas was the most prominent person in the Colesville area during the latter half of the 18th Century. Quaker minister, plantation owner, public servant, dissenter, freer of slaves and family man, he left his mark not only on the future of the area but also on the whole of Maryland.

He was born January 21, 1738, the youngest of five children of Samuel and Mary Snowden Thomas. His two older brothers died at young ages.

Samuel and Mary Thomas owned the largest 18th century plantation in today's Colesville area and were very active in the Sandy Spring Meeting of the Society of Friends. Although the plantation was operated with the help of slaves, there is reason to be believe that his Quaker parents insisted that Evan do his share of field work.

Evan Thomas was a literate person. Where and how he received his education is not known. His parents were sufficiently affluent to hire a tutor or to send Evan away for schooling, or to do both. On the other hand, he may have received his schooling directly from his parents.

The written memorial at the time of his death mentions that Evan was ill as a child, read a number of Quaker writings during that period and became deeply religious. As an adult, he was chosen by his Quaker peers to be a minister, a position awarded to men and women of acknowledged eloquence, "who preached Quakerism to the world and did more than their share in the affairs of Quaker meetings." However, in the 18th century, Quaker ministers were not ordained - they were "called and qualified by God." They were not paid for their services, did not conduct the meetings of worship, and like other members of the meeting, spoke only when the Lord "moved" them to do so.[1]

Plantation Owner

Evan Thomas became a landowner at the age of 26, when he patented 60 acres called *Beaver Dam*.[2] (See Figure 19)

In 1766, the year he married Rachel Hopkins, he patented *Mount Radnor* containing 29 acres.[3] (See Figure 20) *Mount Radnor*, after which

Evan named his entire plantation, was a narrow strip between two of his father's holdings.

In 1768, Evan purchased his father's 1,029 acres of *Snowden's Fourth Addition to His Manor* for the same price his father paid for it twenty years earlier - 100 pounds sterling.[4] In addition, Evan no doubt managed the other 709 acres of his father's plantation which he inherited in 1781 when his father died. At that time, Evan's holdings amounted to 1,829 acres located west of today's New Hampshire Avenue and extending across the Northwest Branch beyond Glenmont. (See Figure 21)

At the start of the Revolutionary War, Evan lived in the only brick house in the Colesville area and was among the wealthier men in Frederick County.

Public Servant

Being a minister did not fully satisfy the aspirations of Evan Thomas, and he enlisted his talents in activities of public service. In 1772, he was appointed a Frederick County Overseer for roads:

From Charles Williams to the lower end of the County and from the main road that leads to Monocacy by Sam Beale's mill to the Northwest Branch from Snowden's Manor to the lower end of the County and from John Rogers race ground to the fork in the road near Edward Owens.

Overseers of roads were usually prominent citizens living nearby their assignment and were responsible for cutting away underbrush, felling trees, draining the worst of the marshes and making heads of rivers, creeks, branches and swamps passable for horses and people on foot. To do that, they were authorized to conscript slaves and other labor from neighboring land owners. They were paid in tobacco.[5]

During the second week of June 1774, Evan Thomas saddled his horse, left his *Mount Radnor* plantation and rode the several miles to Charles Hungerford's Tavern. He was met there by his cousins, Richard Brooke and Richard Thomas, as well as other inhabitants of what was called "Lower Frederick County."

They were meeting to protest the closing of the Port of Boston by the British in March of that year, and they unanimously resolved:

That it is the opinion of this meeting that the Town of Boston is suffering in the common cause of America.

That every legal and constitutional measure ought to be used by all America for procuring a repeal of the act of Parliament for blocking up the harbor of Boston.

That it is the opinion of this meeting that the most effectual means for the securing of American freedom will be to break off all commerce with Great Britain and the West Indies until the said act be repealed and the right of taxation be given up on permanent principles.

This resolution was a bold step. Agreement on nonimportation of goods from Great Britain had been widely supported, and, by 1773, very few goods were being brought into the colonies. However, breaking off all commerce with Great Britain and the West Indies would sharply reduce the incomes of plantation owners like Evan Thomas. Their main cash crop was tobacco and nearly all of it was exported to England or the West Indies.

The meeting also unanimously resolved:

That Mr. Henry Griffith, Nathan Magruder, Dr. Thomas Sprigg Wooton, Evan Thomas, Richard Brooke, Richard Thomas, Zadok Magruder, Dr. William Baker, Thomas Cramphin, Jr., and Allen Bowie be a committee to attend the general committee at Annapolis and of correspondence for the lower part of Frederick County, and any six of them shall have the power to receive and communicate intelligence to and from their neighboring committees.

The meeting in Annapolis which Evan Thomas, his cousins, and the other representatives attended on June 22, 1774, was the First Maryland Convention. Agreement on nonexportations was difficult to attain, and finally a temporary measure was passed which called for prohibition of exports if approved by the other colonies.[6]

There was a strong sentiment among citizens of Maryland to find a peaceful settlement to the growing tension with Great Britain, but on October 15, 1774, the brigantine *Peggy Stewart* anchored in Annapolis harbor with 2,000 pounds of tea aboard. The brigantine's presence provoked those who maintained that the only solution was through forceful resistance, and despite efforts to stop them, they burned the ship.

The Second Maryland Convention met the following November, but adjourned after five days because of poor attendance. With 85 members present, the convention met again on December 8th. Among the resolutions passed, one authorized the organization of military units within the counties.

Henry Griffith, Thomas Sprigg Wooton, Evan Thomas, and Richard Brooke were elected to represent Lower Frederick County at that Second Convention. Evan Thomas refused to serve, a decision that changed the course of his life.[7]

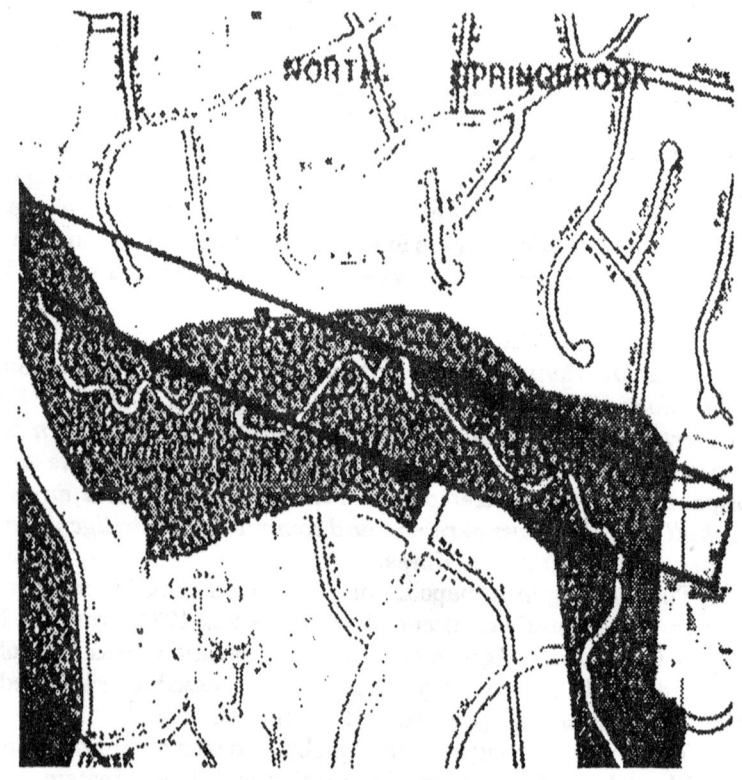

Figure 19:
Evan Thomas's *Beaver Dam*

It contained 60 acres along the course of Northwest Branch. This sketch was overlaid on a 1987 map by the Maryland National Capital Park and Planning Commission. The portions of Northwest Branch that appear below the tract probably eroded to that position since the patent of 1764.

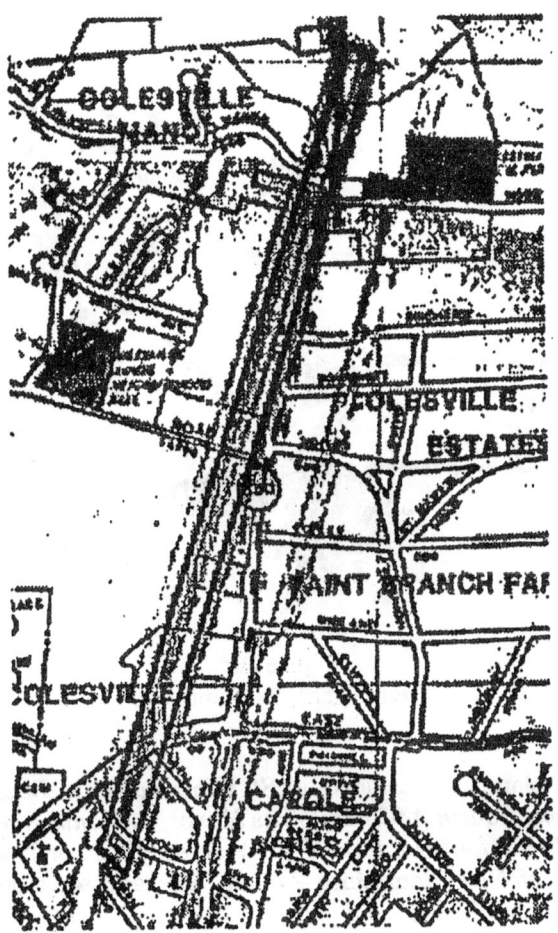

Figure 20: *Mount Radnor* overlaid on a map by the Maryland National Capital Park and Planning Commission.

Patented in 1766 by Evan Thomas, it contained 29 acres and was a narrow strip starting below today's Wolf Drive, crossing the Colesville intersection, and continuing north to Piping Rock Road.

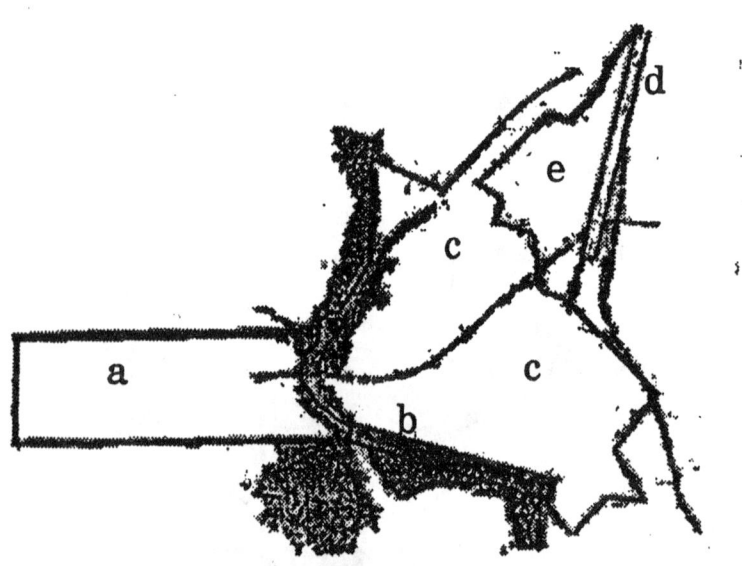

Figure 21:
Evan Thomas's Plantation

This plantation included: a) *St. Winexburgh*, b) *Beaver Dam*, c) *Part Snowdens Fourth Addition to His Manor*, d) *Mount Radnor*, and e) *Part of Beals Manor* for a total of 1,869 acres. (The north-south dotted line is route of New Hampshire Avenue. The east-west dotted line is route of Randolph Road.)

Dissenter

Although Quakers occupied many positions of power and influence during the early decades of Maryland's history, they were constantly attacked for their plain manner of dress and speech, their refusal to take oaths and their opposition to violence of any sort. When Maryland was a Crown colony, they were increasingly barred from holding public office and subjected to taxes in support of the Anglican church, which many refused to pay. Discrimination against them continued even after the proprietorship was restored in 1713. Quakers responded to this treatment by setting themselves apart from society and concentrating introspectively on insuring that each member lived up to the rigid rules of their society.

When Evan Thomas had accepted election to the First Maryland Convention, he had subjected himself to criticism by fellow Quakers for "walking discordantly." His refusal to serve in the Second Maryland Convention probably was hailed by his fellow Quakers as an act of Providence, "bringing him to a sight and sense of his outgoing."

His adherence to Quaker precepts required Evan Thomas to avoid involvement in armed conflict. Quakers believed that there was something divine in everyone, and the end to conflict could be accomplished only by working out differences through negotiations based on love and respect. A Quaker could be loyal to an established government as long as that government did not impose on one's conscience.

Agreeing to and supporting military measures against Great Britain were impositions that Evan Thomas's conscience refused to accept. He and many of other Quakers hoped to remain quiet and maintain their normal lives during the turmoil of the Revolutionary War. They hoped that their example would be a witness to a way of life, which, if followed by all, would take away any reason for war. This was not to be.

At the Maryland Constitutional Convention in July 1775, the delegates adopted the Articles of Association of the Freemen of Maryland. All men of legal age were asked to sign as members of the Association. Committees of Observation were setup in all counties to obtain signatures and to enforce policies of the Association. There were no penalties for nonsigners.

In July 1776, the nonsigners (called non-associators) were required to pledge their good conduct, were subject to higher taxes, could have their arms confiscated and were to be watched carefully. Enforcement was not carried out and the Quakers, as well as others, ignored the requirement.[8]

By October 1777, overt opposition to the war and to the new government of Maryland was especially strong among inhabitants on the eastern side of the Chesapeake Bay (the Eastern Shore). Fear of this opposition stimulated the legislators to pass "An Act for the Better Security of the Government." Every free male over 18 years of age, unless a Quaker, Mennonite, or Tanker, was required to take, repeat, and subscribe the oath of fidelity before March 1, 1778, and had to support the state. Every free Quaker, Mennonite, or Tanker, 18 years of age, was required to affirm, sincerely and truly declare and affirm the words of the oath* and subscribe to it in writing.

Penalties for those who refused to obey the law were:
1. Assessment of treble taxes on real or personal property.
2. Denial of the use of courts to sue or recover debts or damages from exercising or practicing a trade of merchandise.
3. Ban on practicing law and medicine and being a druggist.
4. Ban on preaching and teaching the Gospel, and on teaching in public and private schools.
5. Ban on voting and on holding public and military office.
6. A fine for each offense of 5 pounds sterling for every 100 pounds sterling he is deemed to be worth.[9]

Quaker precepts prohibited the signing of oaths or swearing to them. Their Biblical authority was Jesus's Sermon on the Mount as recorded in the New Testament, Matthew 5:34-37:

But I say unto you, swear not at all; neither by heaven; for it is God's throne

Nor by the earth; for it is his footstool; neither by Jerusalem; for it is the city of the great King;

Neither shall thy swear by thy head, because thou canst not make one hair white or black.

But let your communication be, Yea, yea; Nay, nay; for whatsoever is more than these cometh of evil.

The prohibition on swearing to an oath was repeated in James 5:12:

But above all things, my brethren, swear not, neither by heaven, neither by the earth, neither by any other oath, but let your yea be yea; and your nay, nay; lest ye fall into condemnation.

---

* According to the *Random House Unabridged Dictionary*, "affirm in law" means to declare solemnly before a court, but without an oath.

The words in the Maryland law permitted Quakers, Mennonites, and Tankers to declare (affirm) their agreement with the oath without actually signing or swearing to it, but this compromise was not acceptable to Evan Thomas. He not only refused to comply with the law, but contrary to the ban imposed on non-signers, he also continued his activities as a minister. He visited other Quaker meetings and became a leader in the struggle for freedom of conscience and an eloquent spokesman for the historic Quaker peace testimony.

In August 1778, Evan Thomas was indicted by a Montgomery County grand jury for preaching the Gospel contrary to the law. There were five such indictments, one for June 1, June 4, July 1, July 7, and July 15, 1778 - each time that he had been reported preaching. The informant was his cousin, Richard Brooke. One of the justices to whom the grand jury reported their indictment was Thomas Sprigg Wooten, a co-signer with Evan Thomas of the Hungerford Resolution and a fellow delegate to the First Maryland Convention. Thomas's case dragged on for two and a half years before coming to trial.[10]

In November 1778, Maryland Quakers petitioned the General Assembly to release them from the penalties of the Security Act. The petition was rejected.[11]

Because Thomas refused to support war in any way, and refused to allow the assessment of his property, the sheriff, in 1778, trebled his previous tax assessment and confiscated two horses. In 1779, 13 head of cattle, 24 sheep, 2 oval tables, and one mare were taken away.[12]

In November 1779, Maryland Quakers again petitioned the General Assembly for exemption from the penalties of the Security Act. Again their petition was rejected.[13]

In 1780, Evan Thomas refused to have his property assessed, and therefore, his prior assessment was doubled and the base amount of his taxes tripled. Again he refused to pay because the money would be used to support war, and the sheriff confiscated eight cows and one horse.[14]

In August 1780, Thomas appeared in court and refused to affirm his agreement with the oath required by the 1778 Security Act. A minimum fine of 5 pounds sterling was imposed and he paid it.[15]

The General Assembly, in October of 1780, limited the levy of triple taxes to only those absentees and non-signers of the oath who were attached to Great Britain. The next year the legislators tried to appease Quakers by asking them only to sign a paper saying they were friends to the now established government and that loyalty to Great Britain was not their reason for refusing to sign the oath and not providing accounts of their property. Evan Thomas and many other Quakers refused, saying that they "cannot enter into any engagement or test of this kind in the present unsettled state of affairs."[16]

In March 1781, a jury of the Montgomery County Court found Evan Thomas guilty on all five charges of violating the Security Act. Thomas was fined 198 pounds sterling, nine shillings, and 6 pence for each charge and assessed 731 pounds of tobacco to cover court costs.

Although Thomas appeared in Montgomery County court at his trial, the written judgement of the verdict identifies him as "late of said county." This indicated that Thomas had left Montgomery County, possibly to avoid arrest.

Thomas appealed the five guilty verdicts of the Montgomery County Court to the General Court of the Western Shore of Maryland.

In October 1781, the case was continued to the May term of the next year. In the meantime, the sheriff of Montgomery County had confiscated 4 head of cattle, 4 work oxen, 6 chairs, 1 large looking glass, 12,000 bricks, a kiln, a wagon and cart, a large grindstone, a wheat fan, wheels and shafts, and 150 bushels of wheat in the straw.

The General Assembly, in November of 1781, repealed the penalties for violating the Security Act that prohibited 1) use of courts to sue to recover debts or damages, 2) exercise or practice of a trade, 3) practice of medicine, and 4) except for Methodists, preaching and teaching of the Gospel and teaching in public and private schools.

In May 1782, a jury of 12 persons appointed from Anne Arundel County found Thomas not guilty of violating the Security Act, but he was required to pay back taxes and court costs.

Baker Johnson, Thomas's lawyer, argued at length with the County over the amount of back taxes to be paid, and the case was finally settled in 1791. In addition to the goods already taken by the County, Thomas forfeited 118-3/4 acres of land which were sold at sheriff's sale for £300 to Nicholas Lyddane.[17]

Besides Evan Thomas, only two other male members of the Sandy Spring Meeting, John Thomas and Isaiah Boone, refused to sign the oath. Seven did sign and they were stripped of their membership in the Society of Friends. Richard Thomas, Jr., and Richard Brooke (who reported Evan Thomas's preaching), were disowned by the Quakers because they joined the Maryland militia.[18]

The defection of most of the men in the Sandy Spring Meeting did not lessen Evan Thomas's zeal as a Quaker and a pacifist. He became clerk of the Monthly Meeting held at Herring Creek.** [19]

He also increased his participation in the Yearly Meeting, the central organization for Maryland Quakers. He was a member of the Committee on Sufferings which was formed in 1778 to record financial losses by Quakers resulting from their opposition to war. The committee also collected money and provided other forms of relief to needy Quakers.

Evan Thomas was a member of the committee to answer correspondence from the Philadelphia and London Meetings. He was on the committee to consider important issues. He was named delegate to the Philadelphia Meeting, was appointed assistant clerk to the West River Yearly Meeting, and in 1781, became the clerk. He served as clerk through 1786, during which time the Meeting changed its name from West River to Baltimore Town Year Meeting. He also served as clerk from 1790 to 1792 and again in 1795.[20] It is reasonable to assume that he participated, possibly as leader, in the efforts to have Quakers exempted from the penalties of the Security Act.

In 1795, Evan Thomas presented the Quaker position on slavery to the Maryland General Assembly.[21]

Freer of Slaves

Like most Quakers in rural Maryland during the first half of the 18th century, Evan Thomas and his father operated their plantation with slaves. After finishing the organizational business in a Yearly Meeting at West River, Maryland Quakers frequently boarded slave ships that were anchored nearby and purchased replacements for their labor force.

However, by the middle of the century, Quaker slave holders were being subjected to growing criticism from others in the Society of Friends. As early as 1657, after witnessing slavery in the Barbados Islands, George Fox, the founder of Quakerism, raised the question when he wrote in his journal, "Christ shed his blood for them as well as for you, tasted death for them as well as for you, enlightened them as well as you, ... and his is a propitiation for their sins as well as yours." But it was in

---

** No one formally presided at a Quaker meeting. The clerk listened to the discussion by the members, and when a consensus appeared imminent, devised a written statement, which, after further discussion, sometimes over a period of several meetings, would be accepted by members in attendance and entered into the minutes.

1688, when a group of Friends in Germantown, Pennsylvania, submitted to the Philadelphia Meeting a paper entitled "Remonstrance Against Slavery and the Slave Trade" that the debate among colonial Quakers began in earnest.

John Woolman, a New Jersey Quaker and tailor by trade, became a fervent, eloquent spokesman against the keeping of slaves. He traveled throughout Maryland and the southern colonies preaching the fundamental idea of the brotherhood of all mankind and that no man can be truly free who holds another in bondage.

But Quakers who lived in rural Maryland were reluctant to give up their slaves. They needed hand labor to produce tobacco, to till other crops, to tend livestock and to carry out a multitude of domestic chores about their farmsteads.

Because of the influence of the rural Quakers, opposition to slavery in the Maryland Yearly Meeting grew slowly. In 1768, the record of the Meeting spoke only of the "inconsistency of appointing such Friends the stature of Elders as are in possession of slaves." Two years later, a slightly stronger statement asked Quakers "to be careful toward appointing elders who do not appear to have a testimony in their heart against the practice of slave keeping."

In 1772, the Yearly Meeting achieved a consensus to advise members against owning slaves and set up committees to work towards emancipation. In 1777, the Yearly Meeting prohibited importation, purchase and sale of slaves and required local meetings to disown members who continued the practice. Committees were appointed to work with members who were not conforming with this decision and to report those who would not.

That it took time to carry out such a drastic change is well illustrated by the experience of the Indian Spring Monthly Meeting to which the Sandy Spring Meeting reported. At a 1779 meeting, the subject of disowning slave holders was still under discussion and further consideration was postponed until the next meeting. The matter was still being debated in November of 1780. Finally, in June of 1781, the Meeting decided to disown those who continued to own slaves and appointed two men to visit the nonconformers, try to convince them to change their ways, and report back to the Meeting. As a result, eight members of the Sandy Spring Meeting were disowned.[22]

What part Evan Thomas took in the debates over slavery in the local, Monthly and Yearly Meetings is not known. However, he was a leader in the Yearly Meeting, having been appointed to important committees and was clerk of the meeting in 1781 when the disownment consensus was reached.

How many slaves Thomas owned is not known. Records show that in April 1780, he freed five adult slaves and provided for the freedom of a sixth when the boy reached the age of 21. The procedure he used was known as manumission - the freeing of slaves when they became of age, and it was the only way to do so in accordance with Maryland law.

Although it has been reported that he furnished his freed slaves with patches of land on his holdings, there are no land records to substantiate that claim. It is more likely that the blacks found employment in Baltimore where the shipbuilding industry was booming and demand for labor was high.[23]

Land Disperser

Peaches Lot

By 1777, Evan Thomas's land holdings had grown to 1,877 acres. When he freed his slaves, he literally eliminated the labor force for his plantation. He began to sell sizable parcels of land. The first major sale was made in 1785 to Samuel and Mary Peach. It contained 164.5 acres and was called *Peaches Lot*.[24]

Evidence suggests that *Peaches Lot* contained the residence of Samuel Thomas who died in 1780. The tract was a parcel of the 1,029 acres Samuel Thomas bought from his father-in-law, Richard Snowden.[25] When Evan Thomas bought the 1,029 acres from his father in 1768, the deed specifically exempted his father's residence.[26]

The 1783 Tax Assessment showed that the 1,029 acres contained a brick house (34 x 48 ft.), a frame house, and old houses.[27] Evan lived in the brick house and the frame house probably was the home of his late father.

The deed for *Peaches Lot* also mentioned houses. They probably included the frame house shown in the tax assessment.

Currently there is a brick house on the *Peaches Lot* tract. It was built in the 18th century. Although the original owner has not been fully identified, it appears that the house was built by Samuel and Mary Peach. They were Quakers and the house is of traditional Quaker design for the period. It has an entrance hallway that opens to a room on each side and a stairway leading to bedrooms upstairs. The kitchen was in the basement. This residence, located at 410 Randolph Road, is a designated Montgomery County Historic Site and is on the National Register of

Historic Places. It is now owned by Mr. and Mrs. Robert Barendsen. (See Figure 22)

The frame house (Samuel Thomas's residence) stood in the rear of the current brick one. It was a substantial structure according to William Smith, a 20th century resident of Smithville. Smith helped tear down the building and move timbers to construct the nearby Shepherd residence. He said the frame house was well built and contained features that would not be found in a house for slaves or tenants.[28]

Figure 22: The oldest house in Colesville, at 410 Randolph Road, is located on *Peaches Lot*. It is currently owned by Mr. and Mrs. Robert Barendsen. (Photograph by Joyce Bayley)

Two Farms

By 1792, Thomas had disposed of 694 acres plus the 118.8 acres forfeited to pay his wartime taxes.[29] In 1794 he was granted permission to resurvey the remainder of his holdings, pick up any discovered vacancies, and obtain a single patent for the entire property.

The first resurvey found 167 acres of unclaimed land, but it erroneously included part of *Bealls Industry*, owned by Walter Beall. The resurvey also raised questions about the boundaries of *Beall Christie* as they related to the lands of Evan Thomas and others. In 1795, based on a survey by Thomas Orme, Montgomery County Surveyor, an agreement was reached which relocated the stone markers of *Beall Christie*.[30] Because of these corrections and the correction of other previous survey errors, Thomas obtained 148.5 acres of unclaimed land. He sold it in small parcels to six different buyers, all of whom owned adjoining properties. It is quite probable that the buyers thought they owned the parcels until the more accurate survey by Thomas and Orme showed otherwise.

In 1800, six years after the resurvey was started, a patent for 1,102.5 acres was granted to Thomas and the tract became known as *Two Farms*.[31]

Family Man

Evan Thomas married Rachel Hopkins in a Quaker ceremony, December 26, 1766. Rachel was a daughter of Gerard and Mary Hall Hopkins of South River. She also was a minister and leader in the Sandy Spring Friends Meeting. Their home was *Mount Radnor*, a substantial brick residence built on the narrow strip of land which Evan had patented in 1768. The Sandy Spring Meeting was occasionally held there when the Meeting was devastated by defections during the Revolutionary War.

Like many 18th century families, the efforts of Rachel and Evan to raise a family were scarred by tragedy. Of their eight children, three died in infancy. The five survivors were:

Mary, born in 1768 and married Elias Ellicott in 1786. They established their residence at the corner of Sharp and Lombard Streets, Baltimore, Maryland.

Elias was the third son of Andrew and Elizabeth Ellicott. His father was one of the Ellicott brothers who moved from Pennsylvania to establish Ellicott Mills outside of Baltimore - now known as Ellicott City. The Ellicotts are given credit for transforming much of Maryland agriculture from tobacco production to wheat. As a result of their efforts,

Baltimore became one of the most important ports for the shipment of flour during and after the Revolutionary War. Elias made a living in Baltimore as a merchant-miller, looking out for the various interests of his own as well as those of his brothers.

Evan Thomas gave his daughter, Mary, 165 acres of *St. Winexbergh* in 1788. Less than four years later, she and her husband sold the land to James Pearce for £550. This income was no doubt helpful. When Mary died in 1809, she had born 15 children.

Elias died of a stroke in 1827 at the age of sixty-eight.

Ann, born in 1771, was the second daughter of Rachel and Evan Thomas. In 1790 she married Thomas Poultney, the son of Thomas and Elizabeth Poultney of Philadelphia.[32]

Phillip Evan was born in 1776 and married Elizabeth George of Kent County, Maryland, in 1801. He entered the hardware business in Baltimore with his younger brother, Evan Jr., and his brother-in-law. Originally known as Thomas and George, the firm later became P. and E. Thomas and Sons, hardware merchants and importers. Phillip also entered the banking business and became cashier of the Mechanics Bank.[33]

He was active in the affairs of the Baltimore community, being the first President of the Mechanics and Fire Company, a founder of the Baltimore Library Company, and an organizer of the State Temperance Society. He donated $25,000 toward the construction of Baltimore's Washington Monument.

He was a commissioner for the Chesapeake and Ohio Canal in 1825, but resigned in 1826 because he did not believe the canal would benefit Baltimore. His experience with the C & O introduced him to the politics of grandiose transportation endeavors and gave him an opportunity to appraise Charles Mercer, a leader in developing the canal. Mercer and Thomas became bitter, personal enemies in the struggle to establish a railroad that would doom the economic future of the C & O.

Phillip E. Thomas and George Brown were the "fathers" of the Baltimore and Ohio Railroad, the first long distance rail system in America. Based on an enthusiastic report from Phillip's brother, Evan, about the railroads in England, Thomas and Brown started in 1826 to organize financiers, businessmen, and engineers to construct a railroad from Baltimore across the mountains to the Ohio River. It was a venture for which there were no precedents, no rules, and no certainty of outcome. Their objective was to bring to Baltimore, the grain, livestock, and other trade that was floating down the canal to more southern ports.

Thomas became the first President of the Baltimore and Ohio Railroad in 1827. Through years of struggle against the perils of then unknown feats of engineering, of political maneuver against the formidable opposition of canal interests in Maryland, Virginia, Pennsylvania, and the Federal Government, he successfully led the development of a profitable long distance railroad system that carried both passengers and freight. Exhausted and in ill health, he resigned in 1836.

During all the years of intense business activity, Phillip E. Thomas was a leader in the Baltimore Yearly Meeting of Friends. He was clerk of the Meeting from 1821 to 1832, serving in that position during the traumatic schism of ideologies that split the Society of Friends in two. He was chairman of the Meeting's Indian Affairs Committee from 1808 to the time of his death in 1861. Because of his earnest efforts to help native Americans, he was adopted by the Seneca Tribe and given the name of "Hai-wa-nob", the Benevolent One. He was the representative to Washington for the Six Nations of Indians.

Elizabeth was born in 1779, and in 1797 married Isaac Tyson, son of Elisha and Mary Tyson.[34]

Evan Jr. was born in 1781. He never married. He was a partner with his brother, Phillip, in the hardware business. In 1826 he personally inspected the newly opened English railroad between Stockton and Darlington. In the fall of that year he reviewed his trip at a dinner given for prominent Baltimoreans. A "voluble and impulsive man," he is credited with stimulating the interest of his brother and others in building the Baltimore and Ohio Railroad. He was a member of the six man committee that developed the organizational plans. He designed the earliest example of mechanical brakes for railroad cars. He was still active in the affairs of the B & O when it reached Wheeling, Pennsylvania, in 1853.

Evan Jr. achieved enough fame to be listed in some encyclopedias and history books by inventing a railroad car, called Aeolus. It was propelled by the use of sails, and ran equally well in both directions. He hired a ship captain to pilot it on a test trial and its speed reached 20 miles per hour. Unfortunately, it could move only in the direction toward which the wind was blowing.[35]

In 1824 Evan Jr. wrote a letter to Elias Hicks, a prominent Quaker of that time and friend of the Thomas family. Evan Jr. commented on the advanced age of his parents and the debilities of old age. He recommended "old and pure wine" as a tonic, saying that his "mother's health had improved greatly thereby."

At the time of this letter, Evan Sr. was 86 years old and Rachel was __. Both of them were living in Baltimore.

Just when the Thomases moved from Montgomery County to the city is not known. Deeds list Thomas as being of Montgomery County until after 1800. However, court records state that he was "late of Montgomery County" as early as 1781. In the ensuing years, court records continued this statement and some added that the sheriff should bring Thomas safely to court if he was in the sheriff's bailiwick, i.e. Montgomery County.

Evan died in 1826. The year of Rachel's death has not been found, but it probably was a few years earlier.

Evan Thomas's Legacy

Evan Thomas was the dominant personality and most influential 18th century citizen of today's Colesville area. Like George Calvert, the founder of Maryland, Evan Thomas knew how to use the natural and economic environment to his own benefit. Calvert grew wealthy by providing loyal service to King James I and by capitalizing on the availability of vast riches in the New World. Evan Thomas inherited his wealth and added to it by patenting land previously vacant and by managing his plantation.

Unlike George Calvert, who conformed to the political and religious environment in England during his time, Evan Thomas spent most of his mature years resisting pressure to conform and undertaking efforts to change the social environment around him. His insistence on religious freedom and the right to free speech, even during times of war, contributed to the basic principles of our government today. His position against the institution of slavery and the freeing of his slaves became a part of the slowly developing public pressure that would culminate in the Emancipation Proclamation of 1863.

Notes of Chapter V:
Evan Thomas, Mount Radnor's Eminent Quaker

1.
   - Edward C. Papenfuse, Alan F. Day, Davis W. Jordan, & Gregory A. Stiverson, *A Biographical Dictionary of the Maryland Legislature 1635-1789*, 1979, p. 807.
   - Baltimore Yearly Meeting of Friends, *Memorials to Deceased Friends 1780-1842*, p. 165.
   - John Sykes, *The Quakers*, J. P. Lipincott & Co., New York, NY, 1959, p. 37.
   - Martha C. Nesbitt, et al., Op. Cit. pp. xii, 4.

2. Patent BC & GS 26, pp. 357-358, MD Archives, 1764.

3. Patent BC & GS 29, pp. 340-341, MD Archives, 1766.

4. Deed, Frederick County L, pp. 211-213, 1768.

5. • Court Minutes Book, Frederick County, November 1772.
   • Sir George Leaken Sioussat, "Highway Legislation in Maryland and Its Influence on the Economic Development of the State of Maryland," *Geological Survey 1899 Highway Report*, The Johns Hopkins University Press, Baltimore, MD, p. 112.

6. Jane C. Sween, Op. Cit., pp. 27-28.

7. • Ronald A. Hoffman, *A Spirit of Dissention*, Johns Hopkins University Press, Baltimore, MD, 1973.
   • Jane C. Sween, *Ibid*.

8. Developed from information in:
   • Martha C. Nesbitt, et al., Op. Cit., pp. 27-31.
   • Margaret Hope Bacon, *Mothers of Feminism*, Harper & Row, 1986.
   • Daisy Newman, *A Procession of Friends*, Doubleday & Co., 1972.
   • Ronald A. Hoffman, *Ibid*.
   • Jane C. Sween, *Ibid*.

9. William Kilty, *The Laws of Maryland*, Vol. I, October 1777, Session Chapter XX.

10. • Proceedings, Montgomery County, August Court 1778, p. 95.
    • Proceedings, Montgomery County, March Court 1781, pp. 509-513.
    • Jane C. Sween, *Ibid*.

11. Richard H. Overfield, "A Patriot's Dilemma: The Treatment of Passive Loyalists and Neutrals in Revolutionary Maryland," *Maryland Historical Magazine*, LXVIII, 1973, pp. 141-143.

12. • *Meeting for Sufferings 1778-1841*, Baltimore Yearly Meeting, Religious Society of Friends.
    • Martha C. Nesbitt, et al., Op. Cit., p. 58.

13. Richard H. Overfield, *Ibid*.

14. *Meeting for Sufferings*, Ibid.

15. • Levy List, Montgomery County, August Court 1780.
    • Proceedings, Montgomery County, August Court 1780.

16. Martha C. Nesbitt, et al., Op. Cit., pp. 57-58.

17. - Information of Evan Thomas's record in court was obtained from:
    - Minutes Book, Montgomery County Court, March 13, 1781.
    - Proceedings, Montgomery County Court, 1777-1781, March 1781, pp. 509-513.
    - Docket General Court of the Western Shore of Maryland Oct. 1781, Term #29.
    - *Meeting for Sufferings*, Ibid.
    - Richard H. Overfield, *Ibid*.
    - Judgements of the General Court of the Western Shore of Maryland, May Term 1781, p. 263.
    - Court Record, Montgomery County, 1786-1795, February 20, 1788, pp. 296-306.
    - Proceedings, Montgomery County Court, November 1791, p. 296.
    - Deed, Montgomery County D, pp. 680-681.

18. - Martha C. Nesbitt, et al., Op. Cit, p. 59.
    - Many other Friends defected from Quaker precepts during the Revolutionary War. A notable example: General Nathaniel Greene, second only to George Washington in public esteem, was disowned by the Quakers in Rhode Island for his military service.

19. Martha C. Nesbitt, et al., Op. Cit., p. 59.

20. - West River Yearly Meeting of the Religious Society of Friends, 1779-1781.
    - Bliss Forbush, *A History of Baltimore Yearly Meeting of Friends*, Baltimore Yearly Meeting of Friends Sandy Spring, MD, 1971, pp. 157.

21. Richard H. MacMaster, et al., Op. Cit., p. 135.

22. - Thomas E. Drake, *Quakers and Slavery in America*, Yale University Press, New Haven, CT, 1950.
    - Martha C. Nesbitt, et al., Op. Cit., pp. 79-80.

23. - Deed, Montgomery County A, 1780, p. 481.
    - Martha C. Nesbitt, et al., Ibid.
    - D. Randall Bierne "The Impact of Black Labor on European Immigration into Baltimore's Oldtown 1790-1910," *Maryland Historical Magazine*, Vol. 83, (winter) 1988, pp. 331-345.
    - Tina H. Sheller "Artisans, Manufacturing, and the Rice of Manufacturing Interest in Revolutionary Baltimore Town," *Maryland Historical Magazine*, Vol. 83, (spring) 1988, pp. 3-17.

24. Deed, Montgomery County C, 1785, pp. 51-52.

25. Deed, Prince George's County EE, 1748, pp. 445-447.

26. Deed, Frederick County L, 1768, pp. 211-213.

27. Tax Assessment Book, Montgomery County, 1783.

28. William Smith interview by author.

EVAN THOMAS: MT. RADNOR'S EMINENT QUAKER

29. • Deed, Montgomery County D, 1791, pp. 580-581.
    • Deed, Montgomery County E, 1792, pp. 44-45.
    • Deed, Montgomery County E, 1792, pp. 48-47.
    • Deed, Montgomery County G, 1797, pp. 493-494.
    • Deed, Montgomery County H, 1798, pp. 268-269.

30. Agreement, Montgomery County Land Records F-6, 1795, p. 164.

31. Patent IC P, pp. 27-28, MD Archives, 1800.

32. Information on marriage and first two children of Rachel and Evan Thomas obtained from:
    • William G. Cook, Op. Cit., p. 15.
    • J. Thomas Scharf, *History of Maryland Vol. II*, Traditional Press Hatboro, PA, 1879, p. 46.
    • Charles Worthington Evans, Martha Ellicott Tyson, & G. Hunter Bartlett, *Fox, Ellicott, Evans Family History*, Fox Ellicott, Evans Fund, Cockeysville, MD, 1976.
    • William C. House, *Transcripts of Births, Deaths, Marriages, Disownments and Removals, Excerpts from Certain Friends Meetings within the Baltimore Yearly Meeting*, Indianapolis, IN, 1976.

33. Most of the information on Phillip E. Thomas was obtained from two sources:
    • James D. Dilts, *The Great Road*, Stanford Press, Standford, CA, 1993. Contains too many citations to list.
    • Bliss Forbush, Op. Cit, pp. 58, 61, 83, 158.

34. William G. Cook, Op. Cit., p. 152.

35. • James D. Dilts, *Ibid*.
    • John F. Stover, *History of the Baltimore and Ohio Railroad*, Purdue University Press, West Lafayette, IN, 1987, pp. 13-14.
    • J. Thomas Scharf, Op. Cit., p. ?.
    • *World Book Encyclopedia, Volume 14*, "Railroads," Field Enterprises Education Corp., Chicago, IL, 1959, p. 6,778.
    • William C. House, *Ibid*.

Chapter VI

18TH CENTURY ROADS

The 18th century roads consisted of a north-south route and five private roads leading into that route. (See Figure 23.)

The Road to Bell Town

When frustrated by contemporary bumper-to-bumper congestion, it is difficult to believe that the north-south road through today's Colesville was originally a foot trail travelled by Indians. Later, but still in the years before Colesville became a village, it was a horse track, used by early settlers to go to church, visit neighbors, or reach a store. As early as 1739, the road now known as New Hampshire Avenue was a public road. It is described in Prince George's County court records as the road "from Bell Town by Bells Neck to James Brooke from thence to Monocacy."

Bell (Beall) Town, the southernmost point on this road, was near today's Bladensburg. It was part of a tract known as *Blackash*, and was located on Northwest Branch. In 1732, it contained three ordinaries (inns), a storehouse and stocks. In 1738, the 48 inhabitants requested that silt be cleared from Northwest Branch, apparently an effort to maintain the branch for navigation. In 1742, the residents requested that a bridge be built across the branch and gave up the request for dredging. The reason for their change of mind may lie in action of the Maryland Assembly in 1742. The act called for laying out a new town only one-half mile from Bell Town, near Garrison's Landing, a port for shipping tobacco. The new town became known as Bladensburg.

James Brooke's plantation was the northernmost point of the road. Brooke moved into today's Brookeville area at the age of 18 and patented the *Brooke Grove* tract of 3,164 acres. He married Richard Snowden's daughter, Deborah, and by 1763, his holdings totaled 22,834 acres.

In 1739, the road was used by James Brooke and other planters on the route to transport their tobacco. At that time the route probably was no more than a winding ribbon of cleared forest with sufficient distance between stumps to "roll" huge barrels of tobacco to the port at Garrison's Landing.[1] A barrel was "rolled" by tipping it on its side, a pole through one end and out the other, and connecting the pole ends to shafts in which an ox or horse was hitched.

Maryland law required that these early public roads be marked by a system of notches on trees. A road leading to a church, courthouse or ferry had to be marked on both sides with two notches. In addition, a road to a courthouse had to have a third notch above the other two. The entrance and exit to a church was marked with a "slipe cut," and the entrance to a ferry with three notches, equally spaced.

Road Overseers were appointed to maintain the roads. These were prominent men of the area, and their unpaid responsibility was to keep the roads free of underbrush, remove debris resulting from windstorms and flooding, and fill ruts with tree limbs or trunks. Failure to do so often resulted in fines of 100 pounds of tobacco. Nevertheless, travelers carried axes for clearing unexpected obstacles. James Brooke was the first Overseer for the 1739 route through today's Colesville.

In 1750, while the Colesville area was a part of Frederick County, the route was divided:

The northern part - "from James Brooke's to Chas. Williams." (Chas. Williams owned part of *Bealls Manor*.) The Overseers for this portion were:

1750 - Ignatius Perry (owned 100 acres of *Wolfs Den*)
1756 - James Brooke, Jr.
1770-1776 - Thomas Riggs

For the southern part -"from Charles Williams to lower end of county" - the Overseers were:

1750 - Thomas Case (owned 100 acres of *Bealls Manor* and served on Frederick County grand jury in 1755)
1752 - Thomas Case
1754 - James Odell
1757 - Chas. Williams, Jr.

In 1759, an additional segment was included and the whole southern portion was described as "from Chas. Williams to the lower end of the county and from the main road that leads to Bladensburg by Beall's mill. (The added segment would be today's Lockwood Drive and Colesville Road from White Oak to Silver Spring. Beall's mill was on today's Colesville Road and was later known as Burnt Mills.) The Overseer was Chas. Williams, Jr.

In 1771, two more segments were included with the southern portion and the roads were described as "from Chas. Williams to the lower end of the county and from the main road that leads to Monocacy by Sam Beall's mill to the Northwest Branch, from *Snowden's Manor* to the lower end of the county and from John Rogers race ground to the fork in the road near Edward Owens." The Overseers were Jeremiah Orme in 1771 and Evan Thomas in 1772.

Apparently Evan Thomas was the last appointed Overseer. The above roads, including the southern portion of today's New Hampshire Avenue, were not mentioned in Frederick County court records after 1772. They also were not mentioned in the early Montgomery County list of roads. Montgomery County abandoned the use of Overseers to maintain the roads and adopted direct county maintenance.[2]

During the latter half of the 18th century, roads were cleared sufficiently to allow passage of wagons and eventually carriages, and a deed in 1797 called the north-south route through what is now Colesville the "main road to Bladensburg," - no doubt referring to its connection farther south with the road past Burnt Mills and an east-southwest road that led to the Bladensburg port on the Anacostia River.

Private Roads

In the 18th century, five private roads led into the north-south route through the Colesville area. Of these, three led to single tracts: *Wolfs Den, Drumeldry*, and Evan Thomas's plantation. The other two traversed more than one property.

Travel on private roads, especially those crossing properties of more than one owner, was complicated by the necessity to dismount from a horse or wagon and open and close gates upon entering and leaving. In a short distance, there could be several properties to cross. Also the exact location of the crossing as well as permission to cross was decided by each property owner. At times, of course, gates were left open and the property owner's livestock would stray.

The beginnings of private east-west roadways that passed through today's Colesville intersection can be traced back before the American Revolution. A mill was operating at the site of Valley Mill Park as early as 1773. It no doubt had an access road to the north-south road through the Colesville area.

A second east-west roadway was an access road from Evan Thomas's plantation on the west side of the north-south road. The best information locates Thomas's house near the present-day Randolph Road alignment just west of the United Methodist Church. Inasmuch as Thomas was Road Overseer for the north-south road in 1772, it seems reasonable that he had an access roadway from his house to that road.

18TH CENTURY ROADS

Furthermore, it is known that Thomas had a private roadway leading west from his house, across the Northwest Branch to what is now Georgia Avenue.

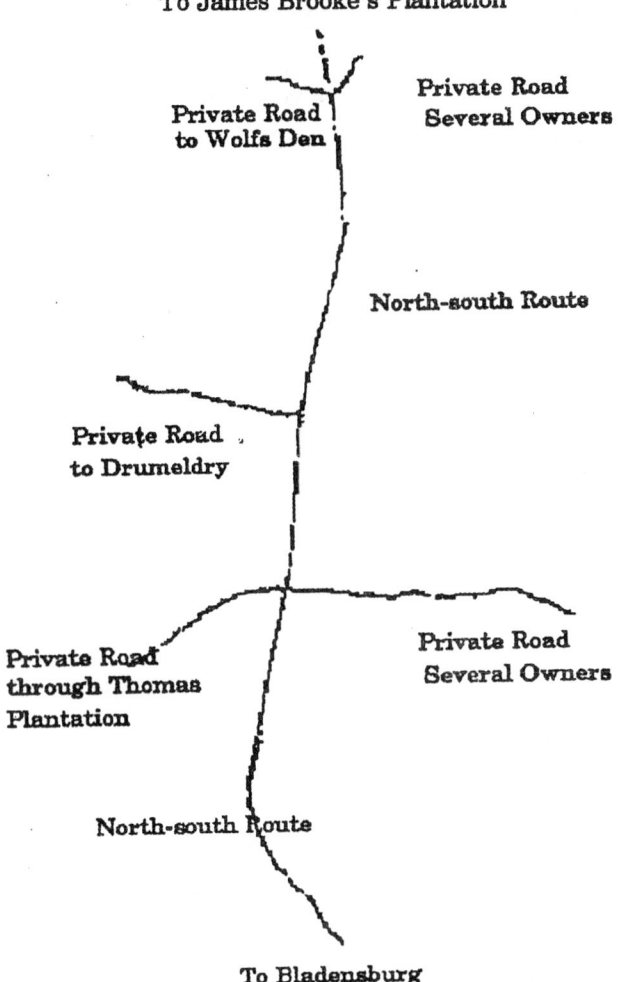

Figure 23: The 18th century roads in the Colesville area.

Notes for Chapter VI: 18th Century Roads

1.
   - Court Records, Prince George's County, March 1738 to June 1740, p. 340.
   - Deed, Montgomery County BS 12, pp. 341-347, 1844.
   - Louise Joy Heinton, Op. Cit., p. 62.
   - R. Lee Van Horn, *Out of the Past, Prince Georgians and Their Land,* Prince George's County Historical Society, Riverdale, MD, 1972, pp. 79, 80.
   - Martha C. Nesbitt, et al., Op. Cit., p. 34.
   - Ray Eldon Hiebert, et al., Op. Cit., p. 11.

2.
   - Court Minutes, Frederick County, November 1750-1772.
   - Louise Joy Heinton, Op. Cit., p. 157.
   - Millard Milburn Rice, Op. Cit., pp. 53, 160.
   - Ray Eldon Hiebert, et al., Op. Cit., p. 7.

INTO THE 19TH CENTURY

Building on the stimulus of the Revolutionary War, activity in Baltimore exploded. During the 1790s, it was the most rapidly growing city on the east coast. Because of its shipbuilding and trade in wheat, flour and other goods, it became the most important port. Demand for labor was high.[1]

In rural areas such as Colesville, farmers no doubt experienced the rise in expectations that affected all common folk after the Revolution - expectations that dissolved in bitter disputes for power between landed members of the Maryland Senate and the less wealthy members of the House of Delegates. Indebtedness rose and taxes increased.[2]

Nearly all the soils in the Colesville area were depleted. Many were severely eroded. Much of the land that was not in crops was covered with brush and trash trees.[3] For this and other reasons, the descendants of the original settlers fled.

Having moved to Baltimore around the turn of the century, Evan Thomas continued to sell his land. By 1816, only 589 acres remained. They became known as *Two Farms Reserve* and were inherited by Thomas's son, Evan Jr. (Details of these land sales are shown in Appendix III.) Thus, the largest single tract in the Colesville area during the latter half of the 18th century had been broken into smaller farm parcels by the end of the second decade of the 1800s.

Jeremiah Berry bought most of *Beall Christie* from the Odells. Samuel Bonifant bought the Lazenby's portion of *Wolfs Den*. Nicholas Lyddane purchased parcels of *Snowdens Manor Enlarged*, *Bealls Manor* and *Mount Radnor*. Dr. Samuel Lukens bought *Drumeldry* and the adjoining acres. Other land owners at the beginning of the 19th century included Richard Jones, Joseph Jackson, James Lee, and John Connelly.

The focus of life in the Colesville area was the individual farm. There was no sense of community. People usually purchased merchandise at the ports of Bladensburg and Georgetown. For many, religious activities outside the home took place at churches south or east of the area. For Quakers, these activities were north at Sandy Spring or east at Indian Spring (near today's Fort Meade).

In the 19th century, wheat production expanded. Grist mills on Northwest and Paint Branches produced flour to use locally and sell in Baltimore. Demand grew for stores, taverns, churches, sawmills, blacksmith shops, postal service and roads.

Notes for: Into the 19th Century

1. Robert J. Brugger, Op. Cit., p. 132.

2. Jane C. Sween, Op. Cit., pp. 33-35.

3. Todd H. Barnett, *Ibid*.

Chapter VII

EARLY MILLS

A Grist and Saw Mill on Northwest Branch

Evan Thomas owned land on both sides of Northwest Branch. Sometime before 1799, he built a mill on the branch. A certificate of survey of that year identified a point "where the main road crosses the branch that leads from Georgetown by Evan Thomas's mill." The metes and bounds of the survey placed the mill slightly south of today's bridge across Randolph Road.[1]

In 1802, Thomas bought 2 and 3/4 acres from Henry Culver. The tract was part of *Addition to Culvers Chance*. It contained a small parcel east of the Northwest Branch between the west boundary of *Two Farms* and the branch. It also contained a long, narrow strip along the west side of the branch between the mill and the dam. Thomas's resurvey for *Two Farms* may have revealed that part of the branch, which he thought he owned, actually belonged to Culver. The transaction was essentially a trade, Culver receiving four acres of *Two Farms* in exchange.[2]

Figure 24: "M" shows location of Evan Thomas's mill.

In 1811, Thomas purchased a tiny parcel of *Berrys Meadow* (.12 of an acre) from Dr. Samuel Lukens.[3] The land was near the dam and this transaction also could have resulted from a boundary error revealed by the resurvey. This deed places the dam more than a mile upstream of the mill. The long channel between the dam and the water wheel at the mill (known as a head or mill race) was necessary to obtain enough drop to turn the wheel and the gears for the grindstones.

Thomas leased the mill to a fellow Quaker, Thomas Brown, from 1803 to 1807. By 1811, Aaron Dyer was operating it. In 1816, Dyer and his wife, Elizabeth, bought the mill from Thomas.[4]

The Dyers sold the mill to Francis Valdenar in 1833. When he bought the mill, Valdenar already owned 540 acres in the Colesville area (including a 154-acre tract known as *Westover* that once was part of *Two*

Farms). He was born in 1797, married Elizabeth Culver, and died in 1884 at the age of 87. His wife, who was born in 1794, died in 1876. They had one daughter, Mary Virginia Harding.[5]

Valdenar sold the mill to Jacob Kemp in 1852.[6] It stayed in the Kemp family for some years and Kemp Mill Road commemorates the mill location. Later owners were Joseph R. Lechlider and Preston B. Ray.[7]

Sometime before 1831, a sawmill was developed by Edward Dawes on an eight-acre parcel of a tract known as *Fine Meadows*. The mill and mill race were just below Valdenar's grist mill on the Northwest Branch. Dawes sold the sawmill to Abraham Dennis. After Dawes's death, his son sold *Fine Meadows* in 1842 to pay off debts. The deed called for protection of the mill race and dam for the saw mill.[8]

As late as 1911, a mill, owned by Lechlider, was operating on the Northwest Branch at the location of the grist and/or sawmill.[9]

The Mills on Paint Branch[10]

NINIAN EDMONSTON'S *HAMBURGH*

Hamburgh was patented in 1765 by Ninian Edmonston, grandson of Archibald Edmonston. It contained 3 and 3/4 acres of previously unclaimed land. The present Valley Mill Park on Randolph Road includes the original site of the tract.

The land formed a natural bowl for damming water from Paint Branch, and although he continued to live in Prince George's County, Ninian built a small mill on *Hamburgh*. It was a breast mill, meaning that the water hit the closely spaced buckets at about midpoint on the wide wheel. It also was single geared, as compared to more powerful double-geared mills. The equipment included a "bolt cloth," showing that the mill made flour from locally grown wheat.

Ninian's dam and pond were located upstream from the mill. Water flowed through a channel or mill-race to the wheel, creating a "drop" which filled

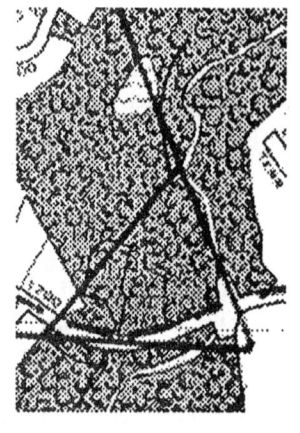

Figure 25: The Triangular *Hamburgh* Patent

the buckets and turned the gears connected to grindstones. (See Figure 26)

Figure 26: Example of a single-geared grist mill powered by a common breast wheel. Water hit the wheel above the axle and forced the wheel and attached gear to turn. (Courtesy of Michael Dwyer)

Walter Beall purchased the mill in 1771. He was a son of Samuel Beall, Jr., who owned the land and mill south of the Colesville area that became known as "Burnt Mills." Walter Beall sold the *Hamburgh* mill to William Murdock in 1774.

During the years immediately preceding the Revolutionary War, over-production of tobacco glutted the market. Property turned over rapidly as business men tried to meet their obligations in the face of falling prices. William Murdock was a Bladensburg merchant dealing in the tobacco trade, and he kept the *Hamburgh* mill only one year, selling it to Richard Sheckles in 1775.

Richard Sheckles, was a planter who added the mill to his plantation. In 1777, he sold it to his son, John, who became the first person to live near the mill. Although there was a growing demand for wheat, there is no evidence that John Sheckles improved the mill to supply flour to the American troops. It continued to be "an old mill."

In 1782, Sheckles wanted to move out to more fertile land in Frederick County and he put his 160-acre plantation up for sale. The advertisement described the property as having "two good dwelling houses, two good tobacco houses, Negro quarters, a grist mill, a still-house, a paled garden, a good apple and peach orchard, all of which are in good repair. There are thirteen bushels of wheat sowed on the land."

Sheckles sold his property to a neighbor, Joseph Perry, and had left the area in 1790. Perry separated the mill from the rest of Sheckles's plantation and sold it to Peter Kemp.

KEMP'S MILL SEAT

Peter Kemp started buying land at the *Hamburgh* mill site in 1793. He was born in Frederick County, the son of a German immigrant. Although his father was a successful farmer, Peter, like several of his relatives, entered the milling trade. His decision to leave the fertile lands around Frederick and set up business among the worn-out farms of the Colesville area may have been influenced by a chance to escape competition in his home county. Also, there were roads nearby that led to the Baltimore markets. He also may have seen an opportunity to use new technology in modernizing the old mill.

Whatever his motives, Peter Kemp was a successful miller. In 1794, he bought additional land for a tail race and purchased acreage of *The James and Mary* above the mill site that could be flooded by a large dam. By 1795, he owned 114.5 acres and consolidated them into one tract called *Kemp's Mill Seat*. He built a new mill closer to east-west road through the Colesville area where it could be fed by a longer head race that would power his overshot wheel. Both the mill and a new brick house were completed by 1799.

The sturdy brick house, which still stands today, was modest in size and typical of the homes in Frederick County. His home was furnished with feather beds, windsor chairs, and an expensive, tall case clock. He had a still house, containing a copper still for making cider and brandy. He and his nephew, Jacob, ran the mill and he had a slave family that did domestic chores and looked after the surrounding farm.

Besides buying land to improve his mill site, Kemp also bought and sold other parcels of land. When he died in 1818, he owned nearly 290 acres besides *Kemp's Mill Seat*.

Peter Kemp willed his property to his wife and upon her death to his nephews, Jacob, John and Peter.

Figure 27: Peter Kemp's house as it appears today at Valley Mill Park. (Photo by Ned Bayley)

DR. WASHINGTON DUVALL BUYS PETER KEMP'S MILL

Figure 28: 1859 etching of "Old Mill on the Paint Branch, Montgomery County, Maryland," by Charles Volkmore, from Goodspeed Collection, Worchester Art Museum. (Copy provided by Michael Dwyer)

Because of the Napoleonic wars between 1793 and 1815, the years that Peter Kemp prospered were ones with a strong European demand for wheat. After 1815, that demand dropped dramatically. By the late 1820s, domestic consumption of flour exceeded exports and New York overtook Baltimore as the leading flour market.

Prices for both wheat and tobacco dropped. Again the local economy was in distress. Many farmers put their fertilely starved farms up for sale.

Dr. Washington Duvall was an exception. In 1835, Duvall purchased the mill from the brothers, Jacob, John, and Peter Kemp. Jacob was in his sixties at the time, and John and Peter were living in Frederick County.

When Duvall bought the mill, wheat was transported directly to larger more commercial mills. Country mills, such as his, ground mostly corn. His mill was Montgomery County's leading producer of corn meal in 1850. Run by a series of tenants, Duvall's mill site also included a sawmill and a blacksmith shop. His mill became a center for the surrounding community where farmers could have their corn ground, their timber sawed, their horses shod, and their equipment repaired.

Duvall also acquired large acreages of land in the Colesville area. Among his acquisitions was the mill on Fairland Road that he purchased from the estate of Dr. Samuel Lukens. Duvall later sold that mill to Thomas Fawcett.

More information on Dr. Washington Duvall is provided in Chapter XIII.

LATER OWNERS OF THE MILL

Dr. Washington Duvall died in 1874, and Franklin Pilling purchased the mill. Forty years had passed since Duvall's improvements, and the mill was undoubtedly in bad need of repair. Pilling invested considerable money "to put the mill in thorough order."

Despite his efforts, the mill did so little business that Pilling lost all his money and the property was auctioned at public sale in 1886. The advertisement for the sale described the property as:

> 22-3/4 acres of land more or less, improved by two dwelling houses, barn, corn house, and other outbuildings, and by a substantial frame mill, 28 x 33 feet, three and a half stories high, the lower story of which is stone. This mill was built in 1879, and fitted up with new and improved machinery, including Poole and Hunt latest improved turbine water wheel. It has three runs of stone, one for wheat, one for corn and one for chop, with all necessary machinery for making a high grade of flour, and has a capacity of two hundred bushels per day. The water supply is ample and the property is in every respect desirable.

Between 1888 and 1900, the mill was owned by a series of persons, most of them residents of Washington, D.C.

THE LANSDALE MILL

On Paint Branch, in the southeast corner of the Colesville area, Isaac Lansdale and Benjamin Berry, Jr., owned a mill. Later owners were John W. Lansdale, Richard Holmes, and Washington Duvall.[11]

FAWCETT'S WOOLEN MILL

In 1723, the certificate of survey for *Snowdens Mill* showed the existence of a mill on the tract, about where Paint Branch crosses today's Fairland Road.[12] This undoubtedly was the sawmill later owned by Dr. Samuel Lukens. It reportedly was on "one of the best lands for sawing timber in the County, and carried out a profitable business."

Lukens's estate sold the mill to Dr. Washington Duvall in 1830. The sawmill, according to court records, had been replaced with a large grist and merchant mill, one capable of manufacturing cloth. Duvall sold the mill to Thomas Fawcett who was already operating it as a woolen mill.

Woolen mills "carded" the tangled, coarse fibers of sheep's wool by straightening them mechanically. By the time he bought the mill from Duvall, Thomas Fawcett had considerable experience with carding wool. He emigrated from Yorkshire, England, a county known for its woolen trade. He also had been engaged in carding at the Lansdale mill on Columbia Turnpike in Prince George's County. When Lansdale was forced out of business because of foreclosure, Fawcett moved his machinery to the mill he purchased from Duvall. He advertised the location as "The Paint Branch Woolen Factory" and besides carding, he manufactured cloth. His mill was a landmark in the community. One of the boundaries of an 1878 deed was "the public road leading from Fawcett's factory" (today's Fairland Road).[13]

Notes for Chapter VII: Early Mills

1. Patent IC P, pp. 27-28, Maryland Archives, 1800.

2. • Deed, Montgomery County K, pp. 203-205, 1802.
   • Deed, Montgomery County K, pp. 270-271, 1802.

3. Deed, Montgomery County P, pp. 217-219, 1811.

EARLY MILLS

4. • Deed (lease), Montgomery County H, pp. 515-520, 1803.
   • Deed (release) Montgomery County ?, 1807.
   • Deed, Montgomery County S19, pp. 467-471, 1815.

5. "Eveleen Carter Notes and Papers" including obituary information from *Montgomery County Sentinel*, July 18, 1884.

6. • Tax Assessment Book, Montgomery County, 1831-1841, p. 82.
   • Deed, Montgomery County JGH 1, p. 377, 1852.
   • Deed, Montgomery County JGH 6, p. 340, 1857.

7. Eleanor M. V. Cook, Op. Cit., p. 138.

8. Deed, Montgomery County BS 11, pp. 291-297, 1842.

9. U.S. Post Office Rural Delivery Service Map G3843 M6P8 1911US, 1911.

10. Most of the information for this section on <u>The Mills on Paint Branch</u> was obtained from Michael F. Dwyer, *The Valley Mill on Paint Branch*, Maryland National Capital Park and Planning Commission, 1984.

11. Eleanor M. V. Cook, Op. Cit., p. 139.

12. Certificate of Survey 337, Maryland Archives, 1723.

13. Deed, Montgomery County EBP 18, p. 451, 1878.

Chapter VIII

EARLY STORES AND A POST OFFICE

Edward Berry's *Coalsville* Store

The name "Coalsville" is first found in the 1804 Montgomery County tax assessment records, which list Edward Berry as owning a 2-3/4 acre tract referred to as *Coalsville*. That it was "Coal" and not "Cole" is insignificant because the two spellings of the family name were used interchangeably in records.

In 1797, after the first *Two Farms* survey, Evan Thomas sold slightly more than 30 acres to Jeremiah Berry. It was part of the unclaimed land included in the patent of *Two Farms*. Despite its being unclaimed land, the deed conveyed "houses, orchards, woods, and underwoods," indicating earlier occupancy. Jeremiah Berry, in 1802, deeded 2-3/4 acres of *Berrys Chance* to his son, Edward Berry, the deed stating that Edward Berry "lives on the tract and keeps a store there."

This was the 2-3/4 acres called *Coalsville* in the 1804 tax assessments. How this tiny tract received its name is a mystery. No record of early settlers in the Colesville area with the name Cole or Coale has been found, yet someone with the name must have run a store there for some years to have the site assume his name.

The name Cole or Coale occurs in the genealogies of Evan Thomas and Jeremiah Berry. Elizabeth Coale Snowden was the grandmother of Evan Thomas and had numerous relatives. The Church Register of Prince George's Parish shows that William Berry married Mary Cole in 1797. However, a clear connection between these Coles and the community's name has not been found.

A current resident of Colesville, Lois Hutchison, has said that her grandfather, Michael Peter, lived in a house which he said was the original Cole house. The building contained the remnant structure of a log cabin. On a joist at the outside entrance to the cellar of the older portion of the house, the letters C-O-L-E were chiseled.

Michael Peter, born in 1844, was a German immigrant and started in this country as a tenant farmer on the land of James Bonifant. Peter's house was on present-day Notley Road, a short distance north of Paula Lynn Drive. The early occupant of the log cabin may well have been a Cole who operated a store on the tract called *Coalsville*.

EARLY STORES AND A POST OFFICE

Figure 29: The Michael Peter house, thought by Peter to be the original "Cole House." It once stood on the northwest corner of today's Notley Road and Paula Lynn Drive. (Courtesy of Culver Hutchison)

When plotted on a present-day map, *Berrys Chance* is a long, narrow strip on the east side of today's New Hampshire Avenue, running north from the middle of Cannon Road to a point about halfway between Colesville Manor Drive and Cape May Road. *Coalsville* was a 2-3/4 acre rectangular plot located at the intersection of New Hampshire and Notley Road. (See Figure 30)

That *Coalsville* was a center of activity in the area is evidenced by the fact that the polling place for the Fourth Election District in Montgomery County was moved there in 1805. When the Columbia Turnpike Company obtained a charter in 1809 to build a road from Georgetown to Ellicott's Mills, subscription books were opened at Edward Berry's store in 1810.

Jeremiah Berry died in 1812 and Edward Berry inherited the rest of *Berry's Chance* and 403 acres of *Beall Christie*.

By 1813, Edward Berry also was dead, and his widow sold the 2 and 3/4 acres of *Coalsville* in a sheriff's sale to John Rabbitt, Jr. The 27 and 1/4 acres of *Berry's Chance* and 403 acres of *Beall Christie* also were sold in that sheriff's sale to Daniel Bussard of Georgetown. In 1816, Bussard bought the parcel named *Coalsville* from John Rabbitt, Jr.

A neighbor of Edward Berry, Patrick Lyddan (Lyddane), may have operated the store at *Coalsville* as late as 1820, possibly renting from Rabbitt and Bussard. Lyddan is listed as a Montgomery County storekeeper for that year; the Lyddan farm was contiguous to *Coalsville* on the west; and with Edward Berry, Patrick Lyddan was an owner of a small piece of land next to the northwest boundary of *Coalsville*.

Although county tax records of 1818 list *Coalsville* as part of Daniel Bussard's property,

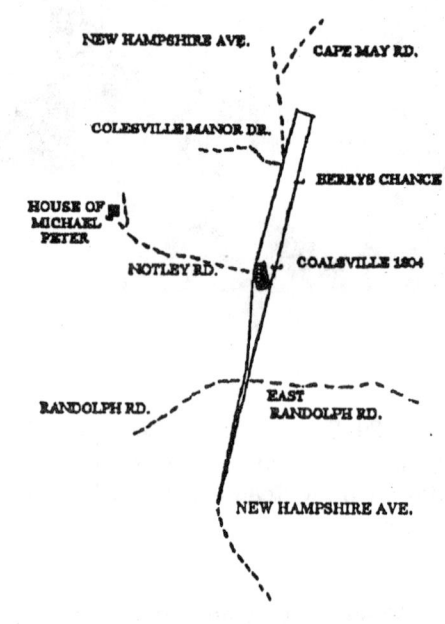

Figure 30: Location of *Berrys Chance*, 1804 *Coalsville* and Michael Peter's house.

when Bussard's son, William, sold his father's holdings in 1832 to the Bank of the United States, no separate mention of the small tract was made in the deed. Also no mention of *Coalsville* as a separate tract is made in subsequent deeds or tax records. Acreage shown for *Berrys Chance* in these documents indicates that the 2 and 3/4 acres of *Coalsville* had been reabsorbed into the original tract.[1]

Rawlings' Store

In 1832, the Bank of the United States owned 403 acres of *Beall Christie*, *Berrys Chance* and a small tract between *Beall Christie* and

EARLY STORES AND A POST OFFICE 83

Beals Manor called *Twilight*.* The total acreage of 447 and 1/2 was sold by the bank to James H. Rawlings in 1835.

The 1837 map of Julius T. Ducatel, State geologist, showed that Colesville had become the name of the community at the intersection of what is now New Hampshire Avenue and Randolph Road. James H. Rawlings owned the land north and southeast of that intersection. Records indicate that at least a blacksmith shop, a store, and a post office were located at the intersection. In a bill of sale of 1843, James H. Rawlings sold his son, Thomas, "two sets of Black Smith tools (including one set complete at the shop at Colesville)." When today's Randolph Road was put under county maintenance in 1844, the plat for the road showed a building on Rawlings's land in the northeast corner of the Colesville intersection.

William Valdenar, son-in-law of James H. Rawlings, was the Colesville Postmaster from 1842 to 1849. He also was a storekeeper. It is reasonable to assume that the building in the road plat was William Valdenat's store and post office.

In 1879, the property, including the store building, was sold to Benjamin Miller, who would hold most of it into the 20th century.[2]

Edward Dawes's Store

Edward Dawes, a resident of Washington, D.C., and also Alexandria, was in the mercantile trade. As early as 1833, he owned a store near Colesville which was stocked with dry goods, groceries, medicines, china glass, and other wares. William Veirs Bouic, a prominent Rockville judge, longtime trustee of the Rockville Academy, and director of the C & O Canal, got his start in life as a clerk in Dawes store.[3]

In 1836, Richard H. Williams worked for Dawes, running the store. Later Dawes rented the store to Williams and his partner, Edward Clarke, selling the stock to them. Still later, the partnership dissolved and Clarke ran the store.

When today's Randolph Road was made a public road in 1844, Dawes store was identified on the plat as being located approximately at the site of the present Holy Family Seminary. The store and the area between it and Northwest Branch were given the name of Claysville. (Claysville also appeared on the 1837 map by Ducatel, but no reference to it has been found since the 1844 plat.)

---

* For further details on *Twilight*, see Appendix I.

Dawes had ties in the Colesville area, having married Ann Pierce, a member of the Pierce family who purchased much of St. Winexberge from Evan Thomas near the beginning of the 19th century. The land was west of Northwest Branch and the family home was between the river and today's Glenmont.

In addition to his buying and selling merchandise, Dawes operated a tannery across the road from his store. The hides were cured in stone lined caves dug into the hillside facing Northwest Branch.

Dawes also was a land speculator. In 1814, he and John Baker, another resident of Washington, D.C., purchased part of *Second Addition to Culvers Chance* that abutted *Two Farms*. Baker later deeded his share of the tract to Dawes. In 1817, Dawes purchased a parcel known as *Fine Meadows* along the Northwest Branch. He bought the 539 acres of *Two Farms Reserve* from Evan Thomas, Jr., purchased *Peaches Lot* from Samuel and Mary Peach, and bought part of *Connellys Lot* as well as tracts outside the Colesville area. The 1837 tax records indicate he owned an eight acre lot containing a saw mill - probably part of the *Fine Meadows* tract on Northwest Branch. He was dead by 1838 and his lands were sold by his son to pay off debts.[4]

Colesville Post Office

A Colesville post office was authorized February 7, 1816. The first Postmaster was James Valdenar and he served until 1823. He returned as Postmaster in 1829 for a seven year term.

Exactly where the first post office was located is not known. The most plausible location is in the store on the tract called *Coalsville*. The tract was purchased by John Rabbitt, Jr., in 1813 and he owned it in February of 1816 when the post office was authorized. If the store was still operating, there is reason to believe the post office was in that store.

In April of 1816, two months after the post office was authorized, Daniel Bussard bought the *Coalsville* tract from Rabbitt. Bussard also owned *Beall Christie, Berrys Chance* and *Twilight* - tracts which were on the east side of today's New Hampshire Avenue and straddled today's Randolph Road. At that time, New Hampshire Avenue was a north-south public road and Randolph Road at the intersection consisted of two east-west private roads. If the post office did not start service until April, Bussard could have opened it in the *Coalsville* store or he could have opened it in a new store at the intersection of today's New Hampshire Avenue and Randolph Road.

EARLY STORES AND A POST OFFICE

There may have been a store and post office at that intersection by at least 1837 when a map by Julius T. Ducatel showed Colesville at the intersection. Also, by that time, the original *Coalsville* tract had disappeared from tax and land records.

There is a high probability that the post office was at the intersection by 1844. From 1842-1849, William Valdenar, a son-in-law of James H. Rawlings, was the Colesville Postmaster. Valdenar was not only a Postmaster but also a storekeeper. During his tenure, the private roads making up today's Randolph Road were put under public maintenance. An 1844 plat of the road shows the intersection as Coalsville and also depicts a building in the northeast quadrant of the intersection on land of James H. Rawlings. It is reasonable to believe that Valdenar's store and post office were in that building on his father-in-law's land.

William Valdenar was succeeded by Hillary Higgins, who served until the post office was discontinued in 1851. The office opened again in 1857, and William F. Lazenby, probably a descendent of the original Robert Lazenby of *Wolfs Den*, was Postmaster. The office was closed in July of 1866, but reopened a month later. John L. Bradford, who owned a store on the southeast corner of the Colesville intersection was Postmaster in 1877 and again in 1879. He died and his widow, Emma K. Bradford, became Postmistress in 1896.[5,6]

Notes for Chapter VIII: Early Stores and a Post Office

1.
   - Edward B. Matthews, *Counties of Maryland*, Johns Hopkins University Press, Baltimore, Maryland, 1907, p. 519.
   - Ray Eldon Hiebert, et al., Op. Cit., p. 107.
   - Orphans Court Docket, Montgomery County, 1798-1824, p. 22.
   - Deed, Montgomery County C, pp. 409-411, 1813.
   - Deed, Montgomery County E, p. 403, 1813.
   - Deed, Montgomery County S 20, pp. 111-114, 1816.
   - Anne W. Cissel, "Public Houses of Entertainment and Their Proprietors 1750-1828, *The Montgomery County Story*, Vol. 30, August 1987, p. 293.
   - Tax Assessment Book, Montgomery County, p. 127, 1813-1830.
   - Deed, Montgomery County BS 4, p. 574, 1832.
   - Tax Assessment Book, Montgomery County, p. 157, 1813-1830.

2.
   - Deed, Montgomery County BS 4, p. 574, 1832.
   - Patent IB O, p. 253 (in Montgomery County Patents, Liber 2).
   - Deed, Montgomery County BS 7, p. 303, 1835.
   - Deed, Montgomery County BS 9. pp. 142-143, 1838.
   - Deed (Bill of Sale), Montgomery County BS 11, p. 525, 1843.
   - Deed, Mongomery County BS 12, pp. 341-347, 1844.
   - Deed (Mortgage), Montgomery County BS 11, pp. 485-486, 1843.
   - Postal Records for Colesville, "Memorandum January 16, 1985", National Archives and Records Service.
   - Deed (Mortgage), Montgomery County BS 11, p. 403, 1842.
   - Deed (Mortgage), Montgomery County BS 11, pp. 485-486, 1843.
   - Deed (Mortgage), Montgomery County EBP 8, p. 133, 1870.

COLESVILLE

- Deed (Mortgage), Montgomery County EBP 14, p. 419, 1876.
- Deed, Montgomery County EBP 20, p. 197, 1870.

3. *Portrait and Biographical Record of the Sixth Congressional District*, Chapman Publishing Co., p. 155, from papers and notes of Eveleen Carter, chairperson, Records and History, Colesville United Methodist Church.

4.
   - Deed, Montgomery County BS 2, p. 502, 1829.
   - Deed, Montgomery County BS 8, p. 28, 1836.
   - Deed, Montgomery County BS 8, p. 30, 1836.
   - Deed, Montgomery County BS 12, pp. 341-347, 1844.
   - Deed, Montgomery County W, p. 568, 1823.
   - Deed, Montgomery County S 19, pp. 83-84, 1814.
   - Deed, Montgomery County T, p. 442, 1817.
   - Deed, Montgomery County W, p. 579, 1823.
   - Deed, Montgomery County BS 7, p. 133, 1834.
   - Tax Assessment Book, Montgomery County, p. 271, 1831-1841.
   - Deed, Montgomery County BS 8, p. 544, 1838.
   - Deed, Montgomery County BS 11, pp. 291-297, 1842.

5.
   - Postal Records for Colesville, *Ibid*.
   - Deed, Montgomery County R, p. 403, 1813.
   - Deed, Montgomery County S 20, pp. 111-114, 1816.
   - Deed, Montgomery County O, pp. 409-411, 1813.
   - Deed, Montgomery County BS 11, p. 485, 1843.
   - Deed, Montgomery County BS 12, pp. 341-347, 1844.

6. **THE POSTMASTERS OF COLESVILLE, 1816-1923**

Date	Discontinuance or Reestablishment	Postmaster or Postmistress
February 7, 1816		James Valdenar
April 12, 1823		John Bailey
December 4, 1824		Lambert Tree
April 5, 1827		Arthur W. Bell
May 5, 1828		Adam Young Jr.
June 18, 1829		James Valdenar
April 25, 1835		James Rawlings
November 7, 1842		William Valdenar
November 21, 1849		Hilleary A. Higgins
August 11, 1851	Discontinued	
November 7, 1857	Reestablished	William F. Lazenby
April 15, 1860		James Hicks Jr.
August 18, 1864		Miss Eliza Fawcett
July 21, 1866	Discontinued	
August 18, 1866	Reestablished	
July 3, 1871		Miss Mary V. Kidwell
January 30, 1877		John L. Bradford
June 10, 1878		George K. Kidwell
January 3, 1879		Levy Fawcett
June 22, 1879		James C. Bean
June 24, 1879		John L. Bradford
December 13, 1896		Emma Bradford
May 23, 1905	Discontinued	
August 3, 1922	Reestablished	Harold L. Bradford

Data obtained from Postal Records for Colesville, National Archives, Washington, D.C., Memorandum, January 16, 1985.

87

Chapter IX

19TH CENTURY ROADS

In the 19th century, the north-south route through the Colesville area became a turnpike. The five private roads leading into the north-south route became public roads. (See Figure 31)

The Washington - Colesville - Ashton Turnpike

In 1816, the State legislature authorized improvement of the north-south route from Colesville to a turnpike that ran from Brookeville to Georgetown. In 1844, the north-south route through Colesville was shown on a road plat as the "Washington Road."
Also in 1816, stock companies were authorized by acts of the Maryland legislature to build and operate turnpikes on specified routes. Many of them were built in the first half of the century, but the Washington-Colesville-Ashton Turnpike was not chartered until 1870. It was surfaced with stone and gravel, and tolls were collected at Sligo, White Oak, Ednor, and Ashton. Fees varied with the type of vehicle, the contents of the load, and the number and kind of animals driven over the road. Toll gate keepers were known for their huge bags of coins needed to make change.[1]

A Public East-West Road

The segment of today's Randolph Road from the Prince George's County line to Georgia Avenue was made a public road in 1844.[2] Prior to that time it was a series of private roadways cutting through 11 different properties. It was known as the Annapolis Road. In the 1890s, a portion of the segment east of Colesville was known as the Smith Village Road.

Good Hope Road

Good Hope Road, leading into the northern part of Colesville, was a series of private roadways until 1856, when it was made a public road. Its name probably was derived from the Good Hope community of which the Good Hope Union United Methodist Church, established in 1870, is the center.[3]

COLESVILLE

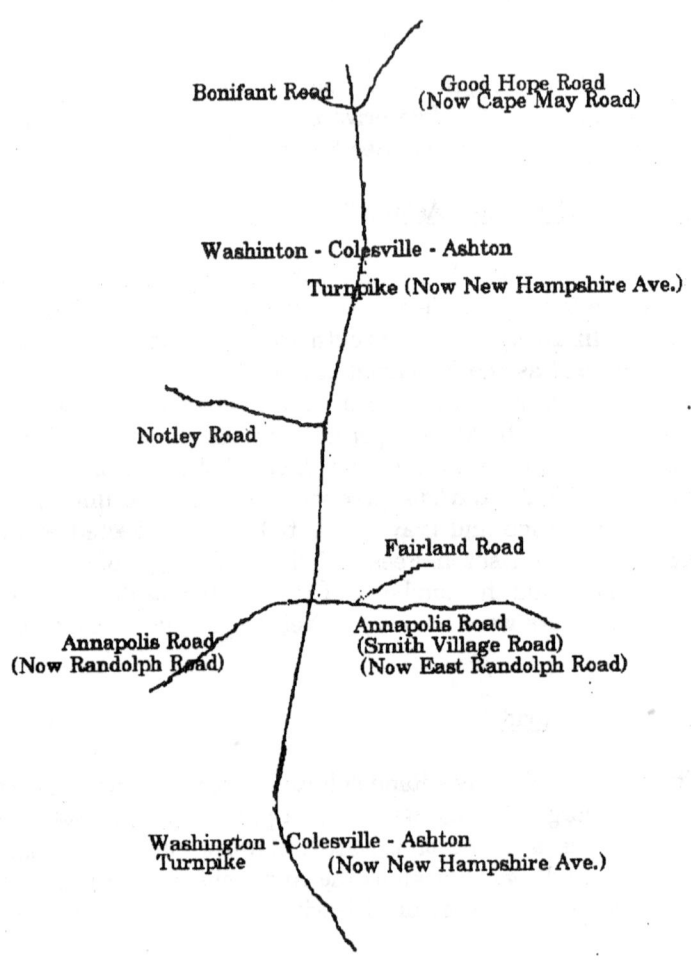

Figure 31: 19th Century Roads in the Colesville Area

Bonifant Road

Bonifant Road cuts across the northern section of Colesville from west to east. For many years, it was a private road of the Bonifant family. In 1871, George Bonifant joined with his neighbors in requesting that the road be put under county maintenance and that it include connection with the Sandy Spring Turnpike (today's Layhill Road). Grades were to be modified and the road straightened. In consideration of these improvements, George Bonifant agreed "to corduroy and make good that portion of the road which traverses the low ground between the dividing line of Bevins and Mullican and the Northwest Branch." He further agreed to pay $100 towards the construction of a bridge across Northwest Branch and "to grade a hill in the line of the road between the bridge and the road known as the Bonifant road."[4]

Notley Road (West)

Notley Road (West) was a private roadway at least as early as 1855 when it ran from Bonifant's road, to the farm of William O. Neal, to John Sharretts' dwelling house on *Drumeldry*, and then to the north-south road which today is New Hampshire Avenue.[5] It is likely that when John Berry owned *Drumeldry* during the latter part of the 18th century, he used a portion of today's Notley Road as a private roadway.

Notley Road (West) is significant for several historical reasons. A girls' finishing school operated at the site of *Drumeldry* in the 1830s. The first Colesville Elementary School was located at the site of Colesville Manor Park and Pumping Station. The house of Michael Peter stood on Notley Road, just north of Paula Lynn Drive. Where Notley Road currently intersects with New Hampshire Avenue, a tract of land called *Coalsville* existed in 1804.

Fairland Road

Although the exact date of its being put under public maintenance has not been found, Fairland Road was shown in a deed of 1878 as the public road to Fawcett's Factory, a woolen mill on the Paint Branch. The road was straightened and a bridge built at the Paint Branch Crossing in 1885.[6]

COLESVILLE

Notes for Chapter IX: 19th Century Roads

1. • J. Thomas Scharf Notes Ms 1599 Ms Sect, Maryland Historical Society Library, Baltimore, Maryland.
   • Ray Eldon Hiebert, et al., Op. Cit., p. ?.
   • Anon "Colesville's History," *The Tamarack Bark*, Vol. 16, March 1984, p. 4.

2. Deed, Montgomery County BS 12, pp. 341-347, 1844.

3. Deed, Montgomery County JGH 5, pp. 140-142, 1856.

4. Deed, Montgomery County EBP 17, pp. 148-150, 1872.

5. Deed, Montgomery County JGH 5, pp. 414-419, 1855.

6. • Deed, Montgomery County EBP 18, p. 451, 1878.
   • Deed, Montgomery County EBP 34, pp. 263-264, 1885.

Chapter X

FEDERAL METHODIST EPISCOPAL CHURCH

Although stores and a post office can give an area identity, the establishment of a well-attended local church with regular meetings can contribute not only to identity but also to a sense of community. About 1805, such a church came into being in the Colesville area.[1] It was known as the Federal Methodist Episcopal Church or the Federal Chapel Meeting House. It was located in the vicinity of today's Meadowood Subdivision on properties of the present 12800 Baker Drive and 11 Thomas Drive. The land was donated by Patrick Orme.

A traveling preacher conducted services every other week. The following excerpt from *The Baltimore Methodist* provides an insight to the life of such a preacher who was known as an *exhorter* or *circuit rider*:

On September 18th, 1829, the exhorter, with saddle bags in hand repaired to a well-known livery stable where a borrowed horse had been prepared for the "circuit rider." Mounted on his fiery steed, with their faces set toward Bladensburg (starting south from Baltimore area on the "Old Turnpike Road.)

Having paid tolls on road and bridge, after lunching by the way out of his well-filled pockets, late in the afternoon, tired, jolted, and sore, he arrived at Bladensburg, then called twenty-eight miles from Baltimore, and was kindly received and entertained at the house of Pro. Miller. In the evening, Friday, Sept. 18, 1829, the Circuit Rider preached in the old meeting house from "The Wages of sin is death," etc., and led the class. Saturday morning came (Sept. 19) ... and the Circuit Rider rode to Washington City for the first time. Revs. Stephen G. Bozel and French S. Evans were pastors at the time-honored "Foundry Station." The former (Rev. Bozel) received the exhorter at the parsonage, provided for his horse, gave him a good dinner, all gratis.

After viewing the Capitol, and other important sights, the Circuit Rider started for the primitive "Federal Meeting House," distant say eight miles. He was welcomed to the comfortable home of Bro. Orme, and after supper (Saturday evening) they repaired to the meeting house where the exhorter led a large class of colored people.

Sabbath morning (Sept. 20) came, and old "Federal" was crowded by a large intelligent congregation. The sermon was founded on "This is a faithful saying," etc. ...
In the afternoon, he rode four miles say to ...

Following the Civil War, Methodist congregations on both sides of the Potomac River formed the Methodist Episcopal Church South and the Colesville church assumed this name. In 1869, a building committee was appointed to replace the Old Federal Meeting House. Members of that committee were: Benjamin Fawcett, Francis Valdenar, John Bonifant, John Winpenny, Sam B. Rhine, William F. Lazenby, James M. Crawford, and Thomas Rawlings. The new building was completed in November 1869 and was called Andrew Chapel Methodist Episcopal Church South. It was built on land donated by Francis Valdenar and his wife, Elizabeth, and was located in the southwest corner of today's Colesville Cemetery on Randolph Road. A frame building, heated by a wood burning stove, it consisted of one large room, with a raised platform for the pulpit and choir, and a vestibule. The chapel served the congregation for the rest of the 19th century and into the 20th.

Notes for Chapter X: Federal Methodist Episcopal Church

1. • Eveleen Carter, Op. Cit., including excerpt from *The Baltimore Methodist*, "A Youthful, Brief Circuit Rider," Vol. 11, No. 10, p. 1, Baltimore, Maryland, October 21, 1880.
   • Eveleen Carter, Centennial 1866-1966, October 1955.

Figure 32: Andrew Chapel Methodist Church
(Courtesy of Eveleen Carter)

Chapter XI

SCHOOLS

The evolution of public education in the Colesville area illustrates the halting steps a society takes when making changes. During the first three decades of the 19th century, there were several private schools in Montgomery County to which the well-to-do could send their children. One of these, a boarding school for girls, was operated at *Drumeldra* on Notley Road. Abraham Brooke was headmaster and his assistant was Elizabeth Hannah Lukens.*

The first public support for schools in Maryland was an act by the General Assembly in 1812. It required banks, as a condition of charter approval, to provide $29,000 annually for schools. The money was to be distributed among the counties. As late as 1830, Montgomery County still had not made use of its share of these funds.

In 1839, the Maryland legislature passed an act to establish primary schools in all the counties. This time the counties were instructed to set up school districts within their election districts. Colesville was in school district 2 of the 5th election district. Residents met at Colesville on September 5, 1839, then adjourned after appointing a census committee. On September 13th, the committee reported that there were 82 "suitable children." The residents levied a $300 tax to support the school and directed that the site be near a spring of water. Three trustees were elected: Thomas Fawcett, George S. Scaggs, and George D. Spencer. County and state funds were not provided and no school was started.

In 1858, Dr. Washington Duvall, Montgomery County delegate to the General Assembly, requested permission to report a bill to establish public schools. In 1860, the legislature passed such a bill. The schools were to be for "all children." Implementation was to be made by a Board of Commissioners, whose members were appointed for two year terms. William H. Farquhar was appointed from the 5th election district, which included Colesville, Olney, and Mitchells' Crossroads (now Wheaton). Farquhar also was elected president of the board.

Within each election district, a two-man board of district commissioners was appointed with the authority to contract for building

---

* Elizabeth Hannah Lukens was the widow of Dr. Samuel Lukens. She later married Abraham Brooke.

schools in their respective election districts. In the 5th district, the members of this board were Francis Valdenar and Caleb Stabler. Shortly after appointment, Caleb Stabler resigned and Thomas Lansdale replaced him. No school was to cost more than $300.

The Board of Commissioners agreed to levy a tax of 10 to 20 cents per $100 value of a resident's property. Each pupil (except the needy) was to pay one dollar per quarter term. The proposed tax created considerable opposition, the most vocal of which came from the well-to-do whose children did not need public schools. Nevertheless, under the leadership of William H. Farquhar, the Board prevailed.

The first Colesville school (No. 6 of the 5th election district) was built about 1860. It was located on the west side of today's New Hampshire Avenue, about two miles north of the Colesville intersection. The first teacher of record was C. H. Mytinger. Originally, the school was open year-round with four terms: summer, fall, winter, and spring. Young children attended the summer session, a time when weather and roads made it easy to walk to and from classes. It also was a time when older children were needed for fieldwork. Women teachers often were employed for the summer session. Older pupils attended school in the fall, winter and spring, and for these terms, qualified teachers were to be males in good physical condition. After one year of operation, the summer session was discontinued because of lack of funds.

Early textbooks included:
Holmes Elementary Speller and Pictorial First Reader
Wilson's Readers
Webster's Common School Dictionary
Cornell's Geographies
Brown's First Lines and Institutes of English
Davies's Arithmetic and Elementary Algebra
Northland's Little Orater and Entertaining Dialogues
Phelp's Natural Philosophy
Onderdock's History of Maryland
Potter and Hammond's System of Practical Penmanship

Later the Holmes and Wilson texts were replaced with *McGuffey's Speller and Readers* and the book by Davies was replaced by *Ray's Arithmetic and Elementary Algebra*. Students had a choice of buying books at cost or paying 75 cents per term for their use.

Funding always was a problem. Raising taxes to meet the needs engendered fierce opposition. The onset of the Civil War, the consequent disruption of families and the demands for resources drained off much of the state and county support. Even after the war, while the county was still trying to heal its division of loyalty between the Union and the Confederacy, the schools struggled to exist. Some schools, including the one in today's Wheaton, were vandalized by Union troops and the county petitioned the War Department in Washington, D.C., for reimbursement of repair costs.

In 1864, the legislature passed a bill that created a new Board of Commissioners with one member from each election district. Joshua Abert was the member from the 5th election district and he also was elected president of the board. In 1865, the Board of Commissioners was made a part of the Maryland State Constitution. William H. Farquhar returned as a member of the Montgomery County board and again became president.

The Board provided $400 in 1868 to build a school at Colesville. This probably was the school that was on the tract of today's Colesville Manor Park on Notley Road. The accompanying photograph, taken in 1899, shows that at least five grades were being taught.[1]

Notes for Chapter XI: Schools

1. The information on schools was obtained from Guy Jewell, *From One Room to Open Space, History of Montgomery County Schools from 1732 to 1965*, Montgomery County Public Schools, Rockville, Maryland, 1976.

Figure 33: Children in five grades pose with their teacher at Colesville School in 1899. The following have been identified (from left to right):

Top Row:
   # 6 - Alice M. Kelly
   # 9 - Bessie Kelly
   #10 - Helen B. Zeigler

Second Row From Bottom: # 1 - Calvin Ray

Bottom Row:
   # 1 - Effie Riggs
   # 4 - Ollie Woodward (holding sign)

(Courtesy of Elizabeth Houston Tucker)

Chapter XII

TWO PROMINENT FAMILIES

The Bonifants - Their First Century in Colesville

When patented in 1718, *Wolfs Den* contained 317 acres. Robert Lazenby bought 217 acres and Ignatius Perry the other 100. Samuel Bonifant purchased Lazenby's portion in 1787.

The tenure of the Bonifants on *Wolfs Den* has lasted for more than two centuries. It is unequaled among families in the Colesville area. They eventually owned all of the tract, but records of their acquisitions are not too clear. One deed showed that the Bonifant share had increased to 234 acres by 1834. A deed in 1841 showed that the Bonifants acquired a large portion of Ignatius Perry's 100 acres of *Wolfs Den*, but the exact acreage was not given. Nevertheless, since 1841, no deed has been found which refers to *Wolfs Den* except as land owned by the Bonifants.

Samuel Bonifant (Bonnifield), from whom the Bonifants of *Wolfs Den* descended, was born in 1721. He was a son of James Bonifant of Prince George's County. He served in Basil Waring's company of the Prince George's County colonial militia. He was a private in the Lafayette corps during the Revolutionary War.

In 1783, according to Montgomery County tax records, Samuel owned 5 horses, 16 cattle, and kept 4 adult slaves with their children. He owned no land in Montgomery County, but probably conducted his farming operation as a tenant. The amount of his personal property was nearly as much as that of Robert Lazenby, from whom he bought the 217 acres of *Wolfs Den*.

Samuel married Sarah Townsend and they had six children. He died in 1810 and was buried in the family cemetery located in the southwest portion of *Wolfs Den* near the Northwest Branch.

Of the five sons of Samuel and Sarah, John was the one who continued to farm *Wolfs Den*. He married Mary Ann Tucker, and they had five sons and seven daughters. John increased the size of the family farm, including the purchase in 1841 of 201 and 1/2 acres containing an additional part of *Wolfs Den*. John lived during the introduction of improved methods for agriculture. His success testifies to his application of practices such as crop rotation and the use of lime and fertilizers.

Of the daughters of John and Mary, Louisa, Elizabeth, Margaret, and Virginia never married. Mary Ann married Thomas Overton Wilson,

Figure 34: Bonifant Family Cemetery. Located south of today's Bonifant Road on land that originally was *Wolfs Den*. Columnar tombstone marks the grave of Samuel Bonifant. (Photograph by Joyce Bayley)

and when she died in 1848, Wilson married her younger sister, Sarah. Caroline married a Dr. Peters and moved to Missouri.

The five sons of John and Mary were Washington, Benjamin, John, James, and George. Washington Bonifant, born in 1812, was a Maryland legislator from 1842-1849. In 1861, President Lincoln appointed him U.S. Marshall.

The Federal Government disarmed the city of Baltimore because of fears that Maryland might leave the Union and put her armed forces under the Confederacy. Marshall Bonifant, backed by 100 soldiers, presented the Union's demands that the city surrender a large quantity of arms. The city met his demands, and several wagon loads of weapons, including 400 muskets and 1,500 pikes, were moved to Fort McHenry.[1]

Washington Bonifant was one of two members of the family on the Union side during the Civil War. During the occupation of Silver Spring by Confederate troops under General Jubal A. Early, soldiers ransacked Bonifant's home, but they were too drunk to burn it down.

Bonifant Street in Silver Spring is named after Washington Bonifant.

Benjamin was born in 1821, graduated from Jefferson Medical College in Philadelphia, settled in Weston, Missouri, and married Matilda Leachman. Like his brother, Washington Bonifant, he sided with the Union during the Civil War. He was a surgeon in the 29th Enrolled Missouri Militia and also the 4th Missouri State Militia.

John was born in 1824, never married, and died in 1870.

James became the owner of *Drumeldry* and his biography is described in a separate section below.

George, was born in 1826 and, following the death of his father, became the owner of the family farm. He married Helen Green in 1875 and built a substantial home on the north side of Bonifant Road near Northwest Branch. It is currently owned by Mr. and Mrs. William Sullivan.[2]

After giving birth to her fifth child, Helen died in 1888 at the age of 31. Of the five children, three never married.

George was a prosperous farmer and expanded his holdings to 600 acres. He also contributed articles to newspapers and magazines. Like his contemporary, Dr. Washington Duvall, he used slaves for domestic and farm labor until 1865.

James and Laura Bonifant of *Drumeldry*

Benjamin Berry sold *Drumeldry* and parcels of *Berrys Meadow* and *Snowdens Manor Enlarged* to Dr. Samuel Lukens in 1803. The combined tracts contained slightly more than 369 acres.

The land changed hands and parcels were sold or added over the years. In 1867, James Bonifant bought the property. It contained 241 and 17/20 acres, including most of the original 225 acres of *Drumeldry*.

James Bonifant, a son of John and grandson of Samuel Bonifant, was born in 1827. In 1860, he married Laura Catherine Craigen, who was born in 1839 in Greenspring, Virginia (now West Virginia). They were married by William Spear, Rector of the Emanuel Parish of Maryland at Fairview, Virginia. Fairview is now part of West Virginia and is located between the western boundary of Maryland and the eastern boundary of Ohio, only a few miles south of the Pennsylvania line. Family tradition states that the couple married in the middle of the Potomac River.

According to oral family history, the *Drumeldry* residence of James and Laura Bonifant was destroyed by fire. They spent too much money rebuilding it and had to sell out to Caroline Brooke in 1883. They moved to Virginia and purchased *Belleville,* a 300 acre farm in Powhatan County.

James and Laura had two sons and four daughters. He died in 1894 in Washington, D.C., and is buried at the Bonifant Family Cemetery near Colesville. (See Figure 34.) Laura died in Potomac, Maryland, in 1921, and is buried in the Craigen family plot of Rock Creek Cemetery, Washington, D.C..[3]

Figure 35: The Bonifant House

Built by George Bonifant after his marriage to Helen Green in 1875. Their daughter, Margaret, who married Thomas Liebig, raised her family there. It is on the north side of Bonifant Road and is now owned by Mr. and Mrs. William Sullivan. (Photograph by Joyce Bayley)

Figure 36: George Bonifant House

Pictured above is the house in which George Bonifant lived prior to building the home shown in Figure 35. His son, George Frederick, lived there. A grandson, Robert, also lived there. Robert's widow, Nancy Bonifant, lived in the house until her death in 1995. It is on the south side of Bonifant Road. The original structure is in the rear. (Photograph by Joyce Bayley)

The Washington Duvalls[4]

Born in 1796, on a tract west of the Colesville area that was known as *Hermitage*, Dr. Washington Duvall was a member of a wealthy and influential family. During the summer of 1814, while visiting Baltimore, he was called into service to defend the city against the British invasion. He remained in service until November of 1814, a member of Captain Nicholas Burke's company in the 6th Maryland Regiment. In later years, he was one those honored as the "Old Defenders" of Baltimore.

He obtained a medical degree from the University of Maryland in 1821 and became "one of the beloved country doctors of Montgomery County." As written by one of his grandsons, "Though he had a down-right manner, he had with it a delightful sense of humor." He was known as a "handsome" dresser.

When he graduated from medical school, he already was a member of the Maryland legislature and was repeatedly reelected. In 1826, he was a member of the Electoral College. In 1850 and 1851, he was a member of the State Convention to revise the Maryland Constitution.

"Doc" Duvall married Eliza Perry in 1822, and settled with his bride on a tract of land called *Rural Felicity* that was owned by James Perry, Eliza's father. It was located across Old Annapolis Road (today's East Randolph Road) from Peter Kemp's mill. They had five children.

The Duvalls were the dominant land owners east of today's New Hampshire Avenue. In 1850, their property included 600 acres of improved land and 1,900 acres of unimproved land. According to the 1850 census, they were one of the wealthiest families in Montgomery County.

Duvall's son, Benjamin, is thought to have managed his father's farm. That they used crop rotation is suggested by the record of their having fields of wheat, corn, oats, and potatoes. Their herds of sheep, milk cows, and swine would have required sizable fields of hay and pasture. They also had the financial capital to purchase lime and fertilizer. Over the years, their labor force included up to 100 slaves.

Dr. Washington Duvall died in 1874; his widow in 1886.

Figure 37: *Drumeldra* (formerly *Drumeldry*)

Drumeldra as James and Laura Bonifant restored it after a fire. It is located on the south side of Notley Road just west of the intersection with Overton Lane. (Photograph by Joyce Bayley)

Notes for Chapter XII: Two Prominent Families

1. Daniel Carroll Toomey, *The Civil War in Maryland*, Toomey Press, Baltimore, Maryland, 1983, p. 20.

2.
   - Patent FF 7, p. 370, 1718, Maryland Archives.
   - Rent Rolls 1651-1772, p. 433, Maryland Archives.
   - Deed, Montgomery County C, p. 424, 1786.
   - Deed, Montgomery County C, p. 683, 1787.
   - Deed, Montgomery County BS 7, p. 9, 1834.
   - Deed, Montgomery County BS 10, pp. 410-411, 1841.

   Genealogy information obtained from:
   - Sallie Gridley, personal communication.
   - George B. Wilson, *The Descendants of Samuel Bonifant of Wolfs Den*, Montgomery County, Maryland, 1980, revised 1983; personal communication.
   - Virginia S. Hooper, *Bon(n)ifield Bonifant Descendants of Male Lines from James Bonevant in Prince George's County, Maryland in 1713*, 1984.
   - Tax Assessment Book, Montgomery County, 1783.
   - Deed, Montgomery County EBP 17, p. 147, 1871.

3. * Deed, Montgomery County L, p. 202-204, 1803.
    * Deed, Montgomery County BS 5, pp. 307-308, 1832.
    * Deed, Montgomery County BS 5, pp. 305-306, 1832.
    * Martha C. Nesbitt, et al., Op. Cit., p. 152.
    * Deed, Montgomery County JGH 2, pp. 440-442, 1853.
    * Deed, Montgomery County JGH 5, pp. 14-19, 1855.
    * Deed, Montgomery County JGH 5, pp. 269-271, 1856.
    * Deed, Montgomery County EBP 6, pp. 132-133, 1867.
    * Deed, Montgomery County EBP 29, pp. 291-293, 1883.
    Genealogy information obtained from:
    * Sallie Gridley, Ibid.
    * George B. Wilson, Ibid.

4. Except as otherwise noted, information on Dr. Washington Duvall was obtained from:
    * Harry Wright Newman, *Mareen Duvall of Middle Plantation*, Washington, D.C., 1952, pp. 515-517.
    * Michael F. Dwyer, Ibid.

Chapter XIII

CIVIL WAR BRINGS CHANGE

During the 1861-1865 War Between the States, the residents of Colesville were certainly caught up in the division among Marylanders about which side to support. The issues were secession from the Union and slavery. Some wished the two issues were separable; they favored the abolishment of slavery but could not bring themselves to separation from the people of the South. Others, including many Methodists, were strong Unionists and against slavery. Still others, particularly those in rural Maryland, needed slaves for their farm and domestic labor and sided with the Confederacy.

The issues were most difficult for the larger Colesville landholders like the Bonifants and the Duvalls. George and James Bonifant were on the side of the Confederacy. A brother, Benjamin, served as a surgeon for Union troops, and another brother, Washington, was a Union marshall.

Dr. Washington Duvall was a delegate to the Maryland General Assembly in 1858. Even if he did not participate, he was exposed to the emotional debates about secession and slavery within the legislature and his community. His own feelings may have been influenced by knowing that Duvalls, probably his relatives, fought on both sides of the war. In one Confederate company, there were six Private Duvalls.[1]

Records give some light on Dr. Duvall's position on slavery. Even though he is reported as treating his slaves well, he did not free them; they were made free when Maryland outlawed slavery in 1864.[2]

Whatever their views, the proximity of Colesville residents to Washington, D.C., and to large numbers of Union troops would have kept them in a constant state of apprehension. When McClellan's troops swarmed out of Washington to meet Lee's invasion of western Maryland, some of them moved up the Brookeville Turnpike before marching west from Olney. That turnpike is now Georgia Avenue, just west of the Colesville area. A store in Sandy Spring, only a few miles north of Colesville, was robbed by Confederate soldiers under Lieutenant Walter Bowie of Mosby's Rangers.[3]

The fears of Colesville residents would have been heightened when Confederate General Jubal Early occupied the area of today's Silver Spring. General Johnson's brigade of Confederate troops drove south from Baltimore to Laurel and then to Beltsville, only a few miles east of Colesville.[4] With troops that close, many of them cavalry, foraging raids

CIVIL WAR BRINGS CHANGE 107

for supplies, cattle, and horses probably invaded the Colesville area. Nevertheless, the major battles were far to the west and north, and no record has been found of Colesville family members who fought in the conflict.

On the other hand, an outcome of the war did affect them directly - the 14th Amendment to the U.S. Constitution, adopted in 1865. It outlawed slavery.[4]

Smith Town

George Smith was born in a family of slaves owned by Dr. Washington Duvall. He spent his early adult life driving teams for Duvall. His wife, Mary, worked in the Duvall house. After he became a free man, George bought three acres from Duvall for a nominal sum. Later, his four sons purchased parcels totalling nearly 100 acres, and other Smith families bought small acreages. Members of the Johnson family also purchased land nearby, some of it from Duvall and some from Benjamin Miller. Soon households of Jacksons and Warners moved into the area. They formed an African-American community that was first known as Smith Town and later as Smith Village. Their tracts were about one mile east of the Colesville intersection, and the road to Colesville became known as the Smith Village Road.

In most African-American communities formed after the Civil War, the homes were close to one another. The residents owned small plots of less than three acres that could provide them with crops sufficient only for subsistence. Their main source of income was from "hiring out" to the farms of former masters or working in nearby towns. In contrast, the homes of Smith Town residents were scattered on larger tracts. Although they did "hire out," they concentrated much of their efforts on truck farming and sold their produce to the growing urban market in Washington, D.C..[5]

Good Hope Methodist Episcopal Church

About 1865, an African-American community developed along Good Hope Road on the northern edge of the Colesville area. In 1872, the community built the Good Hope Methodist Episcopal Church that served as a religious and social center for local African-Americans as well as those from Holly Grove and the developing community of Smith Town. The original structure probably was frame. Today a modern brick church stands on the site.[6]

Schools for African-American Children

In 1872, Montgomery County started a program to provide public education for African-American children. Prior to that time, any education obtained by them was provided by churches or plantation owners. In 1876, the county board set aside $300 for a "colored school" at Colesville. According to William Smith, a lifetime resident of the area, this school was at the site of the original Colesville school - approximately two miles north of the Colesville crossroads on the west side of today's New Hampshire Avenue. Anne Powell was the teacher in 1894. Two years later, an early fall storm damaged the school and the board provided money for repairs. In 1897, hand-me-down desks from the Sandy Spring "colored school" were delivered to the Colesville school.[7]

Joseph Burr - Affluent Resident

Joseph F. Burr started purchasing Colesville area land in 1869.[8] By 1872, he had amassed nearly 1,000 acres. A lawyer in the U.S. Department of the Treasury in Washington, D.C., he and his family lived in a beautiful mansion on the property. It was known as Valley View, contained 24 rooms on three stories, and was heated by fireplaces vented to eight chimneys. The mansion was located on the north side of today's Randolph Road, on the site of today's Holy Family Seminary. Burr was a friend of President Grover Cleveland, who visited Valley View frequently, taking advantage of the rural setting to shoot squirrels.

Burr died in the late 1890s. In 1899, Franklin and Bessie Hobbs and their eleven children moved into Valley View as renters.

Allen Reed's Blacksmith Shop

A blacksmith shop existed near the Colesville crossroads as early as 1843. It was owned by the Rawlings family who also owned large acreages of land north of today's Randolph Road and on both sides of today's New Hampshire Avenue.[9] The shop passed through several hands and was sold with a little over two acres to Allen Reed in 1876.[10] Reed moved to Colesville from the Burtonsville area and renovated the shop. He and his wife had five children. Two of his sons, Edward and Will, became blacksmiths.

Reed bought the shop shortly after the Washington-Colesville-Ashton Turnpike was built. He and his helpers were kept busy with horses whose shoes had been lost or damaged on the rocky roadbed. His shop also undertook wheelwright work - building and repairing wagons. They also took on other jobs that required working with iron.[11]

Figure 38: Valley View
Joseph Burr's Country Mansion Near Colesville. In the 20th century, this house became the home of the Holy Family Seminary. It has been replaced by a more modern structure. (Courtesy of Montgomery County Historical Society)

A Saloon at the Crossroads

A tavern was operated in today's Meadowood area by John T. Baker in 1848.[12] Early taverns were known to provide lodging and meals along with liquor. The first record in the Colesville area of a saloon that served only liquor placed it on the southeast corner of the Colesville intersection and was operated by Tom Bean. He was illiterate and his wife managed the business.

Ed Reed, whose father, Allen Reed, owned the blacksmith shop at the cross roads, remembered:

> *The conditions at the saloon were terrible. Men fought all day. Women and children were afraid to go near. It was not safe. There were times when they stripped each other's clothes, stoned colored people, and fought with hammers and tools they would get from the shop. Conditions were even worse on Election Day.*[13]

The saloon was replaced by a store when John Bradford bought the property in 1880.[14]

Figure 39: Allen Reed's Blacksmith Shop
Allen Reed is the second from left, in boots and with no hat. Edward Reed is on the far right, small barefoot boy. (Made from daguerreotype - courtesy of Russell Reed and Eveleen Carter.)

Notes for Chapter XIII: Civil War Brings Change

1. • Thomas and Joanne Huntsberry, *Maryland in the Civil War Book I, The South* J. Mart Publishers, Bunker Hill, WV, p. 73.
   • Thomas and Joanne Huntsberry, *Maryland in the Civil War Book II, The North* J. Mart Publishers, Bunker Hill, WV, p. 18.

2. • Harry Wright Newman, *Maureen Duvall of Middle Plantation*, Washington, D.C., 1952, pp. 515-517.
   • Vera Foster Rollo, *Your Maryland: A History*, 5th Edition, Maryland Historical Press, Lanham, MD, 1993, p. 279.

3. Daniel Carroll Toomey, Op. Cit., p. 139.

4. Daniel Carroll Toomey, Op. Cit., pp. 124-127.

5. • Everett L. Fly and La Barbara Wigfall Fly, *Northeastern Montgomery County Black History Study*, Entourage, Inc., August 1983, p. 133.
   • Ned Bayley, *Smith Serves as the Living History Book of Colesville*, Free Press, May 15, 1985.

6. Everett L. Fly, et al., Op. Cit., p. 193.

7. Nina H. Clarke and Lillian R. Brown, *History of the Black Public Schools of Montgomery County, Maryland 1872-1961*, Vantahr Press, New York, NY, 1978.

8. Deed, Montgomery County EPB 6, p. 184, 1869.

9. Deed, Montgomery County BS 11, p. 525, 1843.

10. Deed, Montgomery County EBP 16, pp. 80-90, 1876.

11. • Russell Reed - tape provided by Eveleen Carter.
    • Thelma Reed, "The History of Colesville since 1869."

12. Deed, Montgomery County STS 3, p. 574, 1848.

13. Thelma Reed, Ibid.

14. Deed, Montgomery County EBP 23, p. 3, 1880.

THE 20TH CENTURY

Despite social and economic changes caused by the Civil War, Colesville continued to be a rural community of farmers and storekeepers, blacksmiths, millers, and others who provided services to farmers. Except for taxes, markets and prices of farm products, the community was affected very little by events around it. Violent labor riots and rapidly changing industries of Baltimore were primarily topics for conversation among Colesville people. Baltimore remained a market to some extent, but Washington, D.C. was the most important factor influencing changes and growth in Colesville. Jobs, markets, land use, and cultural interests became more oriented to developments in the neighboring capital city. Especially after the 1930s, when activities in Washington mushroomed and new technologies affecting transportation and living in suburban areas became readily available, farming in the Colesville area declined rapidly, residential land use intensified, and the character of the community changed permanently.

Chapter XIV

CHANGING PLACES AND FACES

In the Cemetery

When the Andrew Chapel was built in 1869, a cemetery was laid out nearby. Later two other sections were added. Information from the tombstones in this section is shown in Appendix IV. Except for residents of Smithville buried in the cemetery of the Good Hope Methodist Episcopal Church and a few persons buried in family or other cemeteries, this information provides a census of the families who lived in and around the Colesville area during the latter part of the 19th century and the first part of the 20th. Inscriptions of comfort on some stones and the graves of infants and small children point up the pain associated with living, not just in their days, but in all times.

Figure 40: 1996 view of the original
Colesville Cemetery area.
(Photograph by Ned Bayley)

The cemetery also reveals a change in the lives of Colesville residents. The Lazenby sons were active in the Revolutionary War, but no records have been found which show that people living in Colesville participated in the War of 1812, the Mexican War, the Civil War, or the Spanish-American War. However, graves in the cemetery and military records show that young people from Colesville were members of the armed services that fought the five wars of the 20th century.

The Bradford Store and Post Office

In 1880, John L. Bradford purchased 61 and 5/8 acres in the southeast corner of the Colesville crossroads.[1] The land contained a building that had been a saloon operated by Tom Bean and his wife.

John L. Bradford converted the saloon into a house and store. He and his wife, Emma, operated the store along with the post office. Bradford had been Postmaster in 1877 and was appointed again in 1879. In 1896, Emma was made Postmistress.

John died in 1903 at the age of 68. Emma continued as Postmistress until the post office was closed in 1905. With her son, Harold, she operated the store until 1922, when she died at the age of 77. That same year, Harold reactivated the post office and became the

Figure 41: Emma and Harold Bradford behind their store.
(Courtesy of Chad Leyshon)

Postmaster. His tenure was short-lived; the post office was closed permanently in 1923. After many years of service provided directly from Silver Spring, a branch post office was opened in Colesville in 1970.[2]

Despite the loss of the post office, Harold and his wife, Mary, kept the store in operation. Harold was known among children of that era for giving them sweets when they visited the store with their parents. Mary had the reputation for sternly trying to discourage his largess.[3]

The building that housed the Bradford store was replaced by a Gulf Station and more recently by an Exxon Station.

Cissel's General Merchandise Store

Truman R. Cissel opened a general store in 1898 on the southwest corner of the Colesville crossroads. Born in Howard County, one of 10 children, he opened the Colesville store at the age of 18. Before the widening of today's New Hampshire Avenue in the 1930s, the main entrance to the store was on that road. After the widening, Cissel moved the store entrance and the gas pumps to face today's Randolph Road. He sold the store in 1956. The land was first occupied by a gas station and is now the site of the Equitable Federal Savings Bank.

Cissel was treasurer and member of the vestry of St. Mark's Church in nearby Fairland for 50 years. He was a member of the Colesville Lions Club from 1954 to the time of his death in 1966.

When he died at the age of 85, he had survived all 10 of his brothers and sisters, and his wife, Helen Fawcett Cissel, who died in 1961. At that time there were four granddaughters and 13 great grandchildren.[4]

Ed Reed's Blacksmith Shop[5]

Born in 1871, the son of Allen Reed, Edward L. Reed became the main blacksmith in his father's shop. When his father died, he continued the business. Blacksmithing was hard and sometimes dangerous work. Ed Reed's son, Russell B. Reed, remembers:

"A stranger brought two horses to the shop to be shod. It was winter time so there was room in the shop to bring two horses in to work on them in the warm blacksmith shop. My dad asked the owner if the horses would kick, and he said, "No, they are very mild," and he was sure they would not kick. My dad, in shoeing the two horses, walked behind one of them, and strange as it may seem, the horse kicked his hat off. It didn't hurt him but it did kick his hat off."

When Allen Reed's estate sold the land on which the shop stood, Ed Reed moved it behind his home on today's New Hampshire Avenue. It occupied part of the site of today's Safeway store. Except for Sundays, Ed Reed worked every day of his life. He died in 1949, 17 years after the death of his wife, Bessie.[6]

Figure 42: Cissel's General Store
It was located on the southwest corner of Colesville crossroads, facing today's New Hampshire Avenue. (Courtesy of Katherine Cissel)

Figure 43: Ed Reed stands beside his home that faced today's New Hampshire Avenue. His son, Russell, is on the pony. His daughter, Charlotte, is in the cart near the pony. (Courtesy of Charlotte Reed Stup)

Judge Alfred C. Tolson

Alfred C. Tolson, who owned a farm next to the Bonifant land, was born in 1844 in Prince George's County. At the age of 16, he joined Company B of the Maryland Cavalry on the side of the Confederacy and was taken prisoner during the Battle of Gettysburg. Immediately after the war, he entered the mercantile business in Washington, D.C., then moved to Colesville. He was Judge of the Orphan's Court for twelve years. He died in 1928 at the age of 84. His wife, Catherine, had died in 1916.

One of their children, Elizabeth Ann (known to her family and friends as Ann), was born in 1889. At the age of 85, in an interview with

Hilma Blair, she reminisced about their first automobile. The agent delivered the machine to "the family." He was not allowed to sell it until he taught someone in the family to drive it. Ann had no use for the company policy that required the agent to teach the oldest boy, not her, to drive the car.

In 1911, Ann obtained a license to drive the "family" car. All she had to do was pay a dollar to the Justice of the Peace "or someone" and sign a statement saying she was old enough to drive a car. No demonstration of driving ability was required. When she paid her dollar, she "just took the car out and drove it."

Christopher, a son of Alfred C. Tolson, married Anne R. Canby. She was a member of the Canby family that owned a farm just north of the Colesville area.[7] [8]

The Bonifants[9]

George Bonifant farmed his extensive acres until his death in 1912. At that time the land was divided: an area north of Bonifant Road going to a daughter, Margaret, and an area south of the road to a son, George Frederick Bonifant.

Margaret married Thomas Liebig. They lived in the house built by Margaret's father, George Bonifant, on the north side of Bonifant Road. (See Figure 37) They had two children: Sallie, born in 1916, and Thomas McLean, Jr., born in 1920. Sallie, who lives in the Colesville subdivision of South Stonegate, has been married twice - first to Edgar Glassford and second to Darren Gridley.

George Frederick Bonifant was born in 1882. He married Elizabeth Ann Tolson in 1916. They lived in the house that still stands on the south side of Bonifant Road. (See Figure 38) Their family consisted of two daughters and four sons. The children were still young when George died in 1937, leaving Ann with full responsibility for the family and the farm.[10]

Like other farms in the area, the main crops raised by the Bonifants were corn and wheat. Wheat grain was separated from the hulls by threshing crews who, with their machines, moved from farm to farm. The crews had to be fed, and according to Ann Bonifant, "They ate like wolves! I had to cook for two days before they came!"

For many years, while Ann Bonifant lived there, it was heated by fireplaces and kerosene lanterns provided lighting. Canned goods, including preserves, pickles and jellies, were stored in a fruit cellar below the house. Anne prepared baked goods on a range with water coils in the back. One bitterly cold day, the water in the coils froze and could not circulate. When heated, the stove exploded, hurling metal fragments into the kitchen, and one fragment lodged in Ann's shoulder.

Managing the farm also had its perils. Ann was tending a litter of newborn pigs when the 500-pound sow attacked her. She couldn't escape until her son drove the sow off.

Services of a doctor were hard to obtain. "In those days, you didn't go to the doctor for every little thing that was the matter with you," she told an interviewer. She did the best she could with home remedies, but when absolutely necessary, she drove her buggy to the doctor's office and brought him to her home. He would have a helper bring his own buggy to the house for the return trip.* [11]

Entertainment was primarily a "do it yourself" enterprise. Games and occasional dances such as the Virginia Reel were the most popular. Ann died in 1978 at the age of 89.

Robert Lee Bonifant, a son of Anne and George Frederick Bonifant, was born in 1925. He stayed on the farm, living on the south side of Bonifant Road, and was a member of the staff of the Washington Suburban Sanitary Commission. He married Nancy Cabell Wooding in 1945. They had two daughters and five sons. Robert died in 1983 and Nancy died in 1995. The entire farm has been developed for residential housing.

The Hobbs Family

In 1899, Franklin and Martha Hobbs and their eleven children moved to Colesville from Dayton, Maryland (in Howard County). They rented *Valley View*, estate of the deceased Joseph Burr. In 1910, they moved to the Miller house on the northeast corner of the Colesville intersection. This was a large frame structure with three floors. Franklin farmed the Miller land to the north and east of the house. He died in 1918 at the age of 69. Martha died in 1913 at 52.

Of the eight sons, six remained in the Colesville area. Most of them were dairy and truck farmers:

Lewis Hobbs farmed and operated a roadside stand. He also was a Judge of Orphans Court in Montgomery County.

---

* As remembered by Ed Reed, the blacksmith: "The community doctor was Dr. Richardson. He was a pretty good doctor, but he drank heavily and spent all he made on whiskey. He rode for miles in a horse and buggy or on horseback. He was a bachelor."

Hobbs Drive was named after Claude Hobbs, who owned the land now in the Colesville Estates Subdivision. Claude dealt in cattle, buying, selling, and hauling to the West Friendship and Baltimore markets.

Denton Hobbs, a bachelor, helped his sisters-in-law at butchering time. In addition to slaughter of the animals, the meat had to be cooked, some ground into sausage, and processed for storage. He also helped make apple butter.

William Hobbs was a truck farmer and served as a desk clerk for the Takoma Station of the Montgomery County Police Department. He also worked a short time for the Washington, D.C., government.

Jerry Hobbs, was a hay dealer, trucker, and policeman. He married Margaret Baker.

Charles Hobbs, known to most as Charlie, clerked for a while in Cissel's store and hauled milk in a refrigerated truck from Colesville and surrounding areas to dairies in Washington, D.C.. A description of Charlie's baseball talent follows:

> Love of the game of baseball was common to all the sons of Franklin and Bessie Hobbs, but Charlie is best known for his exploits on the diamond. He and some of his brothers played on the Colesville Cardinals team. According to family lore, "Charlie was known for his sinking fastball. In fact the opposition teams thought it sank a little more abruptly then it should have. Although his strikeout pitch was never proven to be enhanced by a foreign substance, Charlie's pitch caused many a batter to trade his hickory stick for a pine seat.
> Charlie's catcher, Jerry Hobbs, many years later confirmed that Charlie may have had a trick or two up his sleeve, "Charlie threw so hard and the ball dropped so fast that I'd end up with broken fingers and the batter ended up taking a seat."[12]

French Hobbs returned to the Hobbs home farm in Dayton, Maryland. Elmer Hobbs, a dentist, practiced first at Union Bridge, Maryland, and later at Westminster, Maryland.

Of the three daughters, Bessie, the oldest, married James Anderson, who became a prominent farmer in the Colesville area. He taught Sunday School in the Colesville Methodist Church for 35 years. He rented the Westover property (formerly owned by Francis Valdenar). He purchased land on the east side of today's New Hampshire Avenue - across from the Meadowood area. A son of James and Bessie Anderson, James Jr. was a charter member and first president of the Colesville Lions Club.

Grace Hobbs, the youngest child of Franklin and Bessie Hobbs, married Floyd Suthard. He served in the army during World War I. After returning to civilian life, he became a master carpenter, builder, and construction contractor.

Figure 44: Charlie and Grace Hobbs Suthard
The building on the right is the large house that the Hobbs rented on the northeast corner of the Colesville intersection. The horse was a mare named Edna. (Courtesy of Eveleen Carter)

William Smith of Smithville[13]

William Smith was a walking encyclopedia of Colesville history. From Quaint Acres to Briggs Chaney Road, from Northwest Branch to Paint Branch and beyond, he could tell you who owned what and when.

Much of his knowledge came from living and working in Colesville since he was born in 1915. He was one of the Smiths of Smithville, the satellite community, about one-half mile east of Colesville. His grandfather, George Smith, was a founder of Smith Town that later became known as Smith Village and still later as Smithville. William's father, William E. Smith, expanded his original 25 acres by buying another 27 from Cissel, a family that owned a building supply in Silver Spring and operated a general store in Colesville. William and his brother, Branson, raised by their father to be farmers, produced vegetables to sell in the Washington, D.C., markets. In addition, the two brothers ran a saw mill for 25 years.

William's early sources of information about people in Colesville were his school textbooks. Public schools were not integrated when he was a boy. The first African-American school was a small, frame building on Bonifant Road, east of New Hampshire Avenue. In the late 1920s, the Johnson family donated two acres of land and other Smithville residents donated money to build a new school. It was located at the corner of Fairland and Randolph Roads - where the County maintenance buildings now stand. The textbooks of the African-American schools were secondhand. When the white schools introduced new texts, the students turned in their old books, and these were given to the African-American schools. Inside the covers of the old books were the names of white students. William Smith, with his talent for absorbing facts, learned the names of nearly all the Colesville families and their children that lived outside Smithville.

William also learned a lot about Colesville by working throughout the community. Name a subdivision in the area and he had worked there at some time. For example, he remembered clearing the land between today's Mormon Church and Northwest Branch. He helped remove the stone, cave-like structures used for curing hides in Edward Dawes's 19th century tannery. He helped tear down the old frame house behind the historic home now owned by Mr. and Mrs. Robert Barendsen on Randolph Road. The boards from the frame house were used to build *Abre Hill*, the Colesville home of William Shepherd, an attorney for Andrew Mellon.

After his retirement from farming, William Smith and his wife, Lily, continued to live in their farmhouse on the south side of East

Randolph until ___. His father built the house in 1923. Today it is surrounded by newly constructed homes in a subdivision known as Colesville Estates.

Figure 45: William Smith stands beside the house his father built in the 1920. It is now surrounded by newly constructed homes. (Photograph by Joyce Bayley).

Elizabeth McCulloch - Colesville's Venturous Farmer[14]

"I wish to see Senora Padilla. Here is my card." Elizabeth McCulloch extracted a neat calling card from her small, silver clutch purse.

The butler of the Spanish Embassy at 16th and Euclid, Washington, D.C., accepted her card and went upstairs.

Wondering what would happen next, Elizabeth turned nervously toward her freshly washed Chevrolet touring car. She had driven into the circle of the Embassy drive and parked the car dead center in front of the door. She adjusted her very best clothes and made sure her jewelry was properly arrayed.

Senora Padilla, the gracious, well-dressed ambassador's wife, came down the circular stairway.

Elizabeth introduced herself and said, "I have a farm not too far from here and I raise chickens, eggs, strawberries, asparagus, and all kinds of things you can grow in this climate, but I need a market for them. Would you be interested in strawberries so big you have to take two bites to get one in your mouth? Would you be interested in asparagus that's over an inch around and a foot long?"

Senora Padilla replied, "Would I? I would love it!"

"And we also have cows and I have whipping cream or I have regular cream and I have regular milk. We can come in two or three times a week and bring these things fresh from the farm."

"My dear, I have never had such a wonderful offer in my life!"

That was the way Elizabeth McCulloch, Colesville's enterprising farmer, broke through the wholesale price barriers for farm products in 1928. Soon she was selling to the Mexican Embassy next door, then to the British Embassy and several others. Her customers included the Montgomery County Hospital, a rehabilitation center for wealthy topers on what is now U.S. Route 29, and Magruders, who sold groceries and produce to the White House.

One of three daughters of a Methodist minister, a Phi Beta Kappa graduate of Goucher College in Baltimore, she was unwilling to put up with postgraduate studies to prepare for a profession in research. Because of summer experience on a farm, she was interested in agriculture. She persuaded her father to buy the Jerry Hobbs farm of 134.7 acres, about a mile east of Colesville, just off Fairland Road. The farmhouse, built in the late 19th century, stood on a solid foundation of walnut logs, but was in disrepair. The three old barns had not been painted since they were built. Chestnut tree stumps, as high as a man's head, covered most of the land.

Fairland Road was a narrow, primitive dirt track. Elizabeth spent many an evening, after milking the cows, filling the ruts with rocks between their farmgate and Colesville. Otherwise they would never have made it to the Cissel and Bradford stores.

Elizabeth's father taught at Vanderbilt University in Nashville, Tennessee. He commuted at intervals during the school year and spent his summers at the farm. He raised Brown Trout hatchlings and was the first to introduce these fish into Paint Branch.

Because of her father's absence and his other interests, the management of the farm was left up to Elizabeth with the help of her mother. During the first year, they cleared as many of the huge stumps as possible, using dynamite to blow them loose. Even though they had expert advice from a friend in Kensington, they put too much dynamite under one stump and blew it completely over one end of the house.

In the spring, they built a chicken house for 1,000 baby chicks and 800 layers. Elizabeth designed the house herself with an aisle along the back side that opened into the separate rooms. They had trap doors along the aisle for collecting eggs and cleaning roosts without disturbing the chickens.

The first crops consisted of several thousand strawberry plants and an equal number of asparagus crowns. The dairy herd started with four cows and expanded rapidly when a barn was built to house thirty-six more. Eventually the herd contained sixty head and milk was sold both retail and wholesale.

Elizabeth spent a lot of time on horseback during those early years. The gates to the fields were high enough to control cattle but low enough to allow Elizabeth to enter and exit by jumping her horse over them.

Such an enterprise required more labor than Elizabeth and her mother could provide. In those days, as now, many people in West Virginia were desperate for work. She was able to hire married couples, two at a time. Strong and healthy, the men worked in the fields and the women kept the barns and chicken houses clean and tidy.

B. B. Benjamin, a transient, showed up at the farm one day looking for work. Elizabeth didn't need another hand, but her mother liked the looks of the man, and Elizabeth hired him. He was a good worker, strong, unstinting, and always wanting to help, but he stole eggs from the farm and sold them at nearby stores. The first Christmas he was with the McCullochs, he gave them presents of a rake, a shovel, an ax, and several wedges for splitting wood. Later they learned he had stolen the presents from Lawrence White's Hardware in Norbeck. According to Mr. White, B. B. "almost stole him blind!"

As recently as 1986, Elizabeth lived in the renovated farmhouse in the midst of six acres of towering trees at 13826 Castle Cliff Way. The twenty-room house had solid walnut staircases and wainscoting. A long, walnut table and heavy cupboards of the same wood nearly filled the huge dining room. The spacious, comfortably furnished living-room with a stone fireplace led to a library that contained a sixty year-old Steinway grand piano. The library opened onto the paved front porch with tall, plantation style columns.

Elizabeth McCulloch was 80 years old when interviewed by the author. Surrounded by newly built homes on what used to be her land, she looked to the future with the same adventurous gleam in her eyes that she had as a twenty-two year-old ready to start farming.

Figure 46: Elizabeth McCulloch
reads on the porch of her farm home.
(Photograph by Joyce Bayley)

Helen Vierling[15]

In the 20th century era of Colesville, Helen Vierling's name is associated with *Fairview*, *Valley Mill*, and *Drumeldra*. Born in 1886, on New York's Long Island, she married Robert Vierling who worked for the

Waldorf Astoria. Her brother, Captain Winfield Scott Overton, who lived in California, purchased Colesville properties as an investment in 1909. His purchases included *Fairview* and *Valley Mill*, once owned by Dr. Washington Duvall, and the tract known as *Drumeldra*. He told Helen and Robert that they could have one-half interest in the properties if they moved to Colesville and farmed the land for six years.

They accepted his offer and in April of 1914 started south. A wagon carried their belongings and they battled snowdrifts all the way to Colesville. They set up their home at *Fairview* and rented *Drumeldra* to Raymond Stoneburner. Their primary farm enterprises were poultry and dairy cattle. They sold the milk on the Washington, D.C., markets. Also, once a week, Robert hauled a load of eggs to the Silver Spring train depot and shipped them to the Waldorf-Astoria in New York.

When Robert died in 1941 at the age of 57, Helen was left with four daughters and a farm to manage.** Sometimes she worked the fields herself, barefooted, her skirts flying, as she drove a team of horses pulling a harrow or a plow.

When Major Overton's estate was settled, Helen Vierling received *Drumeldra* and *Valley Mill*. She moved to *Drumeldra* in 1946 and entered the real estate business. She developed Drumeldra Hills and deeded *Valley Mill* to her daughter, Mabel McEwan, who operated a day-camp there. Following Mabel's death, *Valley Mill* was purchased by the Maryland National Capital Parks and Planning Commission.

Helen Vierling also purchased property in the southeast quadrant of the Colesville intersection. Some of this land is still owned by her family.

An astute business woman, Helen Vierling knew how to compete with men in hard-ball real estate dealings, but making money was not her only objective. While developing Drumeldra Hills, she tried to retain the feeling of open space as much as possible. Although she could have made the lots as small as one-half acre, she chose to make them not less than one acre. Several lots contained three to five acres.

She reached out a helping hand, financially and spiritually, to people less fortunate than she or who had succumbed to the demands of alcohol. She died in 1982 at the age of 96.

** One daughter died in 1918 during the flu epidemic.

The Hutchisons

John Hutchison was born in 1834. His first land holdings in the Colesville area were 30 acres on the west side of today's New Hampshire Avenue. Unfortunately, the land's title was not clear and he lost it. He later purchased 20 acres between today's Colesville Center and the seminary grounds. He raised corn and other feed for livestock. Ordinarily corn was hoed by hand, but John made a wooden cultivator with metal points and pulled by a horse. John and his wife, Jane Matilda Fling, raised seven children.

John's son, Frank inherited the property and added 10 acres. Frank married Carrie Culver and they had seven children. A son, Culver, inherited the 30 acres. Another, John married Evelyn Vierling and they farmed *Drumeldra*.

Born in 1915, Lois Peter married Culver Hutchison. She was a granddaughter of Michael Peter, the immigrant tenant farmer on *Drumeldra*, who later bought land totaling more than 100 acres. She attended grammar school in the frame building that was on today's New Hampshire Avenue and completed the 11th grade at the Sherwood School between Ashton and Sandy Spring. Her childhood home was on the south side of Notley Road just off New Hampshire Avenue. Her father earned his living as a mechanic and handyman and he was a talented musician. Lois's mother supplemented the family income by boarding children. Swimming in Northwest Branch is among her childhood memories. She also remembers the Hobbs House at the Colesville intersection and Harold Bradford and his wife at the Bradford store and post office. As a child, she could talk Harold out of sweets, but his wife was a forbidding woman. She remembers the Edward Lechlider store at the intersection of today's Cape May Road and New Hampshire Avenue.

Lois and Culver raised four daughters. Culver died in 1994. She still lives in their home on Randolph Road between the Colesville Center and the Morningside Subdivision.

Smitty's Esso[16]

In 1940, when 26 years old, Harry R. Smith moved to Colesville and joined the Montgomery County police force. He married Mae Duvall of the Fairland Duvalls and acquired a ready-made family of two children. They purchased a bungalow on New Hampshire Avenue, between Hollywood and Rosemere Avenues. Mae had a well-paid position with the United States Employment Service in Washington, D.C., and her salary was badly needed to supplement Harry's low pay on the police force. Then Mae was killed in a collision between an Eastern Airlines plane and one of the U.S. Navy.

Figure 47: Smitty's Esso (Courtesy of Harold Smith)

Harry suddenly became a single parent of two children, one a teenager in high school and the other a student in Leonard Hall, a Catholic military school. With equal suddenness, the family income shrank to his meager pay check. In his own words, his pay was "grocery money." He couldn't make payments on the bungalow, let alone meet the other needs of his family. He struggled, and partly because of the leniency of his creditors, he survived.

In 1945, the Meadowood Shopping Center was being developed across the street from Harry's bungalow. A Sinclair gas station was built there and Harry, trying to improve his income, operated the station for three years. Business was not satisfactory, and Harry sought another opportunity. He found it in 1950 at the Colesville intersection.

At that time, the only commercial activities at the intersection were Cissel's General Store, on the southwest corner, and Harry and Mary Bradford's store on the southeast corner. A brick residence on the northwest corner was owned by the Naylors, who worked for the gas company. The other nearest commercial activity, besides Meadowood to the south, was a garage and store operated by John Lancaster and his wife, more than a mile north, at the intersection of today's Cape May Road and New Hampshire Avenue.

The large house on the northeast corner of the Colesville intersection, in which the Hobbs family once lived, had been demolished. Only the foundation of a barn remained to indicate any previous occupancy. In August of 1951, Esso Oil Company built a gas station there and leased it to Harry Smith.

The lease of that station, known as Smitty's Esso, gave Harry Smith a new chance in life. Although Colesville was still a community of farmers, it grew rapidly. So did Smitty's business. Nearly everyone in the area traded there. For many years, today's New Hampshire Avenue was U.S. Route 29, and a large part of Harry's business came from traffic between Washington, D.C., and Baltimore. He was known for his ebullient good nature, providing service with helpful suggestions and unfailing optimism about the future. For a man who had survived tragedy and almost overwhelming financial difficulties, this was a feat that brought him admiration and respect. In 1955, he married Dorothy Plummer, three years his senior, and his present wife.

In the early 1970s, Esso started negotiations to purchase the Naylor property on the northwest corner of the intersection. The company guaranteed Smitty a lease of the new station. Mr. Naylor kept holding out for more money, and the purchase was not achieved until 1979. Smitty, instead of taking the lease, decided to retire.

In 1995, when this author interviewed him, Smitty was living in a spacious home on Harold Road. He was the only living charter member of the Colesville Lions Club, which was formed in 1953. He had served in every office of the club except Secretary. He looked back with pleasure on the oyster roasts and

Figure 48:
Smitty holds a tire sale.

turkey shoots that the club sponsored for years. They were so successful in raising money for charity that when space for shooting was no longer available in the Colesville area, the Burtonsville Lions Club to the north continued them.

Colesville's Mr. 4-H

Shortly after Ed and Naomi Bender moved to Colesville's Paint Branch Farms subdivision in 1951, Ed started a 4-H club for local boys.

His members undertook a variety of projects, but because of Ed's expertise in horticulture, the main emphasis was on gardening. The boys had their individual plots and showed off their products in competition at the Montgomery County Fair. They also worked together in building exhibits and making floats for the fair. Over the many years he led this club, he constructively inspired many boys who grew to manhood and took the lessons they learned into their mature lives.

Ed was appointed to the board of the Maryland 4-H Foundation, and he traveled throughout the state, promoting 4-H and obtaining support from the private sector. In his late years, he and Naomi established a 4-H Horticulture Endowment Fund to provide scholarships for worthy 4-H members.

4-H was not Ed's only contribution to Colesville. As a frequent writer for the *Burtonsville Free Press*, he provided the area with expert advice on gardens, lawns, trees and landscaping. He represented the Paint Branch Farms Subdivision on the Board of the Greater Colesville Citizens Association. In that position, he was a constant watchdog, protecting his neighbors from ill-advised actions within the community or by Montgomery County and State officials. He was a founder of the Colesville Community Strawberry Festival and served on the Board of Directors until his death. In 1991, he received a Certificate of Appreciation from the Maryland State Assembly for his contributions to the community.

Born in Hanover, Pennsylvania, he served in the U.S. Navy during World War II. He obtained a degree in horticulture at Pennsylvania State College, and a master's degree from the University of Maryland. He was an assistant county agent for Montgomery County and served on the staff of the University of Maryland as a vegetable specialist. In 1952, he became the northeastern representative of the American Cyanimid Co., and worked with farmers and agricultural experiment stations on evaluating the safety and effectiveness of agricultural chemicals. He retired from the company in 1982 and turned his energies and talents to 4-H and community activities. He died in June of 1995, at the age of 75, leaving Naomi, his widow, a son, Edward, and three grandchildren.

Notes for Chapter XIV: Changing Places and Faces

1. Deed, Montgomery County EBP 23, p. 3, 1880.

2. Postal records for Colesville, Ibid.

3. From interview by author with Lois Hutchison, longtime resident of Colesville.

4. Eveleen Carter - part of obituary of Truman R. Cissel.

5. Information obtained from Russell B. Reed and Eveleen Carter.

6.
   * Deed, Montgomery County BS 11, p. 525, 1843.
   * S. J. Martinet, Map of Montgomery County, Maryland, 1865.
   * Deed, Montgomery County EBP 16, p. 89, 1876.
   * G. M. Hopkins, Map of Berry District, Montgomery County, Maryland, 1878.
   * Deed, Montgomery County MC 198, p. 280, 190.
   * Deed, Montgomery County MC 198, p. 282, 1908.
   * Anonymous, "Colesville History", *Tamarack Bark*, Tamarack Triangle Civic Assoc., Silver Spring, Maryland, Vol 16., No. 1, March 1984, p. 4.
   * Tombstone data in Colesville Cemetery.

7.
   * Genealogical Abstracts, *Montgomery County Sentinel*, 1800-1934, Vol. 2, M -Z and Index.
   * Interview with Ann Tolson Bonifant by Hilma Blair 1974.

8.
   * William A. Garrett, early american.
   * Father John Sierra, personal communication.

9. Information on the Bonifants obtained from Sallie Gridley, personal communication; and from Hilma Blair interview with Ann Bonifant.

10. Information on Ann Tolson Bonifant was obtained from an interview by Hilma Blair in 1974. At that time Anne was 85 years old.

11. Footnote from Thelma Reed, Ibid.

12. Quotation from material provided by Eveleen Hobbs Carter.

13. The information in this section was obtained by the author in a personal interview with William Smith in 1986.

14. The information in this section was obtained by the author during an interview with Elizabeth McCulloch in 1986.

15. Information on Helen Vierling obtained from Evalyn Hutchison, her daughter, by personal communication and from personal knowledge of the author, and from Michael L. Dwyer, Op. Cit., pp. 28-20.

16. Based on interview by the author with Harry R. Smith on June 1, 1995.

Chapter XV

DEVELOPMENT

Subdivisions

In 1725, no more than nine patents covered the entire area of today's Colesville, and they were held by only five absentee owners. The breakup of these tracts occurred slowly throughout the 18th and 19th centuries and the first two decades of the 20th century. In the 1930s, development for residential and commercial lots began in earnest and increased exponentially. By 1987, the nine original tracts had been subdivided into 29. Each subdivision contained lots of a few acres or less, with most of them being only 20,000 or 10,000 square feet. Nearly every lot had a different owner.

The following excerpt from an article in the November 1985, *Tri-County Free-Press* describes the pace of development as it continued into the 1980s:[1]

> **Colesville in the midst of housing boom**
> If current plans of developers materialize fully, 1,800 new housing units will be constructed in the Colesville area during the next few years. Off East Randolph Road, more than 100 houses, many of them under construction, will surround William Smith's white farmhouse. South of the Colesville Post Office, 34 townhouses are being built.
> On Bonifant Road, east of Northwest Branch, construction has started for 125 new homes.
> The Montgomery County Planning Board recently approved preliminary plans for 150 housing units on 22 acres behind the shopping center on the northwest corner of the New Hampshire Avenue - Randolph Road intersection. The Planning Board also approved preliminary plans for 131 units on 77 acres between Bonifant Road and Colesville Manor Drive.
> In addition, requests are pending to build 159 units between the Holy Family Seminary and the Northwest Branch, 131 units on the Lyons Nursery property facing New Hampshire Avenue and Notley Road, and more than 200 units in 12 other subdivisions.
> The demand for homes in the Colesville area is strong, and people wanting to buy there welcome the rapid development; local

businesses look forward with bright expectations to the expanding population, but existing residents are already experiencing congested roads and overcrowded schools.

The 1994 estimated population of the Colesville area was 17,485.[2] Figure 49 shows the components of this population estimate. Montgomery County is divided into traffic zones. The boundaries of six which approximate the Colesville area are shown in the figure as narrow, solid lines. The north-south dotted line is New Hampshire Avenue. The west-east dotted line is Randolph Road. The broad, solid line on the left is Northwest Branch, and on the right is Paint Branch.

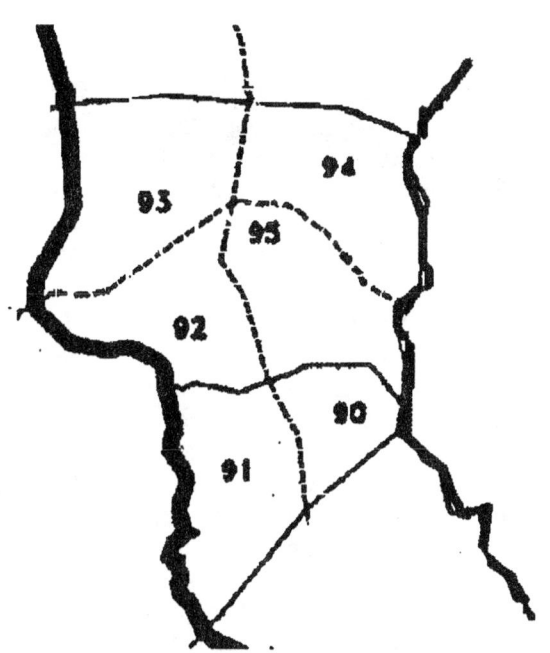

Figure 49: Traffic Zones in Colesville Area

Zone 90 is in the lower right and contains subdivisions from U.S. Route 29 up to and around Jackson Recreation Center. Its 1994 population was 1,311.

Zone 91 extends from U.S Route 29 north into the Springbrook Subdivision. Its 1994 population was 2,865.

Zone 92 includes people living from Springbrook Drive north to Randolph Road. Its 1994 population was 1,985.

Zone 93 is north of Randolph Road north to Bonifant Road. Its 1994 population was 3,246.

Zone 94 is east of New Hampshire Avenue and north of East Randolph, extending up to Good Hope Road. Its 1994 population was 3,946.

Zone 95 is south of East Randolph extending down to about Jackson Road. Its 1994 population was 4,132.

Roads

Figure 50: June 1996. Morning rush hour at Colesville intersection. (Photograph by Ned Bayley)

At the beginning of the 20th century, the Washington-Colesville-Ashton Turnpike and the Annapolis Road that met at the intersection were the two main public roads of Colesville. Three other public roads, which fed into the other two, were Bonifant Road, Good Hope Road, and the Road to Fawcett's Factory.

The turnpike was abandoned in 1911 when citizens of the Colesville District, by a vote of 165 to 89, approved a bond issue of $7,000 to purchase the segment of the road in the Colesville District. They turned it over to the County Commissioners for maintenance. Toll houses were given to the toll gate keepers.

The road became known as Colesville Road and ran from Silver Spring to Ashton in Montgomery County. There also were segments in Prince George's County leading to Bladensburg. In 1961, the leg from White Oak to Colesville was made an extension of New Hampshire Avenue and became MD Route 650. The segment from Colesville to Georgia Avenue at Sunshine was named New Hampshire Avenue in 1964. Only the segment from Silver Spring to the Northwest Branch retained the name of Colesville Road.[3] The New Hampshire Avenue extension through Colesville was widened and lanes were added in the 1960s.

The Old Annapolis Road from Georgia Avenue to Colesville became known as the Colesville-Glenmont Road. In 1961 it was made an extension of Randolph Road that ran east from Rockville.[4] In the mid-1970s, because of rapidly increasing east-west traffic, the road was widened and the bridge across Northwest Branch was moved a few hundred feet north of the original alignment.

The east-west road running from Colesville, once known as Smith Village, then Smithville Road, became known as the Beltsville Road and in 1965, was named East Randolph.[5] Although a bridge spanned Paint Branch previously, traffic had to ford the stream until 1963 when the present bridge was built and the road widened and resurfaced.

The Road to Fawcett's Factory was renamed Fairland Road. Like most side roads, it received very little maintenance in the early part of the century. As late as 1929, farmers had to dump loads of rocks onto the roadbed to drive cars to Colesville. As late as 1955, a one-lane wooden bridge spanned Paint Branch. Heavily loaded gravel trucks roared down the steep twisting approach from the east. Not wanting to lose speed for the next hill, they dared any mere passenger vehicle to deny them right-of-way at the bridge. After several accidents, outraged local residents convinced the Montgomery County Council to order the erection of stop signs at both ends of the bridge. In 1965, the wooden span was replaced with a concrete structure and the approaches widened. In the early 1990s, the entire road was widened and realigned.

Bonifant Road was realigned and widened in 1986. A National Capital Park and Planning Commission staff recommendation to rename the road Bel Pre was rejected after citizens pointed out the historic importance of the Bonifant family. A segment cut off the original road became known as Old Bonifant Road.

Good Hope Road was realigned in 1986 to meet the realignment of Bonifant Road. The truncated segment between New Hampshire Avenue and the new route of Good Hope was named Cape May Road. Unaware of the history of the Good Hope community, the name was selected because there is a Cape May as well as a Cape of Good Hope!

The segment of Notley Road running east from New Hampshire Avenue into Paint Branch Subdivision was developed in 1937. The segment running west from Bonifant into Stonegate Subdivision was built in 1965. Between Bonifant Road and New Hampshire Avenue, traffic on Notley Road has been heavy and hazardous for several years. In 1994, a steep grade was reduced and traffic circles installed.

Police and Fire

In the 18th and 19th centuries, police protection for Montgomery County consisted of the sheriff and his constables. In 1878 there were sixteen constables. Three more were added in 1910 and the force was equipped with bicycles and motorcycles. At that time the speed limit was 13 miles per hour. (This was based on the estimated maximum speed of a horse drawn carriage.)

The Montgomery County Police Department, with headquarters in Rockville, was organized in 1922. The Silver Spring substation was established in 1927. By 1932, there were 32 substations. Officers were equipped with 2-door Model A Fords. The Wheaton-Glenmont Station that serves the Colesville area along with the Silver Spring Station was opened in 1959.[6]

Fire protection in rural areas such as Colesville was a local responsibility - neighbors helping neighbors - well into the 20th century. The 1915 establishment of a fire station in Silver Spring provided some help.

In 1941, a station for the Hillandale Volunteer Fire Department was built just south of the Colesville area. An early volunteer at that station remembers that telephone alarms were installed in a highly audible place, such as a cold air duct, of each volunteer's house.[7]

The Colesville station, a branch of Hillandale, was built near the intersection of New Hampshire Avenue and Randolph Road in 1962.

Utilities

Telephone lines were installed shortly after May 1909. In that year the Chesapeake and Potomac Telephone Company of Baltimore purchased rights of way for the erection of poles and lines.[8]

The Potomac Electric and Power Company (PEPCO) was founded in 1896, but not until 1928 did the company extend lines into rural Montgomery County. Records show that the extension included lines up Georgia Avenue to Olney and Sandy Spring.[9] Ralph Love related to this author how the lines came to Colesville.

Ralph's parents, John Fielding Love and Katherine (Katie) Love, owned a 52 acre truck farm in Colesville. Their land included today's subdivision of Carole Acres and reached New Hampshire Avenue just north of Cannon Road.

Apparently hearing of PEPCO's movement into rural areas, Katie Love approached the company about service to the Love's farm in Colesville. They agreed, provided every landowner along the line paid a fee of $100. That was a lot of money in those days, especially to farmers.

Katie then approached Baltimore Gas and Electric. That company already had lines to Ashton, only a few miles north. If PEPCO insisted on the $100 fee, the Baltimore firm offered to extend their service to Colesville at no cost.

Katie Love went back to PEPCO with this information. PEPCO installed the line to Colesville at no cost to the landowners. The Loves replaced their gas lights with electricity and their neighbors also had electricity available.[10]

Farms in Colesville's outlying area were not so fortunate. Some did not have electric power until the 1940s.[11]

The first water line was laid sometime before 1959, and the first sewer shortly thereafter. Although the purpose of the sewer was to protect public health, citizens protested its installation, fearing it would stimulate development. And it did.

Protection of Natural Resources

In June of 1965, the Montgomery County Council adopted a sediment control program. The introduction reflects the growing concern about soil erosion and sediment in the latter half of the 20th century:

> The people of Montgomery County formed the Montgomery Soil Conservation District in 1945 to combat soil erosion in the county. The District now operates an effective conservation program in the open areas of the county with voluntary cooperation from land owners, farmers, and the many federal, state and local agencies and groups concerned.
> However, excessive quantities of soil are eroding from the areas of the county undergoing development. These losses range up to 2,300 tons per square mile per year in some watersheds; small areas lose soil at many times this rate. This is due to the rolling topography, the intensity of rainfall, the erodibility of the soils, and the extent and duration of exposure of bare soils during development.
> This erosion is removing fertility, cutting rills and gullies, and washing out roads, road banks and fills on the lands affected. The resulting sediment is clogging storm sewers and road ditches, muddying streams, and silting valley lands, lakes, and reservoirs. It also contributes to blocked navigation channels, reduced recreational opportunities, and general unsightliness in the Potomac River.
> Erosion damages are costly to repair, often requiring regrading or replacement of the washed out soil and replacement of damaged pipes and pavements. Sediment damages are also very costly. Sediment is expensive to remove from the water itself and from the channels, reservoirs, or other areas where it is deposited. Sediment limits the use of water for most beneficial purposes.

Public sediment damages are increasing due to increased public ownership of valley lands, the increased use of waters of the county for recreation and water supply, and the expansion of development in the county.

The water pollution aspects of sediment are recognized by the State of Maryland by the inclusion of sediment as a pollutant subject to regulations under the water pollution control laws.

Property owners suffering unreasonable damage from sediment and flooding of property at downstream sites as a result of disturbance of watershed areas upstream often must seek protection from the courts against such damages.

The Interstate Commission on the Potomac River Basin has focused attention on the sediment problem in its Technical Bulletin 1963-1 "A Program for Sediment Control in the Washington Metropolitan Region".

Erosion and sediment control measures developed in the soil conservation district program with the technical assistance of the USDA - Soil Conservation Service and other agencies can be readily adapted to urbanizing areas.

The Washington Suburban Sanitary Commission, Montgomery Soil Conservation District, and Maryland National Capital Park and Planning Commission endorsed and supported the County Council's program.[12]

The initiation of the sediment control program was an important step ahead in the preservation of natural resources. However, overly zealous implementation of waterway erosion control threatened to destroyed small streams such as the tributaries of Northwest and Paint Branches in the Colesville area.

This dangerous situation developed from a problem with storm drainage in the lower part of Montgomery County. When construction took place along Booze Creek and certain streets in the Wheaton area, streams were left open between two lanes of paving. Yet stream channels accumulated trash and children playing in them were subject to injury from broken glass.

A report by a consultant to the Washington Suburban Sanitary Commission in 1964 recommended that this problem be corrected by enclosing all streams if they required a pipe of 72" or less. The Sanitary Commission, Maryland National Capital Park and Planning Commission, and the Montgomery County Public Works Department adopted this recommendation as policy for all streams in the county.[13]

As a result of this policy, the entire length of Bare Branch was scheduled to be piped. The Branch is entirely in the Colesville area and runs from north of Old Bonifant Road, south across Notley Road and into Northwest Branch near Randolph Road. The subdivision of Drumeldra Hills straddles much of the stream.

When Helen O. Vierling and Ned and Joyce Bayley, owners of property along the stream, applied for subdivision approvals in 1966, they were told that enclosure of the stream in a pipe was required. They worked with Edward Shepherd, an engineer living on Springloch Road in Colesville, and developed an alternative plan for the entire stream. The plan called for rip-rap on potentially erodible banks and modification of bends sharper then 45 degrees. This would insure channel retention and protect natural vegetation on both sides of the stream. Other measures would reduce erosion and allow flooding into the natural vegetation thus slowing the current and depositing some of the silt before it reached Northwest Branch.[14] The plan and the subdivision approvals were denied. Six years later, after the national environmental movement had gained momentum, the County and the Commissions relented. In response to negotiations by J. Ambrose Kiley, an attorney living in Paint Branch Farms, the County executed a covenant giving the Bayleys the right to improve the stream in any way they wanted, providing the County would not be held liable for flooding damages.

Today, the branch, now known as Twistin' Creek, meanders through the Bayley property with carefully tailored bends, rip-rap to protect stream banks and three weirs to control erosion. Natural vegetation, including sycamores, tulip poplars and maples, has been maintained along the stream banks. Other property owners, up stream and down, have similarly improved the branch.

Since 1971, the county policy on small streams has changed dramatically. Buffer zones are required on both sides of the streambed. The extent of the buffer zones is related to the severity of adjacent slopes. In the buffer zones, with few exceptions, no structure, impervious surface, or activity requiring grading and clearing are allowed. A conservation agreement is required for persons applying for subdivision approval.[15]

In 1995, the Montgomery County Council adopted a plan to protect the upper Paint Branch. Thirteen million dollars has been committed for purchasing land along the watershed. The plan requires developers to maintain the quality of water in the branch and its tributaries.

One interaction between the increased density of housing and recent efforts to preserve natural areas of grass and trees is the rapid multiplication of white-tailed deer. They are attractive animals, but they have become so numerous that they are a significant threat to traffic safety. They severely damage residential landscaping and gardens. In today's environment, they have no natural predators. Means are being explored to reduce the population.

Notes for Chapter XV: Development

1. Ned Bayley, "Colesville in the Midst of Housing Boom," *Tricounty Free Press*, November 21, 1985, p. 15.

2. • Map of White Oak, Colesville Planning Area, Maryland National Capital Parks and Planning Commission, Silver Spring, Maryland, 1987.
   • Montgomery County Planning Department, Maryland National Capital Park and Planning Commission, Silver Spring, Maryland, 1994.

3. • Jesse F. Nicholson, Memorandum August 28, 1961, MNCPPC, Silver Spring, Maryland.
   • Jesse F. Nicholson, Memorandum July 21, 1964, MNCPPC, Silver Spring, Maryland.

4. Jesse F. Nicholson, Ibid.

5. Jesse F. Nicholson, Memorandum Jamuary 4, 1966, MNCPPC, Silver Spring, Maryland.

6. Donald and Dena Brooks, *A Worthy Innovation, A History of the Montgomery County Police Department*, Montgomery County, MD, pp. 2-19.

7. George Jay, personal communication, 1995.

8. Rights of Way, Montgomery County Lib. 206, pp. 189-200, 1909.

9. Potomac Electric Power Company, personal communication, February 22, 1996.

10. Interview with Ralph Love by Ned Bayley, 1996.

11. Sallie Liebig Gridley, personal communication, February 22, 1996.

12. *Sediment Control Program for Montgomery County, Maryland*, May 1965.

13. John W. Neuman, letter to Helen O. Vierling, May 19, 1967.

14. Helen O. Vierling, Lillian Joyce Bayley, and Ned D. Bayley, *Proposed Master Plan for the Stream Valley of Twistin' Creek, Drumeldra Hills, Montgomery County, Maryland,* January 1967.

15. Planning Department, Environmental Planning Division, *Environmental Management of Development in Montgomery County, Maryland,* Maryland National Capital Park and Planning Commission, 1991, pp. 10-30.

Chapter XVI

SCHOOLS AND CHURCHES

Schools

In 1910, a proposal was made to build an industrial school for African-Americans near Colesville, but no action was taken. The Colesville school for African-American students struggled along with insufficient funds until it was closed in 1914 and the property sold. Students had to go to Spencerville or Burnt Mills. In the 1920s, residents of Smithville donated land and matching money to build the Rosenwald (Smithville) School at the intersection of today's Randolph and Fairland Roads. In 1951, this school had 114 students in grades from kindergarten through sixth. Following the integration of public schools, this building became a county maintenance facility.[1]

Early in the century, African-Americans were restricted to a 5th grade education. Starting in 1927, the United Trustees of Montgomery County, an African-American group, established a two-room high school in Rockville. By 1929, the facility was overwhelmed with students. After struggling with rented facilities, the Trustees obtained some acreage in Lincoln Park and built a high school that provided classes through the 11th grade. Finally, the County School Board decided to improve education for African-Americans and George Washington Carver High School was opened in Rockville in 1950. A Lincoln Junior High School also was created. In 1951, these two schools had an enrollment of 299 and 497 respectively. Until the Supreme Court ordered integration of schools in 1954, these were the only facilities available to African-Americans above the sixth grade.[2]

A large frame elementary school was built about 1906 to replace the one for white students on Notley Road. The new school was located on the east side of today's New Hampshire Avenue between Colesville Manor Drive and Cape May Road.

SCHOOLS AND CHURCHES 145

Figure 51: 1915 class of Colesville School
poses on the steps of frame building that stood
on Colesville Road (today's New Hampshire Avenue).

FROM LEFT TO RIGHT:
Top Row: Catherine Hutchison, Mildred Ray, Sophia Davis, Mr. Watkins (Teacher), Helen Thompson, Lulu Richardson, Maurice Nicholson
4th Row: May Hobbs, Ethel Christopher, Helen Lechlider, Forest Thompson, Harry Woodward
3rd Row: William (Bill) Thompson, Dorothy Cissel, Mary Tucker, Edith Veitch, Clarence Lechlider, Gladys Baker, Louise Hutchison, Mary Hutchison
2nd Row: James Anderson, Edward Lechlider, Estelle Thompson, Irving Davis, Betty Ray, Alvin Wall, Melvin Woodward, Dalton Johnson
1st Row: Joe Bean, Ida Johnson, Richard (Dick) Bean, Catherine Johnson, Ignata Lechlider, Edith Hobbs, Lester Johnson, Donald Hobbs, Amelia Lechlider

In 1930, the frame structure was replaced by a brick building about one hundred yards south on the same side of the road. This building was the site of the Colesville Elementary School until 1964. It is now known as the Community Health Center but also houses a child care unit and the Colesville Clothes and Toy Closets.

In 1951, the enrollment in the Colesville Elementary School was 199. To accommodate the overflow at the Colesville Elementary School, the newly built Colesville Recreation Center immediately behind the school was used as a classroom until the Jackson Road Elementary School was completed.[3] In response to ever increasing needs, Springbrook High School was built in 1960 and White Oak Junior High School (now Middle School) was built two years later. These were followed by four elementary schools: Westover in 1964, William Tyler Page in 1965, Cannon Road in 1967, and Stonegate in 1971.[4]

In 1995, the enrollment of the elementary schools in the Colesville area was 2,005. White Oak Middle School had 908 students and Springbrook High School had 2,033.[5]

In the early days of public education in the United States, many primary and secondary schools were financed and operated by their own school boards. From the start of the first schools in Maryland, these responsibilities have resided in the state and county governments. To offset this lack of local control, each Montgomery County school has had a Parent Teacher Association. The local PTA groups provide communication between the faculty and parents, and through affiliation with other PTAs in the county, they have influence on the quality of education available in the Colesville area. They have been particularly active in efforts to alleviate overcrowding generated by the rapidly increasing population.

Churches

METHODISTS

For more than half the 20th century, the Andrew Chapel Methodist Episcopal Church, South, continued to be the only religious center in Colesville. In 1938, the frame structure was replaced by a brick building that contained a basement used for classrooms, programs, and community dinners. In 1959, the present building at 52 Randolph Road was completed. It was known as the Colesville Methodist Church until 1968, when it became the Colesville United Methodist Church.[6]

SCHOOLS AND CHURCHES

CATHOLICS

The first Catholic organization to locate in Colesville was the Sons of the Holy Family. In 1946, this organization purchased several acres of the Brown farm for a seminary to train priests. The acreage included the Joseph Burr Mansion with its 26 rooms on three stories and eight fireplaces. The mansion deteriorated over the years and was replaced by a more modern structure located in a grove of trees at 401 Randolph Road.[7]

In 1956, the Catholic Archdiocese of Washington, D.C., purchased ten acres in the Springbrook area of Colesville. It was to be the site of facilities for the St. John the Baptist Parish that would serve 175 families in the area.

Four years later, Archbishop Patrick O'Boyle assigned Reverend E. Carl Lyon the task of developing the parish. He was pastor of a church site that consisted of ten acres of trees and brush, a dilapidated, two-story house, a shed and a 20-foot well. The only salvageable items in the buildings were a slipper chair and a Victorian sofa. He had no rectory, no place to hold confessions, and no place to perform mass. He contacted the Sons of the Holy Family to learn if there was a place on the seminary property to hold services, but they were on the process of building a chapel and it would not be ready for several months.

With borrowed funds, Father Lyon purchased a house on Brantford Avenue, near the building site. This was his rectory.

When Father Lyon entered the rectory officially on the afternoon of June 18, 1960, he was met there by a group of ladies who not only greeted him officially but also spent the afternoon preparing the basement chapel for mass and setting up the rectory with furniture, bedding, and food. Among others, these ladies included Rita d'Epagnier, Katherine Haber, Helen Lorentz, Gleaves Steinmetz, and Fran Williams. Thanks to their efforts, the building was ready for confessions scheduled for that evening and mass the next morning. Only one person came to the confession, but the morning mass was well attended.

A master plan was developed for a church, rectory, school, convent, athletic field, parking area, and surrounding grounds. John d'Epagnier of Notley Road provided architectural services and, in addition, designed the cathedral glass window and the exquisite tabernacle. The construction was planned in four stages and the final stage was inaugurated in 1967.[8]

BAPTISTS

In July of 1957, the Kensington Baptist Church surveyed the Colesville area to determine the feasibility of establishing a church there. During July of the same year, the first service of the Colesville Baptist Mission was held in the Colesville Elementary School. In 1959, a three acre building site was purchased at Andrew Drive and Colesville Road (now New Hampshire Avenue). One year later an additional acre was purchased and an architect employed. In May 1960, the Colesville Baptist Mission was constituted as a church and affiliated with the Maryland Baptist Union Association and Southern Baptist Church. In July of 1961, the new building - an education unit - was dedicated. A parsonage was purchased at 1305 Morningside Drive in 1965.

Over a period of four years, plans were developed for a sanctuary, and, in March of 1972, the first services were held in the new building. There were 388 in attendance at the worship service, 275 at Sunday School, and 184 at the evening service.

Church offices were renovated in 1985, and in 1992, renovations were completed for the pre-school area, food service area, Fellowship Hall, decor of the sanctuary, and other portions of the church building.[9]

PRESBYTERIANS

Also in 1957, the Presbytery of Washington City purchased 16 acres of farmland with an old house at 12800 New Hampshire Avenue in Colesville. First Sunday school and worship services were held in a store at the Meadowood Shopping Center. The old farmhouse was made the parish house and was used for the church office and church school classes. By 1959, the Colesville Presbyterian Church was officially organized.[10] The congregation had grown so much that space for worship was moved to a double-store in the shopping center. In the same year, a manse was purchased, a three bedroom rambler on East Holcrest Drive. In January of 1960, the church moved to the newly built Jackson Road Elementary School for Sunday morning services.

On October 30, 1960, the congregation of 195 met for the first time in the newly constructed sanctuary and church school on the acres purchased in 1957. The architect was John Stanley Samperton. Two years later the growing congregation made it necessary to rent space in the White Oak Junior High School for church school classes. In 1965, an addition was constructed to house education classes and enlarge the sanctuary.[11]

SCHOOLS AND CHURCHES 149

EPISCOPALIANS

The Episcopalian Diocese of Washington, D.C., set up a Department of Mission in the early 1950s. In 1957, efforts began to establish a mission in Colesville and a 7.8 acre building site was purchased at the corner of Hobbs Drive and New Hampshire Avenue (then Colesville Road). The first Sunday evening services for the new mission were held in November 1959 in the Colesville Recreation Center on Hobbs Drive across from the mission building site.* Later Sunday morning services were held in the downstairs family room of the vicarage that the mission had purchased on Colesville Manor Drive, about a block from the building site. During that period, church school on Sunday mornings was held in four homes on Colesville Manor Drive. The services of the mission became widely known as the "house church."

John A. d'Epagnier of Notley Road was hired as architect and the mission's chapel was dedicated in October, 1962.

The chapel was named the Episcopalian Church of the Transfiguration.

A history of the mission contains an interesting sidelight on those early years in the new chapel:

> During the first two years in the church building, the congregation could boast a "canine communicant," a large yellow and brown collie named "Sam" who resided across New Hampshire Avenue from the chapel. Sam was a most faithful, regular attendant at services, day after day, Sunday after Sunday. When the narthex doors were open, in he would trot. He would venture from pew to pew until he found the one he preferred - usually one with delighted children to pet him. He was a quiet "worshiper," maintained a regal air and was in all respects a true gentleman. He adopted the church as his own preserve, and the congregation in turn "adopted" him. When in due course he was committed to the Great Beyond, he was missed by all. Sam was gone, but he would never be forgotten.

---

* The Colesville Recreation Center was built in 1959 by the Maryland National Capital Park and Planning Commission.

In 1970, a parish community building was constructed. When the chapel was first constructed, 60 communicants attended the dedication. Five years later the communicants numbered 362.[12]

There were several lay persons who worked diligently over the years to develop the mission, the church, their status as a parish, and the many church activities. Of these, one person was unquestionably the most prominent: Leonidas F. B. Emerson. In 1959, he was asked by the diocese bishop to head a group to canvas the Colesville area for people who would be potential members of an Episcopal mission. Later that same year, the bishop asked him to be the volunteer lay missioner and perform such tasks as necessary to bring a congregation together. He served as lay reader and assisted visiting clergy at evening services during the first winter. He was elected chairman of the Colesville Mission Promotion and Planning Committee that met monthly and conducted the affairs of the mission from January 1960 to May 1961. In the latter month, the diocese granted organized mission status to the Colesville group. Emerson was a member of the committee that drew up the necessary bylaws. Following adoption of the bylaws, Emerson was elected vice-chairman of the Chapel Committee (the vicar was chairman - ex officio). After serving his term as vice-chairman, Emerson continued on the Chapel Committee and as a lay reader at services. When the mission was granted parish status, Emerson was elected Senior Warden of the Vestry. He remained a leader throughout the rest of his active days.

A second prominent lay leader was O. D. Field, a well known realtor in the Colesville area. He was a member of the diocesan Department of Mission in 1957 when the mission for Colesville was started. He worked closely with Emerson during the strenuous days before the mission became a parish and was active in the church throughout his life.

Continued Development of Churches

After the establishment and expansion of the above five churches in the late 1950s, the establishment of churches in Colesville continued at a rapid pace. Seven more recent additions are:
Cambodia Buddhist Society
Chinese Christian Church of Maryland
Church of Jesus Christ of the Latter Day Saints
First Alliance Church
Korean Baptist Church of Washington
New Hampshire Avenue Gospel Church

Washington Spanish Seventh Day Adventist Church

Besides the 12 in the immediate Colesville area, several other churches have been built along New Hampshire Avenue to the north and Old Columbia Pike to the east.

Notes for Chapter XVI: Schools and Churches

1. - Everett L. Fly, et al., *Op. Cit.*, pp. 133-136.
   - Nina H. Clarke, et al., *Op. Cit.*, pp. 24, 29, 20, 37, 45.

2. - Nina Clarke, "The Evolution of Black Education," *Burtonsville Gazette*, March 6, 1995, p. A-29.
   - Board of Education of Montgomery County, *School Enrollment, September 30, 1951*.

3. Leonidas F. B. Emerson, *A Brief History of the Episcopal Church of the Transfiguration During Its First Quarter Century, 1959-1984*, p. 5.

4. Information on school construction was obtained from the Information Office, Montgomery County Public Schools.

5. Montgomery County Public Schools, *Official Report of Enrollment by Grades and School, as of September 30, 1995*, Rockville, Maryland, November 1995.
   The enrollment at each of the elementary schools was:
   Cannon Road   386
   Jackson Road   503
   Walter Tyler Page 403
   Stonegate   338
   Westover   375

6. Eveleen Carter, *Our History*, Colesville United Methodist Church, 1989.

7. - William A. Garrett, *Ibid.*
   - Deed, Montgomery County 1018, p. 200, 1946.

8. Wm. Nolte, Editor, *St. John the Baptist Parish 1960-1965, Twenty-Five Years of Christian Community 1985*, pp. 1-22.

9. - *Historical Highlights Program, Colesville Baptist Church*, May 1985.
   - Dedication Service Colesville, Baptist Church April 5, 1992.

10. After the Colesville Presbyterian Church was officially organized in 1959, a first meeting of the Session was held. Members of the Session were:

Elders-Trustees	Deacons
Robert Jarnagin	Charles R. Baxter
William W. Jones	Robert B. Hammond
John Petersen	Jack A. Richardson

COLESVILLE

Thomas Smith
Charles C. Tevis
Robert O. Wales

Charles E. Taylor
Lucas Voorhees
Fergus Wood

11. • Anon, *Historical Events of the Colesville United Presbyterian Church*.
    • Anon, Colesville Presbyterian Church Firsts.

12. Leonidas F. B. Emerson, Op. Cit., pp. 1-27.

Chapter XVII

CIVIC ORGANIZATIONS

W.C.T.U.

Figure 52: Hall for Colesville Chapter of Women's Christian Temperance Union. Built in 1898, the hall also was used for other public meetings. (Courtesy of Ruth H. Minnick)

In addition to schools and churches, a sense of community was developed by local organizations. In Colesville, the first known of these was the Women's Christian Temperance Union. Organized nationally in 1874 to educate young people about the harm from drinking alcoholic beverages, the Union flourished in the late years of the 19th century and the first two decades of the 20th. Frances Willard, one of the most effective leaders of the movement, spread the organization worldwide. When she died in 1898, she was considered the best known woman of the

19th century. Crowds met her funeral train and flags were lowered to half-mast in Washington, D.C..[1]

The Colesville chapter was active enough in 1898 to be given a tract of land for a public hall. The donors were Benjamin Miller, his wife, Sarah Miller, and Samuel Thomas. If the public use of the site was ever abandoned, the land was to revert to the grantors or the successor owners. The tract was located in the northeast quadrant of the Colesville crossroads, southeast of the present Excel gas station. The hall was not only used for W.C.T.U. meetings, but also for other community gatherings, including the polling place for the 5th Election District.[2]

As a result of the efforts of W.C.T.U. and other prohibition groups, many anti-liquor laws were enacted throughout the country. The movement was given unexpected support by the shortage of grain that occurred during World War I. In 1917, Congress passed the 18th Amendment to the Constitution that was known as the Prohibition Amendment. It was ratified in 1919. The amendment proved unenforceable and was repealed in 1933. With the founding of Alcoholics Anonymous in 1935, emphasis was put on treatment of alcoholics. Activity of Colesville's W.C.T.U. chapters waned. The building had been demolished before 1944, but the group was still holding meetings as late as 1959.[3]

Lions Club

The Lions Club of Colesville is the oldest community organization that is still active. Started in 1953, the members are men and women engaged in business or professions in and around Colesville.[4]

The purpose of the club is to sponsor community activities and to support charities. One of their major fund raising events was an annual Oyster Roast that they held for nearly 25 years. For the past 12 years, they have held an annual Consignment Sale at which landscape, lawn and garden tools and equipment are sold at auction with a commission going to the club. Other fund raising efforts include the White Cane activity and the Coloring Book sales at Christmas time.

The club has supported the Pre-Nursery School for the Blind, Montgomery General Hospital, peewee and junior baseball teams, blood and eye donor programs, and scholarships for specialized schooling. It has sponsored 4-H, scout troops, purchased school band uniforms and provided financial assistance to several elementary schools. Eyeglasses, food, fuel, and other financial assistance have been supplied to the needy. Funds have been provided for police and fire departments, sending children to camp, drug prevention and counseling and local citizen awards. In special projects, it has financed a school in Guatemala and sent funds for tornado relief in Ohio and earthquake relief in Alaska.[5]

Citizens' Associations

Government in Maryland is more centralized than in many states. Montgomery County, of which Colesville is a part, has a population larger than North Dakota. Unlike North Dakota, which has two legislative bodies, Montgomery County is run by a Council of only nine members. Furthermore, many counties in other states are subdivided into townships that also have some authority to make decisions. Township officials have knowledge of local issues and public concerns through personal contacts with the citizenry.

Montgomery County has no townships and except a few incorporated towns, all local decisions are made at the county level. Citizens in communities such as Colesville must deal directly with a complex county bureaucracy or with the County Council, members of which are often complete strangers. Thus local citizens fear that the county government will not understand and will not be responsive to their particular needs.

The Montgomery County government tries to overcome this fear by holding numerous hearings, some of which are held in the localities affected by proposed legislation or rule-making. Recently, the County established five County Services Centers. The one for Eastern Montgomery County is located at the Colesville intersection. This center will try to more fully respond to the issues and concerns of East County citizens. However, these efforts are only partially effective. Citizens in Colesville and other local communities have formed associations to further increase the extent to which their voice is heard at state and county levels.

Colesville has four such associations. The largest is the Greater Colesville Citizens Association (GCCA). It was formed in 1959, when New Hampshire Avenue and Randolph Road were still two lanes wide. New Hampshire was known as Colesville Road and Randolph as the Colesville-Glenmont Road. There was no stop light at the intersection. The only commercial development was Cissel's General Store and Smitty's Esso Station. The issue that stimulated the origin of the association was the imminent introduction of sewer lines into the community. Residents feared the impact of ensuing development. The citizens lost their case but concern about the effect of development remained strong.

At the beginning, the Executive Committee of GCCA consisted of representatives from seven areas. Today, the Executive Board has representatives from 28 areas.[6] GCCA publishes the *Clarion*, a newsletter, for all homes in its areas. In 1959, 700 *Clarions* were distributed. In 1995, the number was 3,200.

Like other citizens associations, GCCA is a watchdog that sounds alarm when impending county or other actions may reduce the community's quality of life. The organization is well known and respected by county and state officials. Unlike its position in 1959 that was to oppose development, the basic position of GCCA today is to guide development as much as possible toward desirable results. The continuing high demand for homes in the area testifies to the unrelenting vigilance of the association and the strong support of the residents.

The Tamarack Triangle Civic Association was formed in 1966. The residents that the organization represents live within the boundaries of East Randolph, Fairland Road and Paint Branch. Although there already were some homes in the area, building on Mimosa Lane in mid-1964 was the beginning of the rapid construction of a 730 home community. The *Tamarack Bark*, newsletter for the association, was started in 1967.[7]

The Valencia Citizens Association was organized shortly after 1969. The community consists of 155 homes in the north-central portion of the Woodlawn Terrace Subdivision. The homes extend southward from the south side of Cannon Road between New Hampshire Avenue and the Cannon Road Elementary School. The association took on a decidedly international flavor when several foreign nationals bought homes there. For some years, a major event was the international lawn party for which homeowners cooked their favorite native country delicacies. Other events have included an annual Halloween parade and contest and an International Holiday Party in December. The association has worked with other organizations in the greater Colesville community on issues and needs to improve the quality of life in Colesville. Robert Aleshire was the organizer and first president of the association. The newsletter of the association is the *Voice of Valencia*.[8]

The Stonegate Citizens Association was organized in 1969. It watches out for the interests of four to five hundred families in the Stonegate Subdivision. An association newsletter is distributed. Block Captains work on issues germane to their areas and when necessary, bring them to the attention of the association trustees.

The Colesville Council of Community Congregations

Combine the efforts of 19 religious organizations, more than 200 volunteers and dedicated leaders and something good is bound to happen. And it did when the Colesville Council of Community Congregations (C4) was formed in 1961. The initial membership was 15 churches and one synagogue. The first joint undertaking of C4 was the establishment of a Clothes Closet to furnish apparel to needy families. Laura Biggs, the manager, opened the closet in the back of the basement stage of the United Methodist Church. Residents of the area and members of the congregations donated clothes, cash and time to supply needy individuals and families with wearing apparel. In 1974, under the leadership of Winifred Dickson, C4 started a toy closet to provide free toys at Christmas time for needy families. Most recently, Laura Biggs started a Baby Closet. In 1994, the C4 closets served 2,600 shoppers for clothes, toys, bedding, and small household goods. The shoppers represented more than 9,800 family members. Besides Laura Biggs, Venita Jackson managed the Clothes Closet for 11 years. In 1994, Diane McManigal and Eva Hannahan became managers of the Clothes and Toy Closets respectively. The closets are operated in the Old Colesville Elementary School building on New Hampshire Avenue.

For 29 years, Colesville Meals on Wheels, a nonprofit corporation sponsored by C4 congregations, has provided meals prepared at Holy Cross Hospital to homebound persons at cost. Sponsored by C4, the original corporation was named C4 Meals and Wheels. Although C4 still sponsored the program, the name was changed recently to Colesville Meals on Wheels.

C4's most recent venture is participation in the Eastern Montgomery Emergency Assistance Network. The network helps people solve temporary rental and energy problems. It combines community, government and client resources to help people become self sufficient.

Current churches and the congregation in C4 are: Church of Jesus Christ of Latter - Day Saints, Colesville Baptist, Colesville United Methodist, Colesville Presbyterian, Epiphany Lutheran, First Alliance, Good Hope Union United Methodist, Heritage Church (Disciples of Christ), Immanuel Church, Liberty Grove United Methodist, Our Saviour Episcopal, Resurrection Catholic Church, Shaare Tefila Congregation, Spencerville Seventh Day Adventist, St. John the Baptist Catholic, St. Mark's Episcopal, St. Stephen Lutheran, Transfiguration Episcopal, and Unitarian Universalist of Silver Spring.[9]

The Colesville Community Strawberry Festival

The citizen associations formed since 1959 had a serious shortcoming. When people turned out in substantial numbers for a general meeting, they were invariably there to protest an action of the County, State or private business. Never did the community as a whole meet socially and for fun. Furthermore, the business and civic groups of the community seldom, if ever, talked to each other.

To remedy these community shortcomings, representatives of the citizens association, the Colesville Lions Club, Sandy Spring National Bank, Colesville Senior Fellowship, Montgomery County Recreation Department and C4 pooled their experience to provide an activity that would bring community families together for fun and increase communication between business and civic groups. Thus the Colesville Community Strawberry Festival was formed and held its first event in 1983.[10]

The festival is usually held the weekend before Memorial Day on the grounds of the old Colesville Elementary School and adjacent Colesville Recreation Center. Activities include the sale of fresh Maryland strawberries by the box, strawberries with ice cream and other refreshments. Local people display and sell their crafts. A plant sale is held by local and nearby nurseries. An auction sells products and services donated to the festival by local businesses. Local businesses also display their wares and services but do not sell them. Churches often have promotional booths. Boy Scouts provide parking and often have a demonstration area. Students from Springbrook High School manage the games for children. Annual Forbes Blair citizenship awards are made to young people who have provided outstanding community services. Exhibits and demonstrations are shown by 4-H clubs, Girl Scouts and local and county service agencies. Clowns entertain youngsters and offer free face painting. Free entertainment is provided. Volunteers carry out these activities. Raising funds is not a purpose of the festival, but to the extent that receipts exceed expenses, money is donated to the charities of the Colesville Council of Community Congregations (C4).

In 1996, the Board of Directors consisted of 32 members including residents, business owners and managers, high school students, scout and 4-H leaders, elected officials and C4. The Board sets the policies of the festival and each member has a responsibility in the management of activities.[11]

CIVIC ORGANIZATIONS

Figure 53: (Courtesy of West Stewart)

Members of the Colesville Senior Fellowship group around their exhibit.

A young Colesville resident has her face painted by a volunteer clown.

Buyers crowd around the strawberry sales table.

COLESVILLE

Notes for Chapter XVII: Civic Organizations

1. Ruth Bordin, *Frances Willard, A Biography*, University of North Carolina Press, Chapel Hill, NC, 1986, pp. 3, 4, 78.

2. Deed, Montgomery County TD 2, p. 307, 1898.

3. Information on the demise of the Colesville W. C. T. U. Chapter provided by Eveleen Carter.

4. Colesville Lions Club

   Charter Members: James M. Anderson, Willard F. Bryan, Edgar L. Burch, George T. Day, William A. Gebicke, Joseph W. Gibson, C. Francis Hammond, Lester W. Harris, Joseph W. Harrison, Arthur L. Irons, Elmer Charles Kane, William R. Love, Horace O. McAlister, Leroy W. Mason, Millard A. Oland, Emory C. Patton, Raymond T. Patton, George R. Ruhl, Ralph George Shure, Harry R. Smith, Charles W. Snyder, Herbert Leroy Stout, Phil A. Thurston, Carroll Trexler and George B. Weller.

   Presidents 1953-1954:
1953-4-5	James M. Anderson		
1955-6	H. O. McAlister	1975-6	James R. Elliott
1956-7	Emory C. Patton	1976-7	Alan J. Ferraro
1957-8	Garnett D. Inscoe	1977-8	Derell C. Wingard
1958-9	Robert D. Ewin	1978-9	Warren P. Morrow
1959-60	George R. Ruhl	1979-80	James P. Garritty
1960-1	Archie A. Biggs	1980-1	Wesley J. Steesy
1961-2	Heywood N. Saunders	1981-2	Charles A. Brown
1962-3	Paul Ruff	1982-3	Robert A. Irick
1963-4	C. Francis Hammann	1983-4	George E. Fox
1964-5	O. D. Field	1984-5	Robert C. Sausser
1965-6	Milton B. Edwards	1985-6	Darrin H. Gridley
1966-7	Harry R. Smith	1986-7	Joseph A. Minnick
1967-8	James McAlister	1987-8	George C. Williams
1968-9	Wallace P. Donaldson	1988-9	Charles J. Berry
1969-70	Jack W. Wise	1989-90	Emory R. Patton
1970-1	Clifton C. Cahall	1990-1	James P. Garritty
1971-2	Henry W. Rohland	1991-2	Charles A. Brown
1972-3	William M. Groff	1992-3	James M. Hastings
1973-4	John E. Patton	1993-4	George E. Gregory
1974-5	Emory R. Patton	1994-95	Pamalee T. Owens
1995-6	Robert A. Smith		

5. *History Lions Club of Colesville, Maryland, Inc., 1953-1994*, Program Colesville Lions Club 12th Annual Consignment Sale, 1995.

6. Presidents of GCCA:
1959-60	Robert J. Miller	1975-76	John J. Kern
1960-61	Pat Hancock	1976-77	Barbara Falkenhayn
1961-62	Ned Bayley	1977-78	Jackie Phillips
1962-63	Boswell Childs	1978-79	George P. Jelen
1963-65	Richard Marsh	1979-80	Raymond Rye
1965-67	Mrs. Frances X. McFadden	1980-81	Richard Groom
1967-68	L. Clark Hamilton	1981-83	Dan Wilhelm
1968-69	Dr. R. G. Lamb	1983-86	Charles Lapinski

1969-70 Dr. Samuel Lazrus
1970-71 Charles Witze
1971-72 Richard C. Hill
1972-75 L. Clark Hamilton
1986-87 Ned Bayley
1987-89 Peter Munson
1989-93 Edward Wetzlar
1993-94 Douglas Redmond
1994-96 Dan Wilhelm

7. *The Tamarack Bark*, March 1984, Vol. 10, No. 1, pp. 7-8.

8. John Bowen, personal communication.

9.
   - Volunteering at C4, Summer 1995.
   - *Tri-County Free Press*, May 18, 1988, p. 25.
   - Don Dickson and Laura Biggs, personnel communications.

10. Members of the 1983 Steering Committee for the Colesville Community Strawberry Festival were:
    Joyce Bayley, GCCA
    Allen Goldberg, Valencia
    Ned Bayley, GCCA Chair
    Rose Klovdahl, C4
    Ed Bender, Paint Branch Farms
    Anne Mathews, GCCA
    Forbes Blair, GCCA
    Joan Mann, Tamarack Triangle
    John Bowen, Valencia
    Charlotte Miller, Colesville Sr. Fellowship
    George Cook, Paint Branch Farms
    George Newett, GCCA
    Don Emel, Sandy Spring National Bank
    Charlotte Note, MC Rec Dept
    Bruno Figallo, GCCA
    Bob Sauser, Colesville Lions Club

11. Members of the 1996 Board of Directors for the Colesville Community Strawberry Festival were:

    Steve Bolen
    Eda Rabineau
    Tracey Kligman
    Sarah Butterfield
    Thelma Richardson
    Cindy Lapinsky
    Paul Daisey, Vice Chair
    Donald Spence
    Robert Lott
    Becky Durfee
    Rosemary Taffs
    Rosins Mason, Chair
    Sheila Hixson
    Valene Tonat
    Harold Miller
    Kay Jones

    Stacey Klatts
    John Bowen
    Norman Rabineau
    Andy Krug
    Ann Carr
    Sally Shelton
    Adrienne Lees
    Dana Dembrow
    Anne Sutton
    Richard Marsh
    Patrick Hancock
    Diane Tseng
    Anne Matthews
    Britta Jones
    John Wnek
    Jennifer Mitchell

EPILOGUE

There you have it: a four century account of the development of the Colesville community. There was no visionary projecting the future, no great plan with goals and means to their achievement. There was no plan at all. The community truly evolved through the interaction of people, their natural resources, their economic and social environments, and time.

The most obvious change over the centuries in the Colesville area is the increase in population. From seasonal use as Indian hunting grounds, the land was populated slowly until the middle of the 20th century. Then houses, businesses, and institutions multiplied so rapidly that roads, schools, and other public facilities could not fully keep up with the need. Obtaining adequate public facilities will always require the concerted effort of civic organizations as open lots and undeveloped land areas continue to be built up with homes and other structures. The use of land and water by the Indians scarcely affected the productivity and quality of natural resources in the area. Degradation of those resources became extensive when settlers and their immediate descendants strove to make a living as farmers without the benefit of modern agricultural and environmental technology. Gradually, starting in the 19th century, improved practices, such as the use of fertilizers, crop rotations and the raising of livestock, reduced some soil depletion and erosion. Nevertheless, runoff from fields and silting of streams continued. In the last decades of the 20th century, an increasing public awareness has resulted in protective measures affecting soil erosion, tree numbers and stream pollution. Despite the enormous amount of houses and other buildings, and the ever increasing paving of streets, driveways and parking lots, there is hope that the environmentally adverse trends of the 19th century and the first five decades of the 20th may be gradually reversed. Even in 1996, the runoff from bare fields has essentially stopped, tree destruction has diminished, and direct efforts are being made to control stream sediment.

History shows an ever increasing quality of life in the Colesville area. In each century of Colesville's development, serious problems confronted the inhabitants. There were no "good old days." Diseases, of local origin and introduced, reduced the Indian population that hunted and fished in the Colesville area. Intertribal warfare and the encroachments of white settlers further decimated the natives. Those that were left fled the area. Early 18th century settlers faced frontier hazards of clearing forested land, crop failure, distance from markets, and primitive transportation. No medical help was readily available for diseases and accidents that disabled and killed. Even in the more affluent families, such as that of Samuel and Mary Thomas, infant mortality was high. Later in that century, the Revolutionary War disrupted their lives. All the Robert Lazenby sons, for example, fought in the patriot forces. Evan Thomas, the Quaker dissenter, did battle in the courts for his rights of free expression. The production of tobacco depleted the soil. Erosion gullied fields, silting streams and rivers. The size of many farms was too small to support sons and daughters of the first generation of settlers. By the end of the century, most of the second generation had left the Colesville area. The frequent turnover of land and mills in the late 18th century and throughout the 19th testified to the wild fluctuations of farm prices and the influence of regional depressions on the Colesville area. People in the 20th century still struggle to stay afloat financially, but the turbulence is not nearly as severe as it was in prior centuries when failure was more the rule than success.

People of diverse races and nationalities are living peacefully together in Colesville and taking part in community activities. Nevertheless, racial and ethnic prejudice is still a problem. The evil of slavery was abolished and measures are in place to increase the rights of minorities and improve their ability to earn and enjoy a satisfactory life, but much more needs to be done.

The role of today's women is a strenuous one. Many share the bread-earning responsibilities in the home and also carry a major load in parenting. But the role of most women in the past was even more strenuous. Wives often bore children until death overtook them. Settlers' wives worked the fields and also carrying on their domestic and family duties. Farm wives of the 19th century obtained water, not from a convenient tap, but from a hand-operated pump, often out in the farm yard. Cooking was on a stove heated by wood fire. Washing was by hand, ironing by a stove heated iron.

The life of men was no less strenuous. Hunting and farm work exposed them to accidents. Transportation was by horse or a horse drawn vehicle. Care and maintenance by those who owned their own horse or horses was for most men a daily chore.

Those who talk wistfully of the "good old days" usually are remembering an incident or two that pleased them when they were young. It is true that the core of living was the family, and some today wish that were still true. People who have such wishes are those whose family life was rewarding. They forget or ignore the violent marriages and child abuse that went unreported in the past.

Is morality less now? To answer that question, one has only to reflect on conditions around the Colesville crossroads saloon during the latter 19th century. Drunkenness, fighting and outright violent prejudice were part of living then and now - perhaps more so back then.

The most important change in the area has been the development of a sense of community. The few Indians that made seasonal hunting excursions responded to community activities of their village far to the south. The first settlers probably had neighborly contacts from time to time, but their social commitments were primarily to churches located to the south, east and north of the area. Their governing centers, Upper Marlboro, Frederick and Rockville were some distance away - a long ride by horseback. During the Revolutionary War, John Berry was a justice on the court that convicted his next door neighbor, Evan Thomas, for not swearing an oath of allegiance and bearing arms. Shortly after the War, the original settlers and their families had left the area. The newcomers were from diverse backgrounds with a common interest restricted mostly to staying alive on worn-out farms.

The establishment of the Federal Methodist Church in 1806 provided the first real opportunity for residents to gather and discuss local concerns. Mills, blacksmith shops, a tavern, stores, and a post office also increased the contacts and sharing of common problems. The naming of Colesville as the polling place for the 5th Election District in 1806 also brought people together.

During the middle and later part of the 19th century, a school was established. There were community meetings to respond to state and county directives for operating it, but for decades these resulted in no action.

The Civil War and the accompanying slavery issue divided residents more sharply than had the Revolutionary War. Families were split between supporters of the Confederacy and the Union. Methodists generally opposed slavery, but their neighbors depended on slave labor to run their farms.

When the war was over and slavery abolished, Smith Town came into being as the first really cohesive sub-community of the area. Its base was the Good Hope United Methodist Church on the edge of the Colesville area, but Smith Town established a separate identity as exemplified by its own ballfield where its team played Sunday afternoons. Later the residents would pool funds and provide land for building an African-American school for their children.

EPILOGUE

The W.C.T.U. (Women's Christian Temperance Union) Hall was built at the beginning of the 20th century. It was the first organized community action effort other than the Methodist Church. In the second half of the 20th century, churches other than the Methodist moved in and started both religious and social service activities. The C4 (Colesville Council of Community Congregations) has pooled resources of 19 churches and a synagogue to provide clothes, food, toys, and financial assistance to the needy.

The Colesville Lions Club, formed in 1953, became a business and professional organization that not only has provided fellowship among its members, but also has carried out substantial fund raising activities for local and regional charities.

Parent Teachers Associations, at each of the elementary and secondary schools, became the focal action groups for people moving into the area with children. These groups joined in local and county efforts to improve education opportunities.

The GCCA (Greater Colesville Citizens Association) and other citizen groups organized to help fill the gap between local needs and county government actions. The Colesville Community Strawberry Festival was established to bring the business and residential community together for family fun and benefit to charities.

All these organizations have brought people together to undertake charitable and civic activities that could not be accomplished by neighbor to neighbor relations. Differences in economic, religious, ethnic, and other points of view will always be present, but the community has the mechanisms in place for airing those differences and taking action toward resolving them. Because of these mechanisms, and despite the problems inherent in a dense population with diverse interests, Colesville today is truly a community. In the 21st century, continued growth of this sense of community can be the most important future influence on quality of life for residents, opportunities for business and management of natural resources.

Finally, the history of Colesville reinforces faith that free people in a democratic country can - despite personal, economic and social disaster - continue to improve their lives from one century to another. Regardless of differences of opinion, religious belief, ethnic culture or life style, they can learn to come together to promote the common good, including management of their natural resources.

Appendix I

TWILIGHT

In 1811, a special warrant was granted to Richard Lyddane to survey 5 acres. He assigned his rights to Daniel Bussard. In 1815, Bussard obtained a patent for 11.625 acres and called it *Twilight*.[1] The unclaimed land probably was discovered after lines for *Beall Christie* were adjusted in 1798.

The land was a slender triangle between the northern boundary of *Beall Christie* and the first line of *Beals Manor*. From north of the old Colesville Elementary School on New Hampshire Avenue, it stretched from east to west.

Appendix II

PERIPHERAL PATENTS

All but two of the patents for tracts on the periphery of today's Colesville area were held by absentee owners. The two exceptions were Henry Lazenby and Samuel Thomas. The Beall family, directly and by marriage, owned five of the patents and the Snowden family owned two. The patents and brief information on them are listed below in accordance with their geographic relationship to the Colesville area. The letter before the name of each patent indicates the general location of the tract as shown on the map in Figure 55.

On the West - from North to South:

A) *Lahill* - acquired in 1716 by James Beall Sr. and containing 1,298 acres.[2]
B) *Culvers Chance* - acquired in 1737 by Henry Culver and containing 100 acres.[3]
C) *Addition to Culvers Chance* - patented by Henry Culver in 1743 and containing 200 acres.[4]
D) *Girls Gift* - patented in 1760 by Henry Lazenby, son and brother of the Robert Lazenbys of *Wolfs Den*. *Girls Gift* contained 100 acres.[5]
E) *Carrolls Forest* - The earliest patent granted on the periphery of Colesville. Awarded in 1694 to Charles Carroll, it consisted of 500 acres on the west side of the Northwest Branch between today's Randolph and Bonifant Roads.[6]

Charles Carroll, the settler, came to Maryland in 1688 as Lord Baltimore's attorney general. When Maryland became a royal colony under Protestant rule in 1691, Carroll, a Catholic, lost his job. He then devoted his talents to land speculation. In these endeavors, he probably was aided by his father-in-law, Henry Darnall, the agent who operated the colony's land office.

In 1712, Carroll succeeded Darnall as the agent in the land office and continued his acquisition and sale of lands. When he died in 1720, he had accumulated sixty thousand acres, including *Carrolls Forest*.[7]

The son of Charles Carroll, the settler, was known as Charles Carroll of Annapolis and managed the family holdings.[8] He requested a resurvey of *Carrolls Forrest* in 1794 because the 1694 patent interfered with an earlier tract called *Hermitage*. As a result, *Carrolls Forrest* was reduced to 290 acres and named *Connelys Lot Resurveyed*.[9]

F) *St. Winexburg* - The second peripheral grant was awarded in 1695 to James Brown for *St. Winexburg*. It contained 500 acres located west of the Northwest Branch, immediately below *Carroll's Forest*.[10]

The starting point for this tract was a bounded white oak which became known as Woodcock's Tree or Oak and was a key surveying landmark in the area for more than a century.[11] The tree was located about thirty feet west of Northwest Branch nearly opposite the intersection of Glenallen Avenue and Kemp Mill Road.

The land of *St. Winexburg* extended west for approximately one mile and a half.

In 1737, James Brown having died intestate, *St. Winexburg* was resurveyed, found to contain 493 acres, and patented by Samuel Thomas.[12]

The history of this tract is a good example of the problems created by surveying errors. In 1745, Samuel Thomas had Allen Bowie, Jr., conduct a resurvey of *St. Winexburg* that found nearly 600 acres of "unclaimed land." However, the resurvey interfered with a 1736 certificate of survey filed by William Beall and James Edmonson, and Thomas could not obtain a patent for the additional acres.[13]

The 1745 resurvey of *St. Winexburg* also is interesting because the listed improvements depict the nature of farmsteads in the first half of the 18th Century: There were:

three plantations and part of another which are as follows: The first plantation is small but very indifferently fenced and has on it two small clap board dwelling houses very old, one old fifty foot tobacco house, one new forty-foot ditto, one very old hen house and one hundred fifty indifferent apple trees. The second plantation is small, the fencing but indifferent, one dwelling house good, one new log house, one old forty-foot tobacco house, one new large ditto thirty-two feet, one small milk house, one hundred sixty apple trees, about twenty cherry trees and a few peach trees. The third plantation with all fencing good, one very good new dwelling house twenty-four feet long and covered with oak shingles, one small clap board ditto, one new milk house, two new fifty-foot tobacco houses, one new corn house thirty-foot long, two hundred young apple trees. The part of a plantation is small with one forty-foot tobacco house and about eighty young apple trees.

G) *Good Luck* - acquired in 1770 by Allen Bowie Jr. and included 101 acres.[14] The north boundary of the tract joined *St. Winexburg*. In 1778, Evan Thomas purchased 50 acres.[15]

H) *Beall and Edmondson Discovery* - acquired in 1746 by William Beall and James Edmonston, containing 894 acres.[16]

On the South:

I) *Second Addition to Culvers Chance* - patented by Henry Culver in 1743 and contained 400 acres.[17] The subdivision of Springbrook Forest now occupies most of the tract. (For a detailed history of this tract see *History of Springbrook Forest and Second Addition to Culver's Chance* by The History Committee of the Springbrook Forest Citizens Association, Montgomery County, Maryland, 1970.)

J) *Addition to Mill Seat* - patented in 1752 by Samuel Beal, Jr. and contained 325 acres.[18] It was resurveyed and increased to 344 acres in 1753. After two more resurveys, the tract had expanded to 508 acres by 1772 and became known as *Bealls Industry*. The tract contained a grist mill that, with the area surrounding it, is known today as Burnt Mills.[19]

On The East:

K) *Bare Garden Enlarged* - patented in 1716 by Archibald Edmonston for 1265 acres.[20]

L) *Deer Park* - patented in 1724 by Archibald Edmonston and containing 682 acres.[21]

170 COLESVILLE

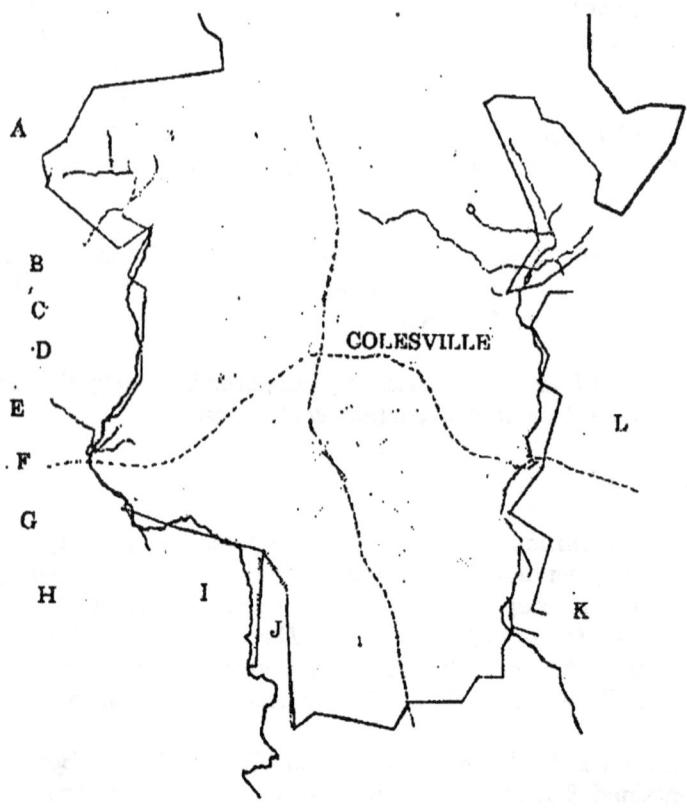

Figure 54: Peripheral Patents,
those external to periphery of the
Colesville area.

Solid lines across the bottom and up the valleys of both branches are the outer bounds of patents within the Colesville area. Upper case letters outside the patents in the Colesville area indicate the general location of the peripheral patents described in the accompanying text.

APPENDIX III

Evan Thomas's Land Acquisitions and Sales

Table 1

LANDS OWNED AND SOLD BY EVAN THOMAS
Prior to Patent of *Two Farms*

Lands Owned Prior to 1800:

Tract Name	Acreage
St. Winexburg	493
Part of Snowdens Fourth Addition to His Manor	1,029
Part of Beals Manor	216
Beaver Dam	60
Mount Radnor	29
Poplar Point	50
Total	1,877

Lands sold before final certificate of survey for *Two Farms* was filed on March 20, 1799:

Year Sold	Sold To	Acreage
From above tracts:		
1785	Samuel Peach	164.50
1788	Mary Ellicott	165.00
1791	Nicholas Lyddane	118.8?
1792	James Pearce	329.37
1792	Joseph Jackson	35.00
From discovered vacancies:		
1797	Jeremiah Berry	30.52
1798	Richard Jones	17.72
1798	Patrick, Michael, & Thomas Lyddane	6.75

Table 2

TWO FARMS LANDS OF EVEN THOMAS
Sales and Acquisitions

Lands sold in 1799 but recorded after certificate of survey for *Two Farms* was filed:

Year	Sold To	Acreage
1799	Patrick Orme	28.25
1799	Robert Peter	56.75
1799	James Pearce	2.42
1799	James Pearce	.88
Total		88.30

Lands sold after patent for *Two Farms* was issued in 1800:

1802	Henry Culver	4.00
1806	Richard Jones	.75
1811	James Lee	48.75
1816	Aaron & Elizabeth Dyer	44.50
1816	John Connelly	39.00
1816	John Connelly	176.25

Lands purchased after 1800:

1803	Henry Culver	2.75
1811	Samuel Lukens	.12

The remaining 589 acres were inherited by Evan Thomas, Jr., and were known as *Two Farms Reserve*.

Appendix IV

ORIGINAL CHURCH CEMETERY
Andrew Chapel, Colesville, Maryland[22]

Catherine E. Baker
1847-1911

Edith S. Baker
1863-1932

Ella M. Baker
1853-1937

R. Lamar Baker
1886-1967

Tyson B. Baker
1858-1920

Katie V. Botele
Born 2-13-1874
Died 10-29-1949

Morgan J. Botele
Born 12-28-1869
Died 2-21-1937

Fannie B. Bowman
1886-1966

Martha A. Bowman
Wife of Allen Bowman
1828-1893

Rosa L. Bowman
Wife of J. B. Bowman
Born 7-14-1820
Died 4-14-1902
There is rest in heaven

Emma R. Bradford
Wife of John L. Bradford
Born 1-3-1845
Died 6-30-1922
At Rest

John L. Bradford
Born 10-24-1835
Died 6-29-1903
At Rest

Grayson B. Burnell
Son of G. B. and Ruth L. Burnell
Died 6-21-1923
Darling boy

Margaret H. Clark
1875-1928

Lula C. Cochran
Born 1-6-1882
Died 12-29-1918

Laurance I. Cochran
Born 12-30-1916
Died 8-14-1918

Samuel A. Cochran
Born 11-28-1914
Died 1-12-1915
Baby

Samuel Iden Cochran
Born 1-30-1875
Died 10-30-1951

Anna A. Cooper-Ashburn
1880-1938

Osborn Crawford
1861-

Rosanna L. Crawford
1867-1921

Thomas Culver
Died 5-10-1891
Aged 76 years
His wife
Ann Matilda Culver
Died 3-2-1892
Aged 71 years

Annie E. Cunningham
Born 9-15-1840
Died 10-30-1930
At Rest

Aged 35 yrs., 7 mos., 22 days, ?

Olena L. Davis
Daughter of John Davis
Born 4-3-1872
Died 1-3-1887

Harry S. Dailey
Born 8-18-1895
Died 12-25-1972

Mildred C. Dailey
Born 12-10-1903
Died 10-16-1987

Diedenover, "Mr. Diddy"
Unmarked
Grave (Buried next to Abraham
Fawcett in Thomas Fawcett lot)

George Dixon
Born 6-10-1852
Died 12-26-1915

Minnie E. Dwyer
Wife of Charles Dwyer
Born 7-1-1863
Died 12-29-1929

Thomas Fawcett
Born 3-6-1794
Died 1-18-1871

Abraham Fawcett
Born 12-26-1830
Died 8-17-1873 or 1879

Lydia Fawcett
Born 6-28-1800
Died 2-14-1874

Benjamin Fawcett
Born 8-26-1823
Died 8-1-1873 or 1879

Marrian Fawcett
Wife of Benjamin Fawcett
Born 2-1-1829
Died 3-18-1892

APPENDIX IV

Eliza Fawcett
Born 6-26-1835
Died 1-8-1871

Joseph Fawcett
Born 8-15-1836
Died 2-20-1871

Martha Fawcett
Born 10-23-1836
Died 12-25-1919

M. Lee Fawcett
Son of Benjamin and
Marrian Fawcett
Born 4-26-1866
Died 2-26-1885

Virginia Fawcett
Daughter of Benjamin and
Marrian Fawcett
Born 7-25-1854
Died 6-4-1935

Gone but not forgotten
Charles F. Gates
Born 2-1-1890
Died 8-8-1923

John W. Gates
1855-1923

Laura V. Gates
1862-1930

William T. Gates
Born 4-1-1892
Died 5-22-1916

Clarence S. Gray
1895-1962

Father
John A. Gray
1891-1939

Mother
Martha A. Gray
1903-1951

Rosa S. Gray
1871-1955

Sacha C. Gray
1904 - 1904

Rest dear brother
Rest Uriah Gray
Born 1-11-1849
Died 11-29-1909
Gone but not forgotten

Vera A. Gray
1901 - 1920

William G. Gray
1903 - 1903

William T. Gray
1852 - 1934

Menoah D. Green
1844 - 1921

Hannah Green wife of Lloyd
Green
Born 10-21-1819
Died 2-7-1858

Lloyd Green
Born 1-7-1803
Died 4-3-1881

John D. Grimes
1842 - 1916

Mary C. Grimes
1850 - 1929

Edith M. Hamilton
1876 - 1954

George E. Hamilton
Born 12-6-1872
Died 4-14-1891

John A. Hamilton
Born 10-1844
Died 6-9-1890

Mary E. Hamilton
Wife of John A. Hamilton
Born 1-12-1848
Died 2-29-1929
At Rest

William Oliver Hamilton
1868-1935

Virginia C. Harding
1883-1962

William F. Harding
1880-1948

Elizabeth A. Hardisty
1842-1930

John E. Hardisty
Born 7-22-1857
Died 6-4-1906
Gone but not forgotten

Rezin W. Hardisty
1836-1907

Denton Hobbs
1879-1954

F. M. Hobbs
Born 3-14-1849
Died 1-4-1918
His faithfulness in Christ

Martha E. Hobbs
Wife of F. M. Hobbs
Born 8-22-1851
Died 3-11-1913
Gone but not forgotten

William M. Hobbs
Son of W.T. and Mae F. Hobbs
Died 8-12-1926

Sarah (Sally) Stump Houston
Unmarked Grave
Died 11-1926

Teresa L. Houston
Born 6-30-1961
Died 12-3-1962

Beulah E. Hutchinson
Born 2-16-1880
Died 12-23-1949

Dallas W. Hutchinson
Born 3-29-1878
Died 10-5-1946

APPENDIX IV

Ada Fowke Jackson
Born 2-20-1844
Died 4-17-1930
Not changed but glorified

Elisabeth B. Jackson
1878 - 1958

Lucile Jackson
Born 8-24-1872
Died 1-24-1883
The Lord gave and the Lord has taken away

T. Lamar Jackson
1873 - 1948

Thomas D. Jackson
Born 1-19-1824
Died 6-10-1890

Father
James L. Johnson
Born 2-28-1850
Died 9-24-1912

Dear Father
James M. Johnson
Born 10-12-1861
Died 12-29-1931

Benjamin H. Kelley
1858-1939

Emma Miller Kelley
1855-1940

Bruce Kelley
Son of B. H. and E. M. Kelley
Born 6-25-1889
Died 6-27-1889

Violet May Leizear
Wife of John S. Leizar
Born 4-16-1884
Died 1-27-1906
Aged 21 yrs., 9 mos., and 11 days

Agnes Emily Leizear
Born 7-24-1884
Died 2-27-1956

Charles H. Leizear
Born 5-13-1883
Died 12-20-1945

E. W. Leizear
Born 8-1856
Died 3-30-1920

Ann F. Kidwell
Born 11-10-1841
Died 1-21-1880
Unmarked grave
From *Scharf's History of Western Maryland*

John Horace Leizear
Born 12-1-1916
Died 9-4-1930

John S. Leizear
Born 10-3-1851
Died 1-23-1918

Violet May Leizear
Wife of John S. Leizear
Born 4-16-1844
Died 1-27-1906
Age 61 yrs., 9 mos., and 11 days

John Samuel Leizear
Died 3-31-1950

Laura V. Leizear
Wife of Charles H. Leizear
Born 10-24-1881
Died 2-2-1915
Loved in life,
In death remembered

Lillian Agnes Leizear
Born 1-19-1885
Died 2-27-1927

Samuel J. Leizear
Born 2-17-1852
Died 4-21-1932

Sarah I. Leizear
Wife of Samuel J. Lizear
Born 9-18-1880
Died 1-1-1942

Clara B. Lindsay
1884-1971

George H. Lindsay
Born 1-9-1852
Died 4-16-1908

Lee H. Lindsay
1877-1953

John F. Lindsay
Son of Lee H. and
Clara B. Lindsay
1916-1920

John H. Lindsay
Buried in Argonne American
Cemetery in France
Born 7-7-1896
Died 10-8-1918
He died that others might live in peace

William G. Lindsay
1891-1934
In God I Trust

Mother
Ruth T. McCullen
1883-1928

Eleanor S. McKeller
Jan. 2-6, 1923

Elizabeth A. McKeller
Dec. 9-31, 1938

Annie E. Miller
1855-1925

Harry Lee Miller
1889-1945

Lewis Miller
1884-1893

Norman Miller
1881-1881

Walter Miller
1888-1888

Wallace A. Miller
1886-1897

APPENDIX IV

Carroll Moore
Unmarked Grave
Born 11-17-1920
Died 4-16-1921

Andrew J. Moran
Born 1-15-1832
Died 11-4-1911
Rest in peace

Infant
John D. Murphy
Died 8-18-1934

In loving memory of
Carl B. Reed
Born 12-25-1884
Died 9-7-1914
Gone but not forgotten

Alice V. Richardson
Born 3-14-1869
Died 6-15-1957
AT REST

Born 12-25-1858
Died 12-17-1939

Richard R. Seek
1899-1953
In God we Trust

William E. Shaw
Born 8-2-1841
Died 7-29-1911

His Wife
Annia Maria Shaw
Born 6-15-1841
Died 12-24-1919

S. Mirriam Shaw
Born 1-9-1867
Died 9-15-1879
Child of W. and A. Shaw

William E. Shaw, Jr.
Born 6-29-1868
Died 10-5-1874
Child of W. E. and A. M. Shaw

Catherine A. Shaw
Daughter of Edwin and
Mary V. Shaw
Born 7-27-1875
Died 9-20-1908

Edwin Shaw
Born 3-4-1858
Died 10-11-1910

Mary V. Shaw
1858-1937
Loved in life
In death remembered

Edna Gertrude Shaw
Born 11-4-1882
Died 2-24-1958

Thomas E. Shaw
Born 2-6-1882
Died 10-2-1945

Mary Louise Stecklein
Daughter of Joseph and
Catherine Stecklein
Born 1-13-1921
Died 2-2-1928
Gone but not forgotten

Catherine Sullivan
Died 4-19-1909
Aged 72 yrs.
Gone but not forgotten

Perry Sullivan
Died 8-2-8-1905
Aged 80 yrs.
Gone but not forgotten

Josephine Talbott
Wife of George W. W. Talbott
Died 7-27-1898
Aged 26 yrs.
May she rest in peace

Anna M. Thompson
Born 10-5-1869
Died 2-8-1951

James M. Thompson
Born 10-13-1860
Died Nov. 2, 1938

Margaret L. Thompson
1885-1966

James M. Thompson
1877-1941

Sarah A. Thompson
Born 2-16-1841
Died 2-12-1905

Cora Lee Thompson
Born 2-13-1890
Died 8-3-1959

Horatio Thompson
1865-1919

Lawrence E. Thompson, Jr.
Son of L. E. and
Laura L. Thompson
Born 5-16-1931
Died 2-22-1944
Gone but not forgotten

William Thompson
Born 7-30-1813
Died 2-6-1900

In memory of our mother
Susan Thompson
Wife of William Thompson
Born 2-1-1813
Died 11-12-1891

Sarah J. Tucker
Wife of William Tucker
Died 12-27-1897
Aged 27 yrs., 7 mos., and 10 days
Gone but not forgotten

Mary Frances Tyler
1886-1953

William Valdenar
1842-1905

Wil Culver Valdenar
Born 3-30-1823
Died 8-9-1852
Let me die the death of the
righteous and let my last end be
like his (Stone moved from
Valdenar family cemetery)

Jacob V. VanHorn
Born 2-11-1844
Died 4-27-1919
At Rest

APPENDIX IV

Sarah A. VanHorn
Born 9-24-1848
Died 2-20-1930

Martha E. VanHorn
Daughter of J. V. and
S. A. VanHorn
Born 7-25-1866
Died 2-22-1885

R. Lee Veitch
1861-1914

Inez S. Veitch
1893-1909

M. Elizabeth Veitch
1865-1963

In memory of Caleb N. Warfield
Born 4-15-1839
Died 3-20-1895
Gone but not

Eliza Ellen Warfield
Wife of C. N. Warfield
Born 1-5-1841
Died 6-3-1914

Darling Sister
Lillian M. Waugh
Born 12-23-1907
Died 5-3-1948

Joan S. Wessells, Jr.
1926-1926

Carrie F. Wheeler
Wife of W. T. Wheeler
Born 8-20-1859
Died 9-11-1887

Martha E. Wheeler
1913-1983
We miss you "Muddy"

The Lord is Risen
Willie T. Wheeler
Born 3-11-1855
Died 4-27-1930

In memory of Noah and Mary
White
Mother died 7-27-1894
Aged 59 yrs., 6 mos., and 28 days
Father died 12-21-1898
Aged 72 yrs., 4 mos., and 28 days
Now is the time

Thelma V. Wright
Born 9-26-1925
Died 12-23-1928
I am thinking of you daughter
Thinking of you in memory just as
I saw you last

Ann J. Zeigler
Born 10-2-1836
Died 4-1-1902

Susie Zeigler
Born 12-12-1861
Died 4-6-1895

COLESVILLE

Notes to Appendices

1. Patent IB O, Montgomery County, Liber 2, p. 253, 1815.

2. Patent FF 7, p. 199, Maryland Archives, 1716.

3. Patent EE 6, p. 14, Maryland Archives, 1737.

4. Patent LG B, p. 684, Maryland Archives, 1748.

5. Patent BC & CS 13, p. 347, Maryland Archives, 1760.

6. Patent B 23, pp. 17-18, Maryland Archives, 1694.

7. • Garrett Power, "Parceling Out Land in the Vicinity of Baltimore 1632-1790, Part I," *Maryland Historical Magazine*, Vol. 87, Winter 1992, pp. 453-466.
   • Michael J. Graham, "The Collapse of Equity," *Maryland Historical Magazine*, Vol. 88, Spring 1993.

8. *Ibid.*

9. • Certificate of Survey 58, Maryland Archives, 1794.
   • Deed, Mongomery County E, pp. 700-702, 1794.

10. Patent C 3, pp. 557-559, Maryland Archives, 1695.

11. Deed, Montgomery County BS 11, pp. 291-297, 1842.

12. Patent EI 2, pp. 528-529, Maryland Archives, 1737.

13. Certificate of Survey 308, Maryland Archives, 1745.

14. Patent BC & GS 38, pp. 490-491, Maryland Archives, 1770.

15. Deed, Montgomery County A, pp. 258-260, 1778.

16. Patent BG & GS 2, pp. 238-239, Maryland Archives, 1746.

17. Patent KI 6, pp. 629-630, Maryland Archives, 1743.

18. Patent BY & GS 4, p. 382, Maryland Archives, 1752.

19. Eleanor M. V. Cook, "The Story of Burnt Mills," *Montgomery County Story*, Vol. 35, No. 4, November 1992, pp. 225-235.

20. Patent FF 7, pp. 349-350, Maryland Archives, 1715.

21. Patent PL 6, p. 4, Maryland Archives, 1724.

APPENDIX IV

22. Information on tombstones provided by Eveleen Carter and Bessie Mae Williams. Monuments for Wil Culver Valdenar and Lloyd, Hannah, and Menoah Green were moved in from family cemeteries.

INDEX

-A-
Abert, Joshua, 96
Abre Hill, 123
Aleshire, Robert, 156
Alexandria, 83
Allen Reed's Blacksmith Shop, 108, 111
American Cyanimid Co., 132
Anacostank, 3, 4
Anacostia River, 2, 3, 4, 14, 66
Anderson, Bessie, 121
  James, 121, 145
  James M., 160
Andrew Chapel, 114, 173
Andrew Chapel Methodist Church, 93
Andrew Chapel Methodist Episcopal Church South, 92, 146
Andrew Drive, 148
Annapolis Road, 87, 136
Appalachian, 2
Ashton, 87, 129, 136, 138
Austin, Gracie, 39

-B-
Bacon, Margaret Hope, 61
Bailey, John, 86
Baker, Catherine E, 173
  Edith S., 173
  Ella M., 173
  Gladys, 145
  John, 84
  John T., 110
  Margaret, 121
  R. Lamar, 173
  Tyson B., 173
  William, 45
Baker Drive, 91
Ballchrist, 13, 16
Baltimore, 57, 58, 69, 74, 76, 91, 99, 102, 106, 113, 121, 131
Baltimore and Ohio Railroad, 58, 59
Baltimore Library Company, 58
The Baltimore Methodist, 91
Baltimore Yearly Meeting of Friends, 53, 59, 60
Bare Garden Enlarged, 169
Barendsen, Mrs., 123
  Robert, 28, 56, 123
Barnett, Todd H., 6, 41, 42, 70
Baron of Baltimore, 9
Bartlett, G. Hunter, 63
Baxter, Charles R., 151
Bayley, Joyce, 56, 99, 101, 102, 104, 124, 127, 141, 161
  Lillian Joyce, 143
  Ned, 75, 112, 114, 136, 141, 142, 160, 161
  Ned D., 143
Beal, Samuel, 169
Beal Christie, 38
Beale, Sam, 44
  William, 21
Beall, 167
  Alexander, 15
  Charles, 12, 14, 22, 39
  Elizabeth, 15
  George, 33
  James, 12, 13, 14, 15, 17, 18, 19, 20, 23, 37, 38, 39, 40, 167
  Josias, 37
  Mary, 14
  Mary Ann, 15
  Ninian, 14, 15, 40
  Samuel, 74
  Sarah, 14

COLESVILLE

Walter, 57, 74
William, 12, 14, 15, 22, 30, 31, 39, 168, 169
Beall and Edmondson Discovery, 169
Beall Christie, 16, 19, 39, 57, 69, 81, 82, 84, 166
Beall Sam, 65
Beall Town, 64
Bealls Industry, 57, 169
Beall's Manor, 13, 65, 69
Beall's Mill, 65
Beals Manor, 15, 16, 22, 35, 39, 40, 83, 166
Beals Manor, Part of, 48, 171
Bean, Dick, 145
  James C., 86
  Joe, 145
  Richard, 145
  Tom, 110, 115
Beaver Dam, 43, 46, 48, 171
Bel Pre Road, 137
Bell, Arthur W., 86
Bell Town, 64
Belleville, 101
Bells Neck, 64
Beltsville, 106
Beltsville Road, 136
Bender, Ed, 131, 132, 161
  Edward, 132
  Naomi, 131, 132
Benjamin, B. B., 126
Berry, 39
  Benjamin, 36, 38, 78, 100
  Charles J., 160
  Edward, 80, 81, 82
  Eleanor, 38
  Eleanor Bowie, 37
  Jeremiah, 39, 69, 80, 81, 171
  John, 36, 37, 38, 89, 164
  Mary, 80
  William, 80
Berrys Chance, 80, 81, 82, 84
Berrys Meadow, 71, 100
Bevins, 89
Bierne, D. Randall, 62
Biggs, Archie A., 160
  Laura, 157, 161
Birmingham Manor, 24
Blackash, 64
Bladensburg, 64, 65, 66, 69, 74, 91, 136
Blair, Forbes, 159, 161
  Hilma, 119, 133
Bolen, Steve, 161
Bonifant, 106, 118
  Ann, 119, 120
  Ann Tolson, 133
  Anne, 119, 120
  Benjamin, 99, 100, 106
  Caroline, 99
  Elizabeth, 98
  Elizabeth Ann, 119
  George, 89, 99, 100, 101, 102, 106, 119
  George Frederick, 102, 119, 120
  Helen, 100, 101
  James, 80, 98, 99, 100, 101, 104, 106
  John, 92, 98, 99, 100
  Laura, 100, 101, 104
  Laura Catherine, 100
  Louisa, 98
  Margaret, 98, 101, 119
  Mary, 98, 99
  Mary Ann, 98
  Matilda, 100
  Nancy, 102
  Nancy Cabel, 120
  Robert, 102
  Robert Lee, 120
  Samuel, 35, 69, 98, 99, 100

INDEX

Sarah, 98
Virginia, 98
Washington, 99, 100, 106
Bonifant Road, 21, 30, 89, 99, 100, 101, 102, 119, 123, 134, 135, 136, 137, 167
Bonifant Street, 100
Bonnifield, Samuel, 35, 98
Boone, Isaiah, 52
Booze Creek, 140
Bordin, Ruth, 160
Botele, Katie V., 173
  Morgan J., 173
Bouic, William Veirs, 83
Bowen, John, 161
Bowie, Allen, 45, 168, 169
  Walter, 106
Bowman, Allen, 173
  Fannie B., 173
  J. B., 173
  Martha A., 173
  Rosa L., 173
Boyd, T. H. S., 5
Bozel, Stephen G., 91
Bradford, 125
  Emma, 86, 115
  Emma K., 85
  Emma R., 173
  Harold, 115, 116, 129
  Harold L., 86
  Harry, 130
  John, 110
  John L., 85, 86, 115, 173
  Mary, 116, 130
Bradford Store, 115
Brantford Avenue, 147
Briggs Chaney Road, 123
Brooke, Abraham, 94
  Caroline, 101
  Deborah, 24, 64
  Elizabeth Hannah, 94

  James, 24, 35, 64, 65, 67
  Richard, 44, 45, 51, 52
Brooke Grove, 64
Brookeville, 64, 87
Brookeville Turnpike, 106
Brooks, Dena, 142
  Donald, 142
Brown, 147
  Charles A., 160
  George, 58
  James, 168
  Lillian R., 112
  Thomas, 71
Brugger, Robert J., 5, 11, 28, 41, 70
Bryan, Willard F., 160
Buckley Downs, 19
Burch, Edgar L., 160
Burke, Nicholas, 102
Burnell, G. B., 173
  Grayson B., 173
  Ruth L., 173
Burnt Mills, 65, 66, 74, 144, 169
Burr, Joseph, 108, 109, 120
Burtonsville, 108
Burtonsville Free Press, 132
Burtonsville Lions Club, 131
Bussard, Daniel, 82, 84, 166
  William, 82
Butterfield, Sarah, 161

-C-

C & O Canal, 83
C4, 158
Cahall, Clifton C., 160
California, 128
Calvert, Anne, 9
  Benedict Leonard, 11
  Cecil, 10, 24
  Charles, 11
  George, 7, 8, 9, 10, 11, 60

Cambodia Buddhist Society, 150
Canby, Anne R., 119
Cannon Road, 81, 138, 156
Cannon Road Elementary School, 146, 151, 156
Cape May, 137
Cape May Road, 22, 81, 129, 130, 137, 144
Cape of Good Hope, 137
Carole Acres, 19, 138
Carr, Ann, 161
  Lois Green, 11
Carroll, Charles, 167, 168
Carrolls Forrest, 167, 168
Carter, Eveleen, 79, 86, 92, 93, 111, 112, 122, 133, 151, 160, 183
  Eveleen Hobbs, 133
Case, 40
  Thomas, 65
Castle Cliff Way, 126
Catholic Archdiocese of Washington, D.C., 147
Charles, 7
Charles Hungerford's Tavern, 44
Charles I, 8, 9, 10
Chase, Addie Bell Baggerly, 40
Chesapeake and Ohio Canal, 58
Chesapeake Bay, 1, 2, 50
Childs, Boswell, 160
Chinese Christian Church of Maryland, 150
Christopher, Ethel, 145
Churches - See religious organizations.
Cissel, 121, 123, 125
  Anne W., 85
  Dorothy, 145
  Helen Fawcett, 116
  Katherine, 117
  Truman R., 116, 133

Cissel's General Merchanside Store, 116
Cissel's General Store, 117, 130, 155
Clagett, Eleanor Bowie, 37
Clark, Margaret H., 173
Clarke, Edward, 83
  Nina, 151
  Nina H., 112, 151
Claysville, 83
Cleveland, Grover, 108
Cloverly, 25
Coale, Elizabeth, 24
Coalsville, 80, 81, 82, 84, 85, 89
Coalsville Store, 80
Cochran, Laurance I., 173
  Lula C., 173
  Samuel A., 174
  Samuel Iden, 174
Cole, 80, 81
  Mary, 80
Colesville, 2, 3, 5, 7, 12, 13, 15, 22, 24, 25, 26, 30, 33, 34, 36, 37, 38, 39, 40, 43, 44, 47, 56, 60, 64, 65, 66, 67, 69, 71, 74, 75, 77, 78, 80, 83, 84, 85, 87, 88, 89, 91, 92, 94, 95, 96, 98, 101, 102, 106, 107, 108, 110, 113, 115, 116, 117, 118, 119, 120, 123, 125, 128, 129, 130, 131, 132, 134, 135, 136, 137, 138, 139, 140, 141, 142, 144, 146, 147, 148, 149, 150, 151, 153, 154, 155, 159, 162, 163, 164, 167, 170, 173
  Strawberry Festival, 132, 158, 159, 161, 165
  Greater Colesville Citizens Association, 132, 155, 165
  Pumping Station, 89
Colesville Baptist, 157

INDEX 189

Colesville Manor Subdivision, 26
Colesville Mission, 148
Colesville Cardinals, 121
Colesville Cemetery, 92, 114
Colesville Center, 129
Colesville Clothes and Toy Closets, 146
Colesville Council of Community Congregations, 157, 158, 165
Colesville Elementary School, 89, 146, 148, 158, 166
Colesville Estates Subdivision, 121, 124
Colesville Lions Club, 116, 121, 131, 158, 160, 165
Colesville Manor Drive, 81, 134, 144, 149
Colesville Manor Park, 89, 96
Colesville Meals On Wheels, 157
Colesville Methodist Church, 121, 146
Colesville Park Estates, 19
Colesville Post Office, 84, 134
Colesville Postmaster, 85
Colesville Presbyterian Church, 148, 157
Colesville Recreation Center, 146, 149, 158
Colesville Road, 65, 136, 145, 148, 149, 155
Colesville School, 97, 108, 145
Colesville Senior Fellowship, 158, 159
Colesville United Methodist Church, 22, 86, 146, 157
Colesville-Glenmont Road, 136, 155
Columbia Turnpike, 78
Columbia Turnpike Company, 81
Community Health Center, 146
Connelly, John, 69, 172

Connellys Lot, 84
Connelys Lot Resurveyed, 168
Cook, Eleanor M. V., 29, 79, 182
  George, 161
  William C., 42
  William G., 28, 63
Cooper-Ashburn, Anna A., 174
Craigen, Laura Catherine, 100
Cramphin, Thomas, 45
Crawford, James M., 92
  Osborn, 174
  Rosanna L., 174
Cromwell, Oliver, 8, 24
Culver, Ann Matilda, 174
  Carrie, 129
  Elizabeth, 72
  Henry, 71, 167, 169, 172
  Thomas, 174
Culvers Chance, 167
Culvers Chance, Addition to, 71, 167
Culvers Chance, Second Addition to, 84, 169
Cunningham, Annie E., 174

-D-

Dailey, Harry S., 174
  Mildred C., 174
Daisey, Paul, 161
Darnall, Henry, 167
Davis, Irving, 145
  John, 40, 174
  Olena L., 174
  Sophia, 145
Dawes, Ann, 84
  Edward, 72, 83, 84, 123
Day, Alan F., 60
  George T., 160
Dayton, 120
Deer Park, Archibald, 169
Dembrow, Dana, 161

Dennis, Abraham, 72
D'epagnier, John, 147
  John A., 149
  Rita, 147
Dickson, Don, 161
  Winifred, 157
Diedenover, Mr. Diddy, 174
Dilts, James D., 63
Disciples of Christ, 157
Dixon, George, 174
Donaldson, Wallace P., 160
Drake, Thomas E., 62
Drumeldra, 94, 104, 127, 128, 129
Drumeldra Hills, 128, 141
Drumeldry, 13, 16, 18, 25, 37, 38, 66, 69, 89, 100, 101, 104
Ducatel, Julius T., 83, 85
Duffy, John, 41
Dunkin, William, 40
Durfee, Becky, 161
Duvall, 106
  Benjamin, 103
  Doc, 103
  Eliza, 103
  Mae, 129
  Washington, 76, 77, 78, 94, 100, 102, 103, 105, 106, 107, 128
Dwyer, Charles, 174
  Michael, 73, 76
  Michael F., 79, 105
  Michael L., 133
  Minnie E., 174
Dyer, Aaron, 71, 172
  Elizabeth, 71, 172

-E-

Early, Jubal, 106
  Jubal A., 100
Early mills, 71
Early stores, 80
East Holcrest Drive, 148

East India Company, 9
East Randolph Road, 27, 103, 134, 135, 136, 137, 156
East Springbrook, 17, 23
Eastern Branch, 14
Eastern Montgomery Emergency Assistance Network, 157
Easy Purchase, 13, 16, 17, 20, 39, 40
Easy Purchase, Addition to, 13, 16, 20
Ed Reed's Blacksmith Shop, 116
Edmonson, James, 168
Edmonston, Archibald, 12, 15, 72, 169
  James, 169
  Mary Ann, 15
  Ninian, 72
Edmundson, Archibald, 17
Edna, 122
Ednor, 87
Edwards, Milton B., 160
Ellicott, Andrew, 57
  Elias, 57, 58
  Elizabeth, 57
  Mary, 57, 171
Ellicott City, 57
Ellicott Mills, 57
Ellicott's Mills, 81
Elliott, James R., 160
Emanuel Parish of Maryland, 100
Emel, Don, 161
Emerson, Leonidas F. B., 150, 151, 152
Epiphany Lutheran, 157
Episcopalian Church of the Transfiguration, 149
Episcopalian Diocese of Washington, D.C., 149
Equitable Federal Savings Bank, 116

INDEX

Esso Oil Company, 131
Established Church of England, 7
Estep, Alexander, 40
Evans, Charles Worthington, 63
   French S., 91
Ewin, Robert D., 160

-F-

Fairknoll, 27
Fairland, 116, 129
Fairland Road, 25, 27, 77, 78, 89, 123, 125, 137, 144, 156
Fairview, 127, 128
Falkenhayn, Barbara, 160
Farquhar, William H., 94, 95, 96
Fawcett, Abraham, 174
   Benjamin, 92, 174, 175
   Eliza, 86, 175
   Joseph, 175
   Levy, 86
   Lydia, 174
   M. Lee, 175
   Marrian, 174, 175
   Martha, 175
   Thomas, 77, 78, 94, 174
   Virginia, 175
Fawcett's Factory, 89, 136, 137
Fawcett's Woolen Mill, 78
Fawlings, Thomas, 92
Federal Chapel Meeting House, 91
Federal Meeting House, 91
Federal Methodist Church, 164
Federal Methodist Episcopal Church, 91
Ferraro, Alan J., 160
Field, O. D., 150, 160
Fife, 14
Figallo, Bruno, 161
Fine Meadows, 72, 84
First Alliance, 157

First Alliance Church, 150
Fling, Jane Matilda, 129
Florida, 2
Fly, Everett L., 112, 151
   La Barbara Wigfall, 112
Forbush, Bliss, 62, 63
Fort Mchenry, 100
Fort Meade, 69
Foundry Station, 91
Fox, George, 24, 53
   George E., 160
   William Lloyd, 28
Francek, Thomas, 5
Frederick (town), 164

-G-

Garrett, Elizabeth, 39
   William A., 133, 151
Garrison's Landing, 64
Garritty, James P., 160
Gates, Charles F., 175
   John W., 175
   Laura V., 175
   William T., 175
Gebicke, William A., 160
George, Elizabeth, 58
George Washington Carver High School, 144
Georgetown, 69, 71, 81, 82, 87
Georgia Avenue, 67, 87, 106, 136, 138
Gibson, Joseph W., 160
Girls Gift, 167
Glassford, Edgar, 119
   Sallie, 119
Glenallen Avenue, 168
Glenmont, 44
Goldberg, Allen, 161
Good Hope Methodist Episcopal Church, 107, 114
Good Hope Recreation Center,

159
Good Hope Road, 22, 87, 135, 136, 137
Good Hope Union United Methodist, 87, 157
Good Hope United Methodist Church, 164
Good Luck, 169
Gould, Clarence P., 28
Graham, Michael J., 182
Gray, Clarence S., 175
  John A., 175
  Martha A., 175
  Rosa S., 175
  Sacha C., 175
  Uriah, 175
  Vera A., 175
  William G., 175
  William T., 175
Greater Colesville Citizens Association, 155, 165
Green, Hannah, 175, 183
  Helen, 100, 101
  Lloyd, 175, 176, 183
  Menoah, 183
  Menoah D., 175
Gregory, George E., 160
Gridley, Darren, 119
  Darrin H., 160
  Sallie, 104, 119, 133
  Sallie Liebig, 142
  Sallile, 105
Griffith, Henry, 45
Griffiths, George F., 42
Grimes, John D., 176
  Mary C., 176
Groff, William M., 160
Groom, Richard, 160

-H-

Haber, Katherine, 147
Hall, Mary, 57
Hamburgh, 72, 74
Hamilton, Edith M., 176
  George E., 176
  John A., 176
  L. Clark, 160, 161
  Mary E., 176
  William Oliver, 176
Hammann, C. Francis, 160
Hammond, C. Francis, 160
  Robert B., 151
Hancock, Pat, 160
  Patrick, 161
Hannahan, Eva, 157
Harding, Lucy, 33
  Mary Virginia, 72
  Virginia C., 176
  William F., 176
Hardisty, Elizabeth A., 176
  John E., 176
  Rezin W., 176
Harold Road, 131
Harris, Lester W., 160
Harrison, Joseph W., 160
Hastings, James M., 160
Heinton, Louise Jorner, 28, 42
  Louise Joy, 68
Henriette Maria of France, 7
Heritage Church, 157
Hermitage, 102, 168
Herring Creek Monthly Meeting (Society of Friends, Quakers), 35, 53
Hicks, Elias, 59
  James, 86
Hiebert, Ray Eldon, 85, 90
Higgins, Hillary, 85
  Hilleary A., 86
Hill, Richard C., 161
Hillandale, 138
Hixson, Sheila, 161

INDEX

Hobbs, 129, 130
  Bessie, 108, 121, 122
  Charles, 121
  Charlie, 121
  Claude, 121
  Denton, 121, 176
  Donald, 145
  Edith, 145
  Elmer, 121
  F. M., 176
  Franklin, 108, 120, 121, 122
  French, 121
  Grace, 122
  Jerry, 121, 125
  Lewis, 120
  Mae F., 176
  Margaret, 121
  Martha, 120
  Martha E., 176
  May, 145
  W. T., 176
  William, 121
  William M., 176
Hobbs Drive, 19, 121, 149
Hoffman, Ronald A., 61
Holly Grove, 107
Hollywood Avenue, 129
Hollywood Park, 23
Holmes, Richard, 78
Holy Family Seminary, 83, 108, 109, 134
Hooper, Virginia S., 104
Hopkins, Elizabeth, 36
  G. M., 133
  Gerard, 57
  Johns, 36
  Mary, 57
  Rachel, 43, 57
House, William C., 63
Houston, Sally, 176
  Sarah Stump, 176
  Teresa L., 176
Huntsberry, Joanne, 112
  Thomas, 112
Hutchinson, Beulah E., 176
  Dallas W., 176
Hutchison, Carrie, 129
  Catherine, 145
  Culver, 81, 129
  Evalyn, 133
  Evelyn, 129
  Frank, 129
  Jane Matilda, 129
  John, 129
  Lois, 80, 129, 133
  Louise, 145
  Mary, 145
Hyslop, Stephen G., 6

-I-

Immanuel Church, 157
Indian Spring, 69
Indian Spring Country Club, 18
Indian Spring Monthly Meeting, 54
Indians, Algonquins, 4
  Anacostank, 5
  Nacotchtanks, 3
  Piscataway, 2, 3, 4
  Seneca, 2, 59
  Susquehannock, 2, 4
Inscoe, Garnett D., 160
Irick, Robert A., 160
Irons, Arthur L., 160

-J-

Jackson, 107
  Ada Fowke, 177
  Elisabeth B., 177
  Joseph, 69, 171
  Lucile, 177
  T. Lamar, 177

Thomas D., 177
Venita, 157
Jackson Recreation Center, 135
Jackson Road, 136
Jackson Road Elementary School, 20, 146, 148, 151
James and Mary, The, 15, 16, 23, 25, 74
Jamestown, 4, 7, 9
Jarnagin, Robert, 151
Jay, George, 142
Jelen, George P., 160
Jennings, Francis, 5
Jewell, Guy, 96
Johnson, 107, 123
  Baker, 52
  Catherine, 145
  Dalton, 145
  General, 106
  Ida, 145
  J. C., 6
  James L., 177
  James M., 177
  Lester, 145
Jones, Britta, 161
  Kay, 161
  Richard, 39, 69, 171, 172
  William W., 151
Jordan, Davis W., 60
Joseph Burr Mansion, 147

-K-
Kane, Elmer Charles, 160
Kelley, B. H., 177
  Benjamin H., 177
  Bruce, 177
  E. M., 177
  Emma Miller, 177
Kelly, Alice M., 97
  Bessie, 97
Kemp, Jacob, 72, 75, 77

John, 75, 77
Peter, 74, 75, 76, 77, 103
Kemp Mill Road, 72, 168
Kemp's Mill Seat, 75
Kensington, 126
Kensington Baptist Church, 148
Kern, John J., 160
Kidwell, Ann F., 177
  George K., 86
  Mary V., 86
Kiley, J. Ambrose, 141
Kilty, William, 61
Klatts, Stacey, 161
Kligman, Tracey, 161
Klovdahl, Rose, 161
Korean Baptist Church of Washington, 150
Krug, Andy, 161

-L-
Lahill, 13, 167
Lamb, R. G., 160
Lancaster, John, 130
Lansdale, Isaac, 78
  John W., 78
  Thomas, 95
Lansdale Mill, 78
Lapinski, Charles, 160
Lapinsky, Cindy, 161
Laurel, 24, 106
Lawrence White's Hardware, 126
Layhill Road, 89
Lazenby, 32, 33, 36, 39, 69, 115
  Alexander, 34
  Ann, 31, 33
  Elias, 34
  Elizabeth, 34
  Henry, 30, 31, 33, 34, 167
  Joshua, 34
  Lucy, 33, 34
  Martha, 33

Mary, 40, 41
Robert, 30, 31, 33, 34, 37, 85,
   98, 163, 167
Thomas, 34
William F., 85, 86, 92
Lazrus, Samuel, 161
Leachman, Matilda, 100
Lechlider, Amelia, 145
   Clarence, 145
   Edward, 129, 145
   Helen, 145
   Ignata, 145
   Joseph R., 72
Lee, 106
   James, 69, 172
Lees, Adrienne, 161
Leizar, John S., 177
Leizear, Agnes Emily, 177
   Charles H., 178
   E. W., 177
   John Horace, 177
   John S., 177
   John Samuel, 178
   Laura V., 178
   Lillian Agnes, 178
   Samuel J., 178
   Sarah I., 178
   Violet May, 177
Leonard Hall, 130
Leyshon, Chad, 115
Liberty Grove United Methodist, 157
Liebig, Margaret, 101, 119
   Sallie, 119
   Thomas, 101, 119
   Thomas Mclean, 119
Lincoln Junior High School, 144
Lindsay, Clara B., 178
   George H., 178
   John F., 178
   John H., 178

Lee H., 178
Willliam G., 178
Lions Club of Colesville, 154
Lockwood Drive, 65
Lombard Street, 57
London Meeting, 53
Lorentz, Helen, 147
Lott, Robert, 161
Love, John Fielding, 138
   Katherine, 138
   Katie, 138
   Ralph, 138, 142
   William R., 160
Lukens, Elizabeth Hannah, 94
   Samuel, 69, 71, 77, 78, 94, 100, 172
Lyddan, Patrick, 82
Lyddane, Michael, 171
   Nicholas, 52, 69, 171
   Patrick, 82, 171
   Richard, 166
   Thomas, 171
Lyon, Father, 147
   Reverend E. Carl, 147
Lyons Nursery, 134

-M-

McAlister, Horace O., 160
   James, 160
McClellan, 106
McCullen, Ruth T., 178
McCulloch, Elizabeth, 124, 125, 126, 127, 133
McEwan, Mabel, 128
McFadden, Mrs. Frances X., 160
McKeller, Eleanor S., 178
   Elizabeth, 178
McManigal, Diane, 157
MacMaster, Richard H., 62
   Richard K., 41
Magruder, Elizabeth, 15

Nathan, 45
Zadok, 45
Manakee, Harold R., 5
Manard, Russell B., 11
Manito, 4
Mann, Joan, 161
Marsh, Richard, 160, 161
Martinet, S. J., 133
Maryland National Capital Park and Planning Commission, 3
Maryland Route 650 (new Hampshire Ave.) 136
Mason, Leroy W., 160
   Rosins, 161
Mathews, Anne, 161
Matthews, Anne, 161
   E. D., 6
   Edward B., 85
Meadowood, 110, 121
Meadowood Shopping Center, 130, 148
Meadowood Subdivision, 91
Mechanics and Fire Company, 58
Mechanics Bank, 58
Mellon, Andrew, 123
Mercer, Charles, 58
Methodist Episcopal Church South, 92
Mill Seat, Addition to, 169
Miller, 120
   Annie E., 178
   Benjamin, 83, 107, 154
   Charlotte, 161
   Harold, 161
   Harry Lee, 178
   Lewis, 178
   Mary Reading, 28
   Norman, 178
   Pro., 91
   Robert J., 160
   Sarah, 154
   Wallace A., 178
   Walter, 178
Millican, 89
Mimosa Land, 156
Minnick, Joseph A., 160
   Ruth H., 153
Mitchell, Jennifer, 161
Mitchells' Crossroad, 94
Monocacy, 64
Monocacy River, 44
Montgomery County Recreation Department, 158
Moore, Carroll, 179
Moran, Andrew J., 179
Mormon Church, 123
Morningside Drive, 148
Morningside Subdivision, 129
Morrow, Warren P., 160
Mosby, 106
Mount Radnor, 43, 44, 47, 48, 57, 60, 69, 171
Munson, Peter, 161
Murdock, William, 74
Murphy, John D., 179
Myers, Valentine, 40
Mytinger, C. H., 95

-N-

Naylor, 130
Neal, William O., 89
Nesbitt, Martha C., 28, 41, 42, 60, 61, 62, 68
Neuman, John W., 142
New Hampshire Avenue, 17, 19, 25, 26, 38, 44, 48, 64, 66, 81, 83, 84, 89, 95, 103, 108, 116, 117, 118, 121, 123, 129, 130, 131, 134, 135, 136, 137, 138, 144, 145, 148, 149, 151, 155, 156, 157, 166
New Hampshire Avenue Gospel

Church, 150
New York, 76
Newett, George, 161
Newman, Daisy, 61
  Harry Wright, 28, 105, 112
Nicholson, Jesse F., 142
  Maurice, 145
Niebert, Ray Eldon, 41, 68
Nolte, William, 151
Norbeck, 126
North Springbrook Subdivision, 26
Northwest Branch, 2, 5, 15, 18, 21, 30, 31, 32, 34, 35, 44, 46, 64, 65, 67, 69, 71, 72, 83, 84, 89, 98, 100, 123, 129, 134, 135, 136, 140, 141, 167, 168
Note, Charlotte, 161
Notley Road, 18, 80, 81, 89, 94, 96, 104, 129, 134, 137, 144, 147, 149

-O-

Odell, 39, 69
  Elizabeth, 39
  Gracie, 39
  James, 38, 39, 65
  Martha, 33
  Martha Brewer, 33
  Mary, 38
  Thomas, 35, 38, 39
Ohio, 101
Ohio River, 58
Oland, Millard A., 160
Old Annapolis Road, 103, 136
Old Bonifant Road, 137, 141
Old Colesville Elementary School, 157
Old Columbia Pike, 151
Old Federal Meeting House, 92
Old Salem Village Subdivision, 26

Old Turnpike Road, 91
Olney, 94, 106, 138
Orme, Jeremiah, 40, 66
  Patrick, 91, 172
  Thomas, 57
Our Saviour Episcopal, 157
Overfield, Richard H., 61, 62
Overton, Major, 128
  Winfield Scott, 128
Overton Lane, 104
Owens, Edward, 44, 66
  Pamalee T., 160

-P-

P. and E. Thomas and Sons, 58
Padilla, Senora, 124, 125
Page Elementary School, 19
Paint Branch, 23, 25, 27, 69, 72, 76, 78, 89, 123, 125, 135, 137, 140, 141, 156
Paint Branch Crossing, 89
Paint Branch Estates, 23, 27
Paint Branch Farms, 19, 131, 132, 141
Paint Branch Subdivision, 137
Paint Branch Woolen Factory, 78
Papenfuse, Edward C., 60
Patton, Emory C., 160
  Emory R., 160
  John E., 160
  Raymond T., 160
Patuxent River, 2, 4, 24
Paula Lynn Drive, 80, 81, 89
Peach, Mary, 55, 84
  Samuel, 55, 84, 171
Peaches Lot, 55, 56, 84
Pearce, James, 58, 171, 172
  John, 14
  Sarah, 14
Peggy Stewart, 45
Perry, Eliza, 103

Ignatius, 31, 65, 98
James, 103
Joseph, 74
Peter, Lois, 129
  Michael, 80, 81, 89, 129
  Robert, 172
Peters, Caroline, 99
  Dr., 99
Petersen, John, 151
Philadelphia, 58
Philadelphia Meeting, 53, 54
Phillips, Jackie, 160
Pierce, Ann, 84
Pilling, Franklin, 77
Piney Branch, 3
Piping Rock Road, 47
Plummer, Dorothy, 131
Poplar Point, 171
Porter, Frank W. III, 5, 6
Post Office, 80
Potomac, 101
Potomac River, 1, 2, 4, 92, 101, 139
  Eastern Branch, 2
Poultney, Ann, 58
  Elizabeth, 58
  Thomas, 58
Powell, Anne, 108
Power, Garrett, 182
Presbytery of Washington City, 148
Price, Mary, 14
Prince Charles, 8

-Q-
Quaint Acres, 17, 123
Queen Elizabeth, 7
Quinn, David B., 5, 11

-R-
Rabbitt, John, 81, 82, 84

Rabineau, Eda, 161
  Norman, 161
Raleigh, Sir Walter, 7
Ramsey, John, 40
Randolph Road, 3, 19, 23, 26, 36, 48, 55, 56, 66, 71, 72, 83, 84, 85, 87, 92, 108, 116, 123, 129, 134, 135, 136, 138, 144, 146, 147, 155, 167
Rawlings, 108
  James, 86
  James H., 83, 85
  Thomas, 83
Rawlings' Store, 82
Ray, Betty, 145
  Calvin, 97
  Mildred, 145
  Preston B., 72
Redmond, Douglas, 161
Reed, Allen, 108, 110, 111, 116, 117
  Bessie, 117
  Carl B., 179
  Charlotte, 118
  Ed, 110, 116, 117, 118, 120
  Edward, 108, 111
  Edward L., 116
  Russell, 111, 112, 118
  Russell B., 116, 133
  Thelma, 112, 133
  Will, 108
Religious Organizations (churches, etc.):
  Andrew Chapel Methodist, 93
  Andrew Chapel Methodist Episcopal, 146
  Andrew Chapel Methodist Episcopal Church South, 92
  Baltimore Yearly Meeting (Quakers), 53, 59, 60
  Cambodia Buddhist Society, 150

INDEX

Catholic Archdiocese of Washington, D.C., 147
Chinese Christian Church of Maryland, 150
Church of England, 7, 10, 13
Church of Jesus Christ of the Latter Day Saints, 150, 157
Colesville Baptist, 157
Colesville Baptist Mission, 148
Colesville Council of Community Congregations, 157, 158
Colesville Methodist, 121, 146
Colesville Presbyterian, 148, 157
Colesville United Methodist, 22, 86, 146, 157
Disciples of Christ, 157
Epiphany Lutheran, 157
Episcopalian Church of the Transfiguration, 149
Episcopalian Diocese of Washington, D.C., 149
Federal Chapel Meeting House, 91
Federal Meeting House, 91
Federal Methodist Church, 164
Federal Methodist Episcopal, 91
First Alliance, 150, 157
Good Hope Methodist Episcopal, 107, 114
Good Hope Union United Methodist, 87, 157
Good Hope United Methodist Church, 164
Heritage Church, 157
Herring Creek Monthly Meeting (Society of Friends, Quakers), 35, 53
Holy Family Seminary, 83, 108, 109, 134
Immanuel Church, 157

Indian Spring Monthly Meeting, 54
Kensington Baptist, 148
Korean Baptist Church of Washington, 150
Liberty Grove United Methodist, 157
London Meeting, 53
Methodist Church, 165
Methodist Episcopal Church South, 92
Morman, 123
New Hampshire Avenue Gospel, 150
Old Federal Meeting House, 92
Philadelphia Meeting, 53, 54
Presbytery of Washington City, 148
Resurrection Catholic Church, 157
St. John the Baptist Catholic, 157
St. Mark's, 116
St. Mark's Episcopal, 157
St. Paul's, 14
St. Stephern Lutheran, 157
Sandy Spring Friends (Quakers), 24, 36, 43, 52, 53, 54, 57
Seventh Day Adventist on New Hampshire Avenue, 17
Shaare Tefila Congregation, 157
Society of Friends, 53, 59
Sons of the Holy Family, 147
Spencerville Seventh Day Adventist, 157
Transfiguration Episcopal, 157
Unitarian Universalist of Silver Spring, 157
United Methodist Church, 66, 157

Washington Spanish Seventh
  Day Adventist, 151
West River Meeting of Friends,
  35
West River Yearly Meeting, 53,
  62
Resurrection Catholic Church,
  157
Rhine, Sam B., 92
Rice, Millard Milburn, 41, 42, 68
Richardson, Alice V., 179
  Dr., 120
  Jack A., 151
  Lulu, 145
  Thelma, 161
Riggs, Effie, 97
  Thomas, 65
Roads, 64-68, 87-90
Robinson, Stitt, 6
Rockville, 136, 164
Rockville Academy, 83
Rogers, John, 44, 66
Rohland, Henry W., 160
Rollo, Vera Foster, 11, 112
Rosemere Avenue, 20, 129
Rosenwald School, 144
Rover's Content, 14
Ruff, Paul, 160
Ruhl, George R., 160
Rural Felicity, 103
Rye, Raymond, 160

-S-

Safeway, 117
St. John The Baptist Catholic,
  157
St. John The Baptist Parish, 147
St. Mark's Church, 116
St. Mark's Episcopal, 157
St. Paul's Church, 14
St. Stephen Lutheran, 157

St. Winexburg (Winexberge,
  Winexbergh, Winexburg, etc.)
  35, 36, 48, 58, 84, 168, 169,
  171
Sam, 149
Samperton, John Stanley, 148
Sandy Spring, 24, 35, 69, 106,
  129, 138
Sandy Spring Colored School, 108
Sandy Spring Friends Meeting,
  57
Sandy Spring Meeting, 52, 53, 54
Sandy Spring Meeting of Friends,
  24, 36
Sandy Spring Meeting of the
  Society of Friends, 43
Sandy Spring National Bank, 158
Sandy Spring Turnpike, 89
Sappington, Thomas, 38
Saunders, Heywood N., 160
Sauser, Bob, 161
Sausser, Robert C., 160
Scaggs, George S., 94
Scharf, J. Thomas, 63, 90
Schools, 94, 144
Seek, Richard R., 179
Seneca Tribe, 59
Seventh Day Adventist Church
  on New Hampshire Ave., 17
Shaare Tefila Congregation, 157
Shannon Drive, 18
Sharp Street, 57
Sharretts, John, 89
Shaw, Annia Maria, 179
  Catherine, 179
  Edna Gertrude, 179
  Edwin, 179
  Mary V., 179
  S. Mirriam, 179
  Thomas E., 179
  William E., 179

INDEX

Sheckles, John, 74
　Richard, 74
Sheller, Tina H., 62
Shelton, Sally, 161
Shepherd, 56
　Edward, 141
　William, 123
Sherwood School, 129
Sherwood Forest Manor
　Subdivision, 26
Shure, Ralph George, 160
Sierra, Father John, 133
Silver Spring, 65, 100, 106, 116, 123, 128, 136, 138
Sioussat, Sir George Leaken, 61
Sligo, 87
Smith, Branson, 123
　Captain John, 2, 4
　Dorothy, 131
　George, 107, 123
　Harold, 130
　Harry, 130, 131
　Harry R., 129, 133, 160
　Lilly, 123
　Mae, 129, 130
　Mary, 107
　Robert A., 160
　Thomas, 152
　William, 134, 56, 62, 108, 123, 124, 133
　William E., 123
Smith Town, 107, 123, 164
Smith Village, 27, 107, 123, 136
Smith Village Road, 87, 107
Smithville, 56, 114, 123, 144
Smithville Road, 136
Smithville School, 144
Smitty's Esso (station), 129, 130, 131, 155
Snowden, 13, 167
　Deborah, 24, 64
　Elizabeth, 24
　Elizabeth Coale, 80
　Mary, 24, 35, 43
　Richard, 12, 24, 25, 26, 27, 35, 36, 55, 64
Snowden's Fourth Addition to His Manor, 16, 25, 26, 35, 36, 44, 48, 171
Snowden's Manor, 44, 65
Snowden's Manor Enlarged, 25, 69, 100
Snowdens Mill, 16, 25, 27, 78
Snyder, Charles W., 160
Society of Friends, 53, 59
Sons of The Holy Family, 147
South River, 57
South Stonegate Subdivision, 26, 119
Sowndes, Chris, 40
Spear, William, 100
Spence, Donald, 161
Spencer, George D., 94
Spencerville, 144
Spencerville Seventh Day Adventist, 157
Sprigg, Sarah, 14
Springbrook, 17, 147
Springbrook Drive, 135
Springbrook Forest, 169
Springbrook High School, 146, 158
Springbrook Manor, 17
Springbrook Subdivision, 135
Springbrook Villa, 17
Springloch Road, 141
Stable, Caleb, 95
State Temperance Society, 58
Stecklein, Catherine, 179
　Joseph, 179
　Mary Louise, 179
Steesy, Wesley J., 160

Steinmetz, Gleaves, 147
Stewart, West, 159
Stiverson, Gregory A., 60
Stoneburner, Raymond, 128
Stonegate, 21
Stonegate Citizens Association, 156
Stonegate Elementary School, 21, 146, 151
Stonegate Subdivision, 26, 137, 156
Stout, Herbert Leroy, 160
Stover, John F., 63
Stup, Charlotte Reed, 118
Sullivan, Catherine, 180
  Mrs., 100, 101
  Perry, 180
  William, 100, 101
Sunshine, 136
Susquehanna River, 2
Suthard, Floyd, 122
  Grace, 122
Sutton, Anne, 161
Sween, Jane C., 41, 61, 70
Sykes, John, 60

-T-

Taffs, Rosemary, 161
Talbott, George W. W., 180
  Joseph, 180
Tamarack Triangle Civic Association, 156
Taylor, Charles E., 152
Tevis, Charles C., 152
Thomas, Ann, 58
  Elizabeth, 24, 36, 58, 59
  Evan, 36, 40, 42, 43, 44, 45, 46, 47, 48, 49, 51, 52, 53, 54, 55, 57, 58, 59, 60, 62, 63, 66, 67, 69, 71, 80, 84, 163, 164, 169, 171

  Even, 172
  John, 24, 52
  Lawrence B., 28, 41
  Mary, 24, 35, 36, 43, 57, 58, 163
  Phillip, 59
  Phillip E., 58, 59, 63
  Phillip Evan, 58
  Rachel, 43, 57, 58, 60, 63
  Richard, 44, 45, 52
  Samuel, 24, 25, 35, 36, 40, 42, 43, 55, 56, 154, 163, 167, 168
  Thomas and George, 58
Thomas Drive, 91
Thompson, Anna M., 180
  Bill, 145
  Cora Lee, 180
  Estelle, 145
  Forest, 145
  Helen, 145
  Horatio, 180
  James M., 180
  L. E., 180
  Laura L., 180
  Lawrence E., 180
  Margaret L., 180
  Sarah A., 180
  Susan, 180
  William, 145, 180
Thurston, Phil A., 160
Tolson, Alfred C., 118, 119
  Ann, 118
  Anne R., 119
  Catherine, 118
  Christopher, 119
  Elizabeth Ann, 118, 119
Tonat, Valene, 161
Toomey, Daniel Carroll, 104, 112
Townsend, Sarah, 98
Transfiguration Episcopal, 157
Tree, Lambert, 86
Trevelyan, G. M., 7, 11

INDEX

Trexler, Carroll, 160
Tri-County Free-Press, 134
Trundle, John, 40
Tseng, Diane, 161
Tucker, Elizabeth Houston, 97
  Mary, 145
  Mary Ann, 98
  Sarah J., 180
  William, 180
Twilight, 83, 166
Twillight, 84
Twistin' Creek, 141
Two Farms, 57, 71, 72, 80, 84, 171, 172
Two Farms Reserve, 69, 84, 172
Tyler, Mary Frances, 180
Tyson, Elisha, 59
  Elizabeth, 59
  Isaac, 59
  Martha Ellicott, 63
  Mary, 59

-U-

U. S. Route 29, 131, 135
Unitarian Universalist of Silver Spring, 157
United Methodist Church, 66, 157
Upper Marlboro, 164

-V-

Vabare Branch, 141
Valdenar, Elizabeth, 72, 92
  Francis, 71, 92, 95, 121
  James, 84, 86
  Wil Culver, 180, 183
  William, 83, 85, 86, 180
Valencia Citizens Association, 156
Valley Mill, 127, 128
Valley Mill Park, 27, 66, 72, 75
Valley View, 108, 109

Valleybrook, 17
Van Horn, R. Lee, 68
Vanhorn, J. V., 181
  Jacob V., 180
  Martha E., 181
  S. A., 181
  Sarah A., 181
Veitch, Edith, 145
  Inez S., 181
  M. Elizabeth, 181
  R. Lee, 181
Vierling, Evelyn, 129
  Helen, 127, 128, 133
  Helen O., 141, 142, 143
  Robert, 127, 128
Virginia, Fairview, 100
  Greenspring, 100
Virginia Company, 9
Volkmore, Charles, 76
Voorhees, Lucas, 152

-W-

Waldman, Carl, 6
Wales, Robert O., 152
Wall, Alvin, 145
Walley View, 120
Walsh, Richard, 28
Walstad, Mary, 14
Walter Tyler Page Elementary School, 151
Warfield, C. N., 181
  Caleb N., 181
  Eliza Ellen, 181
Waring, Basil, 98
Warner, 107
Washington City, 91
Washington Road, 87
Washington Spanish Seventh Day Adventist Church, 151
Washington, D.C., 1, 84, 101, 106, 107, 113, 118, 121, 123, 124,

128, 129, 131
Washington-Colesville-Ashton
   Turnpike, 87, 108, 136
Waters, William, 40
Watkins, Mr., 145
Waugh, Lillian M., 181
Weller, George B., 160
Wessells, Joan S., 181
West Friendship, 121
West River Meeting of Friends,
   35
West River Yearly Meeting, 53,
   62
West Virginia, 126
  Fairview, 100
  Greenspring, 100
Westover, 71, 121
Westover Elementary School,
   146, 151
Wetzlar, Edward, 161
Wheaton, 94, 96, 140
Wheeler, Carrie F., 181
  Martha E., 181
  W. T., 181
  Willie T., 181
Wheeling, Pennsylvania, 59
White, Lawrence, 126
  Mary, 181
  Noah, 181
White Oak, 17, 65, 87, 136, 142
White Oak Junior High School,
   146, 148
White Oak Middle School, 146
Wilhelm, Dan, 160, 161
Willard, Frances, 153
William Tyler Page Elementary
   School, 146
Williams, 40
  Bessie Mae, 183
  Charles, 44, 65
  Fran, 147
  George C., 160
  Richard H., 83
Wilson, George B., 104, 105
  Mary Ann, 98
  Sarah, 99
  Thomas Overton, 98
Wilstach, Paul, 41
Windham Manor, 23
Wingard, Derell C., 160
Winpenny, John, 92
Wise, Jack W., 160
Witze, Charles, 161
Wnek, John, 161
Wolf Drive, 47
Wolfs Den, 15, 16, 21, 30, 31, 33,
   35, 65, 66, 69, 85, 98, 99, 167
Women's Christian Temperance
   Union, 165, 153
Wood, Fergus, 152
Woodcock's Tree, 168
Wooding, Nancy Cabel, 120
Woodlawn Terrace, 19,
   23
Woodlawn Terrace Subdivision,
   156
Woodward, Harry, 145
  Melvin, 145
  Ollie, 97
Woolman, John, 54
Wooten, Thomas Sprigg, 51
Wooton, Thomas Sprigg, 45
Wright, Thelma V., 181

-Y-

Young, Adam, 86

-Z-

Zeigler, Ann J., 181
  Helen B., 97
  Susie, 181